Religious Freedom in Church and State

Religious Freedom
in
Church and State

A Study in Doctrinal Development

by
PIUS AUGUSTIN, O.S.B.

HELICON
Baltimore—Dublin

Helicon Press, Inc.
1120 N. Calvert Street
Baltimore, Maryland 21202

Helicon Limited
20 Upr. Fitzwilliam Street
Dublin 2, Ireland

Library of Congress Catalog Card Number 66-26479

Nihil Obstat:	Carroll E. Satterfield Censor Librorum
Imprimatur: ✠	Lawrence Cardinal Shehan Archbishop of Baltimore September 13, 1966

PRINTED IN THE UNITED STATES OF AMERICA

To the courage and scholarship of

JOHN COURTNEY MURRAY

whose pioneering work in this field

has been so essential to the

Declaration on Religious Freedom

of the

Second Vatican Council

Contents

Introduction 11

Part I. Growth Curve to Modern Times

Chapter One: The New Testament 17
1. Church-State Relations 19
2. Freedom of Conscience 27

Chapter Two: The Fathers of the Church 34
1. Early Patristic Teaching 36
2. The Golden Age 40
3. Freedom of Conscience and the Fathers 67

Chapter Three: The Middle Ages 85
1. The Medieval Reality 88
2. Theologians and Canonists 109
3. The Nature and Dignity of Conscience 125
4. The Permanent Medieval Legacy 135

Part II. The Modern Age

Chapter Four: Three Hundred Years 147
1. The Intellectual Background 149
2. The Political and Sociological Situation 156
3. The Catholic Position 166

Chapter Five: Pope Leo XIII 178
1. Church-State Autonomy 185
2. Church-State Cooperation 191
3. Human Freedom and Church-State Theory 207

Chapter Six: Pope Pius XII 218
  1. Beyond Politics 222
  2. The New Universalist Teaching 226
  3. Perspectives on the Past 240
  4. The Ideal Church-State Relation? 254

Chapter Seven: Pope John XXIII and Vatican II 269
  1. The New Papal Diplomacy 272
  2. Universalism Achieved 276
  3. The End of an Era 287
  4. Declaration on Religious Freedom 301

Chapter Eight: Foundation for Progress 313

Bibliography 317

Index 323

Religious Freedom in Church and State

Introduction

The Second Vatican Council has yielded many doctrinal and moral fruits which undoubtedly will serve God's people well in its task of re-speaking Christ's truth and comfort in terms relevant and meaningful to our times. It produced no new doctrinal definitions. Its historic significance will rather lie, beyond a doubt, in the *development* which it gave to so many doctrinal and moral principles. The Council's whole purpose was an *aggiornamento*. This "bringing up to date" is necessarily founded on, and centers in, development and growth in many areas of Christian teaching. Few of these doctrinal advances achieved by the Council are more striking and significant than the teachings of the Declaration on Religious Freedom. Here, progress of far-reaching effects has been achieved, and none more important than those in the area of Catholic church-state doctrine.

Christian church-state relations and religious liberty have always been closely allied by their very nature. Today, however, in the minds of many of the world's most learned men, the Catholic Church's teachings on these two points are more contradictory than complementary. The Church, they are convinced, stands for a repression of civil religious freedom. This conviction has become rooted in men's minds over the past several centuries. It has become so deeply rooted that it has contributed as much as any other single factor to the great schism which we now see and feel between our modern civilization and Christian culture. This age of democracy finds authoritarianism hard to tolerate.

11

With the promulgation of the Declaration on Religious Freedom, the fundamental cause for suspicion has been removed. The Church has affirmed its support of religious freedom in clear and unambiguous terms. But the significance of this fact has not yet been comprehended by Catholics, much less by other Christians and by western society in general. I suspect that most of general western society will interpret the declaration as simply a move of expedience: the Church has reversed its former position regarding the duty of States to proclaim and protect it because not to do so would have meant a complete loss of influence. The popes of the last century defended civil repression of non-Catholic religions. The Council reversed this teaching, they assume, for pragmatic reasons alone. But this is simply not true. The Council's epoch-making declaration was the end result of a centuries long, *unidirectional* development. Demonstrating that this document was not a simple reversal of position is of course no easy task. It requires a deep, honest examination of the whole history of Christian church-state doctrine and practice.

The evolving Christian notion of the human conscience and its dignity has had, throughout its history, a profound effect on church-state doctrine. Hence, any study of church-state development must be made in the light of the concomitant growth of the Christian concept of human freedom and rights. Christ's own beautiful respect for man took centuries to penetrate through individual consciences into the civil statutes of the western Greco-Roman political structures of our civilization. It is the purpose of the present study to follow this development. It is an investigation of the growth curve of Christian church-state doctrine in the light of a growing realization of human dignity and freedom.

The Council's Declaration on Religous Freedom, with its great consequences for Catholic church-state doctrine, is not the result of a few years of discussion by the fathers at the Second

Vatican Council. It is one of the results of Christ's leaven patiently working in the human milieu during these past two thousand years. It is my hope that this essay will do at least some small bit toward bettering the spirit of Christian brotherhood by bringing to light the actual historical concatenations of events and beliefs, and tracing their development and growth. This, I believe, will remove a great deal of resentment on all sides, and help to open up and make more fruitful a healing dialogue.

I would like to express my sincere gratitude to my kind and very able mentor, Bernard Häring, C.SS.R., and to the librarians of the Abbeys of Maredsous in Belgium, of Montserrat in Spain, and especially of Sant'Anselmo in Rome, for their kind and patient assistance. Also, I am greatly indebted to Kassius Hallinger, O.S.B., of Sant'Anselmo, and to the help and encouragement offered by my confreres and friends.

PART I

Growth Curve to Modern Times

Chapter One

The New Testament

Christ is the divine Word of God. He is the living and life-giving Logos. Scripture is the word of God in an analogous sense. Both proceed from the same divine source. Both illumine man's being with the light and the life of God. Like the perfect Word, the "word of God" carries the very power of God. They are the source of the inner conversion which makes the "new man." They are likewise the source of that external activity which has in many ways changed the face of the earth.

For theology, the Scriptures are the foundation. The theologian begins with the Scriptures in the building up of his spiritual edifice. The Christian, guided in his reading by the Spirit living in himself and in the Church, finds in the Scripture his instruction and inspiration.

When church-state relations are discussed, therefore, it is normal to begin with the New Testament. Part One of this study presents the first nineteen hundred years of Catholic church-state doctrine in a historical perspective. This history begins with Christ. The Scriptures are both the chronological and the causal beginning of a Christian system of relations between civil and religious authority. And, if one stops to consider for a moment, this particular area of Christian thinking furnishes yet another graphic proof of the massive moving force of the "word of God."

Up until the Christian era the direction of both religious and

17

civil affairs was to a large extent combined. Church and State,[1] while not really one, were united under one authority. The Roman emperor was also the Pontifex Maximus. The Jewish theocracy had Yahweh as its leader in both its wars and its religion. It was a constant characteristic of practically all the great civilizations that religion and State tended to fuse at their topmost echelons. They tended to have either a deified king or a regal high-priest. But this condition of thousands of years was reversed in one stroke. With Christ's coming, the two were stated to be clearly distinct (though this was not immediately clear to all Christians). Still, even outwardly the trend was reversed.

Christ's kingdom was something basically "other." As described in the parables of the kingdom and in other references, the kingdom of God was something vastly richer, larger and more beautiful than kingdoms in this world. But the empire of the Caesars was not belittled. It was recognized and even defended by Christians. When Christ's kingdom seemed to conquer in the West, this essential duality began to be incorporated into law. Though often obscured by one or other of the two parties, and occasionally almost obliterated, this distinction remains in force today. One could say that the two-edged sword of the word of God was the one instrument capable of the division.

While essentially two, Church and State are in no way essentially contradictory. But the fact that Church and State are distinct entities according to the New Testament does more than demonstrate the power of the word of God. It furnishes one of

1. The term "State" is, of course, not to be taken here in its literal sense. It is technically accurate only when used to describe the modern national entities with their central authorities. However, we are concerned with church-"State" relations and so, throughout this work, the word is to be understood in its broad, unrestricted sense. But this must not prevent us from understanding clearly that the term will stand for political entities of vastly differing natures as we pass from one era to another. These differences are extremely important for our theme, and they will be pointed out as the need arises.

the two basic truths of the entire Christian position on church-state relations. The other truth of religious freedom is complementary. But let us see what the New Testament tells us about these two propositions.

1. CHURCH-STATE RELATIONS

Distinction between the two societies begins with Christ's own words. "Render to Caesar the things that are Caesar's and to God the things that are God's" (Mt 22:22; Mk 12:17; Lk 20:25). The religious leaders who framed the question which elicited this answer clearly showed the mentality of their age. The Hebrew saw an obligation to pay taxes to a theocracy in which the civil ruler and God were more or less one. The Roman empire, too, under whose yoke the Pharisees chaffed, did not make a sharp distinction between Caesar and the gods.[1] And so even the shrewdest and best of Abraham's sons were totally unprepared for Christ's way out of their dilemma. It was an answer worthy of the Son of God: simple and so evident that it allowed room for no retort. Its bearing on our subject is clear enough. If Caesar deserved only "the things that are Caesar's," then his realm was essentially distinct from that of God.

This same concept was taken up by Christ's disciples and developed. Paul tells his converts that civil authority must be obeyed as a divinely established authority, and respected. "Let

1. The "State" in the time of Christ was, for the whole western world, the Roman empire: that is, a monarchical, comparatively totalitarian system. Yet it possessed the most highly developed and smoothly functioning judiciary and legal structure ever known to man up till those times. It was this administrative and judiciary excellence that conditioned the respect which the writers of the New Testament tendered to Rome. For a thorough treatment of this complex and important "State," see F. Adcock, *Roman Political Ideas and Practice* (Ann Arbor, 1959) and L. Homo, *Roman Political Institutions* (London, 1929). They give many valuable insights into the Christian attitude towards public political power as reflected in the New Testament and early patristic writing.

everyone submit himself to the ruling authorities, for there
exists no authority not ordained by God. And that which exists
has been constituted by God" (Rom 13:1). Hence we have
affirmed clearly if indirectly the second basic foundation mentioned above. If Christians are to recognize and respect the
authority of the State, then that society embodies nothing fundamentally incompatible with the nature and aims of Christ's
kingdom. The same truth is contained in Christ's statement
about rendering Caesar's things to Caesar. Such a rendition
could be possible only if doing so did not damage the divine
society which Jesus was in the process of setting up. Paul further instructs Titus to pray for civil rulers: "Remind the faithful
to be subject to rulers and authorities" (Tit 3:1). Peter also
demands full obedience to State authority (1 Pet 2:13-17). From
the Christian side at least then, relations between the authorities
should be friendly and constructive.

But must the State return this favor? *Can* the State understand the kingdom of God? Does the New Testament teach that
the State can and should recognize the existence of another
public power on a different level from its own? This is the crucial part of the whole problem of church-state relations today.
The two founding principles mentioned above are fairly evident
and evoke little debate. But the question as to whether the State
can and should recognize the Christian religion as the true religion stands ultimately as the central problem. The various
answers by thinkers of every degree of belief and unbelief are
basically three. In order to appreciate the scriptural position it
is essential to understand these varying viewpoints.

First, at one extreme lie those atheists and agnostics who favor
a totalitarian State. They begin by denying even the possibility
of religious truth, and then deny that the State has any real
obligation at all to recognize religion.

The second group can be called the "separationist" school.
We will speak here only of the Christians who have this church-

state conviction. These men believe that one form or other of separation between Church and State is more consonant with basic Christian principles than the various forms of union which have existed in the past.[2] They do not attempt to set up any one system as being the Christian ideal. They simply argue that any type of real union cannot avoid a basically unchristian force exerted against citizens whose consciences require them to dissent from the established religion. In general, they contend that the State, by its nature, cannot make a supernatural act of faith or declare religious truth.

The third category is the "unionist" school of thought, which cites the long tradition of the Church as proof that the ideal form of church-state relations is a formal union of the State with Christ's own true religion. Both of these last two schools appeal to the Scriptures as the foundation for their respective views.[3]

But what does the New Testament say about this whole problem of the State's power and duty to recognize religion? As a matter of fact neither Christ nor his disciples speak of the problem. That Jesus allowed for legitimate and distinct places for both societies is clear. That both Peter and Paul demanded recognition of the State and due submission to it leaves little room for doubt. But regarding the State's duty to return this recognition, we find no direct reference. Actually, this is not to be wondered at, for the New Testament centers on the Christ and on the nature of his kingdom, and never dwells on the political.

Though not treating this problem explicitly, the inspired

2. Examples of the school are: J. Maritain, *Les droits de l'homme et la loi naturelle* (Paris, 1945); C. Journet, *The Church of the Word Incarnate*, II, "The Apostolic Hierarchy" (London, 1955), pp. 193-330; Joseph Lecler, *L'Eglise et la souveraineté de l'Etat* (Paris, 1946); John Courtney Murray (see the articles listed below, n. 1, sect. 5); and many others.

3. Among the followers of this conception are: F. Martinez, *Naturaleza juridica y derechos de la Iglesia* (Pamplona, 1945); A. Cardinal Ottaviani, *Ius Publicum* (Tipografia Vaticana, 1939, two vols.); Joseph Fenton (see articles listed below, n. 1, sect. 5); and others.

Christian writings do not leave us without some unmistakable guidelines. A condemnation of the atheistic State (including the first of these three theories) is clearly present. In the Apocalypse, John speaks of the "beast of the abyss" which the whole world worshipped:

> "Who is like the beast," they said, "and who can fight against it?" . . . It opened its mouth to utter blasphemies against God, to blaspheme his name and his tabernacle and those who dwell with him. It was empowered to make war on all the saints, and to conquer them and it was given authority over every tribe, nation, tongue, and people (Apoc 13:4-7).

Though the image is obscure and apocalyptic, exegetes agree that it clearly refers to the Roman empire and its totalitarian policies towards the newborn Christian Church.[4] Representing such a State as "the beast" is as clear a condemnation as one could want.

The representatives of the second, "separationist," theory support their beliefs with a scriptural argument which at first sight is quite impressive. Many, presuming that the State as such cannot make an act of faith and espouse religious truth, argue that the Lord himself implied as much. Jesus warned his disciples that they would be brought to trial by civil authorities because of their teachings: "They will try to hand you over to courts of justice and to flog you in their synagogues; you will even be brought before governors and kings for my sake" (Mt 10:17-18). And he himself was crucified by an uncomprehending State. Paul, explaining his belief before the Roman governor, Festus (Acts 26:24), was judged a fool. He was imprisoned several times and finally executed.

Jesus' warning was unqualified, argue the extreme separationists. Does it not indicate a basic inability on the part of civil

---

4. See O. Cullmann, *Dieu et César* (Paris, 1956), pp. 77-90; also H. Schlier, "L'Etat selon le Nouveau Testament," in *Lumière et Vie*, IX (Sept.-Oct.: 1960), 118-122.

authority to comprehend religion? Further, it is argued, Jesus and his apostles, in their turn, make light of earthly kingdoms. Jesus emphasized that his kingdom was in heaven, and insisted that Christians ever remember the passing nature of the earthly city: "Here indeed we have no lasting city; but we are in search of the city that is to come" (Heb 13:14). It seems plausible then—they reason—that Jesus and the apostles, knowing the blindness of the State to their "heavenly city," emphasized its "other-worldness" to avoid any overly ambitious notions about their compatibility.

Let us examine briefly these scriptural indications in their context and in their compatibility with other important related passages. First of all, in Matthew 10:18, Jesus ended his warning by affirming that these trials would be opportunities for making converts of the kings themselves. "It will be your chance to testify to Jew and Gentile." If the hearer were congenitally deaf to supernatural testimony it would seem that there would be little use in testifying. The fact that both Pilate and Festus chose not to "hear" the testimony given does not imply that, as civil judges, to hear would have been impossible.

The most indicative passage, however, is found in John's gospel, chapter eighteen. Here we have a positive indication that the Lord did expect States to understand, to some degree at least, the nature of his kingdom. While being tried for his life by Pilate, Jesus presented his kingdom and kingship as it was: "My kingdom is not of this world" (Jn 18:26). When Pilate refused to become involved in the question of religious truth and abandoned the truth in abandoning Jesus, the Lord immediately judged him guilty.[5] His life depended on Pilate recognizing the supernatural nature of his kingdom. When Pilate

5. See H. Schlier, *Die Zeit der Kirche* (Freiburg, 1956), pp. 1-16: "The State, though here open to religious truth and neutral regarding it, cannot of itself find this truth. Nevertheless, it is dependent on him who is the truth."

failed, Jesus (paradoxically enough) rendered judgment on the judge. It was clearly a case of Church vs. State, and Jesus insisted that there was no incompatibility between the two: "I am a king" (18:38). Generally such an affirmation would be treason and punishable by death. "But my kingdom is not a worldly one." And therefore no claim to a share in Caesar's royalty was involved. In order to release Jesus, Pilate had to recognize *officially* that there was room for such a different king-ship. When he refused to do so, he received Christ's censure as being among those who were unjustly causing his death. There is, therefore, little doubt that Jesus intended that the State recognize religion as a legitimate entity to be respected and allowed to flourish.

But did Jesus expect Pilate to recognize him as the Son of God and to use his office of procurator to place the official stamp of credence on his teachings? This is the line of thought of our "third school." Pilate could not have done that even if he believed with all his heart. Christ's censure did not fall upon him for failing to do this. It seems that Jesus was asking only that defer-ence which is due any innocent religious belief. This would have required only a natural reverence on the emperor's part. Failure to give even this surely merited Christ's blame. But this does not prove that the New Testament evidence is *against* the opinion that full adherence to Christ's Church is possible for the State. It is merely negative evidence. Chapter eighteen of John's gospel does not indicate that such adherence is either good or bad. This much, however, *is* indicated: Jesus himself demanded that the State recognize the legitimacy of his teachings, and *his right to spread them*. It is doubtful that he demanded full and formal credence. Thus the New Testament simply furnishes no definite answer to the central bone of contention between the second and third schools of Christian church-state thought. It does not give clear evidence as to whether the State can and should recognize and defend Christ's religious truth. What it does clearly say is that the State has no right to *suppress the teaching* of religious truth.

As to Paul's insistence on the ephemeral nature of this life, no aspersion on the State is intended. These texts simply expose clearly a basic quality of Christianity: its eschatological orientation. Professor Cullmann explains admirably this facet of New Testament church-state doctrine.[6] The primitive Church, he shows, lived constantly in the hope of the second coming of Christ. Whether this coming be near or relatively distant, the hopes and loves of Christians should be centered there. The present order of things, including the State, took on for the early Christian community an appearance of transitoriness because of this fact.

We cannot, therefore, condemn as against the Scriptures the basic contention of either the second or the third school of thought. They are divided as to whether or not the State has the power to recognize true religion. As we have seen, exegesis can do little toward the solution of this problem.

What is there in Scripture to indicate the precise relations between the two societies, granting that they cede to each other initial mutual recognition? Does the New Testament favor separation of Church and State as that phrase is understood by most modern Christians? Or does it favor union of Church and State as that term is used by many Catholic theologians: a union of close cooperation? From every indication there exists in the inspired writings not even an indirect affirmation of either the one or the other. Jesus seems to have left the solution of this problem—as of countless others—to the inspiration of his Spirit working within his Church. Only hints as to the broadest outline of a solution can be found.

One boundary for the extent of cooperation by the State can be seen. It is evident that the use of the brute force of State arms was not included in Christ's method of building up or of

6. Cullmann, *op. cit.*, pp. 91-96.

conserving his Church. Neither was the use of any dazzling display of physical power sanctioned. Jesus steadfastly rejected the urgings of his disciples to employ or accept such means of persuasion. He ordered Peter: "Put your sword back into its place. All those that use the sword will die by the sword" (Mt 26:52). He rebuked the "sons of thunder" for suggesting the use of lightning bolts. "Lord, do you want us to order fire to drop from the sky and consume them? But Jesus turned upon them with a stern rebuke" (Lk 9:54). He preferred the interior force of love, of suffering, and of the action of his Spirit. "No one can say 'Jesus is Lord,' except under the influence of the Holy Spirit" (1 Cor 12:3). Only when all external force is absent is there assurance that love and the spirit are the real motives for asserting the truth.

The pros and cons of this whole discussion center on the problem of religious liberty. What is religious liberty? At what point does State recognition of religion become an illicit moral pressure on unbelievers and on other religions? One can go to ludicrous lengths in either direction in answering this question. One can say that any official mention of God by the State is illicit pressure. And if so, is not any public preaching of the Gospel equally damaging to one's freedom? Or, one can say that baptism at the sword's point does not really take away one's power to say "no." The New Testament speaks often of liberty. St. Paul preaches freedom so often that he can justly be termed the "apostle of freedom." But there is equal evidence of a balancing doctrine of authority.

None of the texts on either freedom or authority have to do with church-state relations. Nevertheless, freedom is a central problem for the present essay, and the general New Testament doctrine of authority vs. freedom sheds much light on what must be a genuinely Christian balance between the two in the realm of Church and State. This teaching on religious liberty is a second and final broad scriptural guideline as to how the two tendencies, "separationist" and "unionist," can be reconciled. It is also the final New Testament doctrine of great importance in the realm of relations between the civil and the sacred, which are of interest in our essay.

2. FREEDOM OF CONSCIENCE

The Christian notion of freedom, particularly freedom *(eleutheria)* as presented in St. Paul, is one of Paul's central themes.[1] It is one of the most essential facets of the Christian message. Unfortunately, it is also one of the most frequently misunderstood doctrines.

In this age of democracy we hear about freedom from every rostrum, radio and television set. This is good. But the type of freedom preached would more often than not be unrecognizable to the Man who proclaimed: ". . . then you will know the truth and it will make you freemen" (Jn 8:32). To associate the freedom preached by Jesus and his disciples with the "freedom" to do what we please, to make our own self the center of the world, is really to misunderstand the Gospel. Paul's idea of freedom is not a simple absence of restraint. It is the freedom to be a slave of Christ. It is a liberation from the Jewish Law and from the "law" of sin.[2] It is an experience (not distinct from the original act of faith in Christ) founded in his cross-won power to free us from our sinful natures and to make us whole and just.

We realize our helplessness before the "old man" as Paul did. But through that passover of baptism, through a mystical configuration with Christ crucified, buried and risen, we are freed

1. L. Cerfaux, "Condition chrétienne et liberté selon saint Paul," in *Structures et Liberté: Etudes Carmelitaines* (Brussels, 1958), pp. 244-252. See also A. Cardinal Bea, "Religiöse Freiheit und Wandlungen der Gesellschaft," in *Stimmen Der Zeit* (February, 1964), 322-323: "The freedom of the Christian is actually one of the strongest themes running through his epistles."

2. See A. Bea, *op. cit.*, 322, and another article of his, "San Paolo, araldo et eroe della libertà," in *La Civiltà Cattolica*, LV (1960), IV, 3-14.

from our slavery. At last we are free to give ourselves wholly to God in love. "Unhappy man that I am! Who will rescue me from this body doomed to death? Thanks be to God! Through Jesus Christ our Lord [rescue is effected]" (Rom 7:24-25). The Law of the Jews was also like a bondage. Now Paul is free from all his bonds. "But now we have been set free from the Law, having died to that by which we were held down, so that we may render service which is new and according to the spirit" (Rom 7:6).

As usual with Paul, the idea of freedom here is essentially supernatural. His freedom is not merely philosophical.[3] Nevertheless, it is evident that this type of "freedom of the sons of God" has a definite bearing on the question of freedom of religion and religious "tolerance."[4] Whence did the Christian tradition of love and respect for individual freedom arise if not from here? Of all the interests between Church and State, this matter of freedom from coercion by the State in matters of religion is the most debated. The great importance of the problem demands a close examination of the pertinent scriptural references.

It is Paul's type of freedom which gives the Christian his great dignity. Before Christ, man was cut off from God and suffered an inescapable frustration. He was harried by the Law and by his own unruly self, and did not know where to turn for relief. Now, man is freed and made capable of a humble pride. Through Christ's death and love he is given strength gradually to break the bonds of the "old man" completely, and thereby become a whole and healed man. Once again, with Christ's strength, man can see his goal and then pursue and win it. Man has been remade: redeemed. He is independent, in a Christian sort of way. He need no longer rely blindly on the direction of the Law,

3. See H. Schlier, *op. cit.*, pp. 193-206.
4. See L. Cerfaux, *op. cit.*, 250, and A. Bea, "Religiöse Freiheit": "Who can deny that in Paul's concept of freedom the actual essence of freedom itself is expressed?"

for now the "law of Christ" (Gal 6:2) guides his thoughts and decisions.

This being so, man not only *can* follow his own Christ-guided conscience; he *must* do so. But with this maturity comes responsibility; and with responsibility comes decision and action. Paul himself says as much. In his epistle to the Romans we see some of his Roman converts having trouble, throwing off their pagan (or Jewish?) habits. Paul declares that they should follow their consciences even though they be erroneous. He judges that they sin if they act in spite of consciences which forbid them to lay these observances aside (Rom 14). Such was the extent of the responsibility and maturity of Christians. Such has been the general consensus of opinion among most of the Church's teachers.

It is the constant presumption everywhere in the Bible that one has a free will. Not being philosophical texts, the Scriptures do not treat explicitly of the matter. But the constantly recurring theme of merit and reward vs. guilt and punishment clearly presumes freedom. Hence the freedom and responsibility of man were not treated as Christian innovations by Paul. He recognized that non-Christians were also free and responsible for their actions. He tells the Romans that the pagans, though without the Law, would be judged by the law "written in their hearts" (Rom 2:15).

All civilizations have, in various degrees, recognized that man is free in will and therefore responsible, and because responsible, deserving some degree of respect and civil liberty. It was because this love of liberty was so strong among his hearers, both Greek and Hebrew, that Paul illustrated the splendor of the "new man" in terms of liberty and slavery.[5] In effect he says to the non-Romans: "You know that all men deserve freedom to

5. L. Cerfaux, in the article cited above, declares that this concept of liberty was decisive in Paul's policy of adapting Christ's message to Greek minds (p. 251).

follow their own lights. All of you, both Greek and Jew, share a common hatred of Roman fetters. But you were held in a yet narrower bondage when you were slaves to your carnal appetites and to the unredeeming law of Moses. Rejoice then, in the glorious freedom of the sons of God! Now you are really free! And this new freedom is of such great importance that the mere civil freedom which you long for pales by comparison."

St. Paul, it seems, saw this new freedom not as something essentially different from the other, the civil, type. He never thought in terms of natural and supernatural. Though this distinction is not incompatible with his thought, it is surely of a later period of Christian thinking. There are clear indications that this is also true of his doctrine on freedom. The "freedom of the sons of God" was a flowering and completion of the natural freedom which went before it and stood beside it, but it is not essentially and artificially separate from it. Hence, though he advised slaves to be subject to their masters, he still seems to have taken upon himself the privilege of "freeing" Onesimus, the run-away slave of Philemon, asking that he be received back as "a dear brother" (Philem 1:16).

The whole tone of the New Testament shows forth the same spirit. It was impossible for the earliest Christians to throw down a whole social order and abolish slavery. Still, the power of the Gospel message drives unerringly toward the full maturation of man's potential for unfettered and unpressured love of God. Why did Christ completely reject force of any kind in his kingdom? Was it not because the divine creator of our human psyche saw plainly that total love and total self-giving is possible only when the act of giving is totally free?

While the presence of this theme of "freedom in order to love God" is unmistakable in the Christian message, it is not unqualified. It is tempered with the idea of authority: the authority of basic revealed truths taught by Christ and his disciples. Man wins his freedom from sin slowly and laboriously, and in this life he is never totally emancipated from his bonds. Only Adam and the citizens of heaven are really free, since there are absolutely no fetters holding them back from the object of their desires.

The New Testament writers saw clearly the moral impossibility of man being wholly free in this life. Even after re-birth man remains ignorant and the "flesh"—Paul's *sarx*—remains powerful; it throws both knowledge and desire into conflict and disorder. Christ himself recognizes the necessity of a State authority.

Neither is it by accident that the Lord speaks of the *kingdom* of God. The main attribute of a kingdom of any kind is a government: an authority. It keeps order within its boundaries. In this manner, and even more explicitly in other places in the gospels, Christ taught the need for authority in his Church. To Peter he gave the keys of the kingdom and on him he built his Church. Binding and loosing and keeping the gates of hell at bay presume authority. Authority always implies powers of restriction and powers of punishment. Both of these run contrary to some modern notions of freedom. Neither is contrary to the notion of freedom in the New Testament. Indeed, they are integral parts of the idea.

In his first epistle to the Corinthians, Paul excommunicates the incestuous man with summary authority. He takes away his right to associate with members of the community. John deals just as authoritatively (not "authoritarianly") with gnostic heretics (1 Jn 2:18-30). His words are not demonstrative of broadminded tolerance. He does not hesitate to call error by its name. This passage and similar ones in both John and Paul are frequent. Error and heresy for them are not just a case of sincere difference of opinion. But if Paul and John connect a *personal* lapse from the truth with sinfulness, still, they neither say nor imply that such sin permits force as a remedy against it. Also one must

remember that Paul and John did allow for a subjectively blame-
less error in some cases. (We have already heard Paul's words
to the new converts still clinging to pagan taboos.)

Exegetes, Catholic and Protestant, are in agreement that the
teaching on freedom found in the inspired writers of the Christian covenant is difficult to understand in all its subtle nuances.
Few will deny, however, that it has influenced profoundly the
individual Christian's concept of his own dignity and right to
freedom. Surely what is needed today is a general rediscovery
of the scriptural notion of freedom with its balancing comple-
ment of authority.[6] We will see when we look at the opinions of
the Fathers of the Church that the same regard for freedom was
immediately taken up and defended, and never completely lost
sight of, even when the major occupation of the Fathers had
become the battle with heresy.

The present state of knowledge concerning the New Testament
doctrine on church-state relations leaves much room for investigation, as is easily seen from this necessarily brief summary. In
the Scriptures, however, we see clearly an appreciation for the
State, a dedication to the Church, and a general idea as to what
form concrete relations between the two should take. Christ
foresaw the expansion of his little flock into a huge throng.
Indeed, he explicitly sent his apostles out to effect this growth:
"Go, therefore, and make all nations your disciples: baptize
them in the name of the Father and of the Son and of the Holy
Spirit" (Mt 28:19). Jesus intended that his whole doctrine be
brought to bear on whatever situation might be encountered.
He adds: ". . . and teach them to observe all the commandments
I have given you." He also evidently foresaw the difficulty that
would be encountered in preserving this teaching whole and
unpolluted in so many and different nations, down through so

6. See J. L. McKenzie, S.J., *Authority in the Church* (New York, 1966).

many changing ages. For he concludes with encouragement and an assurance of divine assistance. "And mark: I am with you at all times as long as the world will last." We must then work patiently in his light and strength as best we can.

Chapter Two

The Fathers of the Church

Patristic doctrine is considered by Christians as enjoying a privileged place in the ranks of authentic Christian teaching. After the Scriptures themselves, no group of writings is more highly respected. It is a body of writing by men closest in time to Christ, who cooperated closely with the Spirit as it guided the first steps of the new Church. They are therefore considered by all Christians as being worthy of trust and obedience.

In the areas of church-state doctrine and of religious liberty the writings of the Fathers are of truly immense importance. They contain within their scope the experiences of the Church under each of the three possible degrees of acceptance by the State: total rejection, total neutrality, and total accord. Everyone agrees that abstract theory is of relatively little value until it is subjected to the test of concrete practice. Further, the infinite complexities of concrete and individual social, cultural, and religious experience exert great influence on the formation and development of theory of any kind, including Christian doctrine. Indeed, what is theory but the formulation of the experience of the truth?

Both the Old and the New Testaments are nothing other than the inspired history of the people to whom God chose to reveal himself. The experiences of the Fathers in church-state relations and their formulations of these experiences in the light of Christ's teachings are but a continuation of this divine history of God's relations with men. They, of course, do not enjoy that intimate guidance which we call inspiration, but they do share in the same Spirit's assistance to a lesser degree. In fact, during its first five hundred years the Church experienced successively all the difficulties involved in living under persecution, under religious freedom, and finally under a State totally Christianized. This fact alone makes patristic times the most valuable source of all for truly Christian thinking on this problem.

There is still another reason for the special value of the patristic writings. It was during the fourth and fifth centuries that church-state relations took on the definite and settled shape which was to endure up to modern times. It is often thought that the so-called "union of Church and State" (a confusing and inaccurate phrase, as we shall see) was a product of the middle ages. Actually the close cooperation between the two societies was effected in its essentials during a single life-span, in which several of the greatest Fathers lived and wrote. Augustine, John Chrysostom, Gregory of Nyssa and Ambrose were witnesses and founders of the beginnings of the relationship. The middle ages saw only a continuation and evolution of a system which can in all accuracy be termed patristic.

For these reasons, therefore, it has been necessary to give to the patristic period a greater share of consideration. It is the fountainhead of Christian church-state relations as such. This is not to say that all the Fathers were happy with their situation in all its details, nor that any of them gave their consent to its abuses—nor even that the most representative of them saw no difficulty in defending it as such. We will see in the following pages what were their attitudes to this and other problems. We shall likewise see to what a striking extent the patristic church-state doctrine, like that of other ages, was a child of its times. And we shall see how existing circumstances forced the very leader of Christianity to all the boundaries set by Christ himself —and sometimes a little beyond them.

1. EARLY PATRISTIC TEACHING

As the name implies, the apostolic fathers were either in direct
contact with the apostles themselves or were closely linked to
them by teachers who had enjoyed such direct contact. During
this period relations with the State (which was synonymous
with the Roman empire) were practically non-existent for the
nascent Church. It had been under almost constant persecution
since Nero's reign, and it was not to know any long period of
peace until a considerable time after the last apostolic father
had ceased to write. Hence it is not surprising to find almost no
progress in church-state theory. When no relations exist, why
bother to speculate about what they should be?

The Fathers of this period contented themselves with echoing
the Scriptures. Besides a strong affirmation of the right of the
Christian assembly to exist and to function normally—an affirmation sealed in the very blood of the Fathers—there are several
clear references to the rights of the State which was their persecutor. These witnesses take a form almost identical to their
prototypes already seen in Paul. Clement of Rome in his first
letter to the Corinthians writes:

> Thou, O Master, through Thy transcendent and indescribable
> sovereignty hast given them the power of royalty, so that we,
> acknowledging the honor and glory conferred upon them by
> Thee, may bow to them, without in the least opposing Thy will.
> Grant to them, O Lord, health, peace, concord, and firmness, so
> that they may without hindrance exercise the supreme leader-
> ship Thou has conferred on them.[1]

Similarly Polycarp of Smyrna writes to the Philippians:

> Pray therefore for kings and men of power and rulers, and for
> those who persecute and hate you, and for the enemies of the
> cross . . ."[2]

1. Translation from *Readings in Church History*, ed. Colman Barry, I
(Westminster, Md., 1960), p. 20. Cf. Funk, *Patres Apostolici*, I (Tubingen,
1901), 179-80.
2. C. Barry, *ibid.*, p. 25. Cf. Migne, *Patres Graeci*, V, 1020. (Hereafter

In St. Ignatius of Antioch we find the same eschatological spirit regarding earthly kingdoms which we saw earlier in St. Paul: "Of no use to me will be the farthest reaches of the universe or the kingdoms of this world. I would rather die and come to Jesus Christ than be king over the entire earth.[3]

During this opening chapter of the patristic age, then, we find only a reflection of the Scriptures. And this state of development was adequate for the small and struggling Christian community of the early second century.

The apologists, following closely after the apostolic fathers, and representing a movement of evident human and divine dynamism, bear witness to Christian faith before their persecutors. Among their testimonies we find another stone added to the edifice of Christian church-state teaching: that of freedom of conscience and of religion. They accepted as a starting point the previously established doctrines of the divinely given right of both the State and the Church to exist and to exercise their respective functions. They then defend their right to worship God according to their beliefs. Beginning timorously with no more than an affirmation, each succeeding apologist adds breadth and depth to the concept.

The Roman prided himself on his broadmindedness in religious matters. Roman governors usually allowed the citizens of conquered lands to keep their gods, and even helped matters by worshipping these newly acquired divinities themselves. But one stipulation was insisted upon: the official Roman cult had to be given its place alongside the older divinities. This was generally a happy arrangement. The peoples of Greece, Egypt, and Babylonia had no strong objections to enriching their temples in this fashion. It worked well for Rome as it was a strong

---

Migne's *Patres Graeci* will be indicated by P.G.; *Patres Latini* will be indicated by P.L.)

3. Barry, p. 25. Cf. Ignatius, *Ep. to the Romans*, P.G., V, 691.

unifying force, allowing for peaceful communication between the conquered and the conqueror. In an extraordinary gesture of liberality the Jewish nation was even allowed to forego the cult of the Roman gods since it was an ancient religion and totally forbade syncretism to its people. But the same liberality was resolutely and constantly refused to the new Christian cult. They were almost immediately branded as enemies of the State and as atheists because they refused all recognition to the Roman demand of governing the way men worshipped.

It was this Roman broadmindedness that the first apologists appealed to. Around the year 150 A.D. Justin Martyr, one of the first and perhaps the greatest of the apologists, made the following appeal in a defence addressed to the emperor:

> . . . although we do no evil we are killed as evildoers. On the other hand, others worship trees, streams, mice, cats, . . . Each in turn, because he does not worship the same object, considers the other to be irreligious. The only thing which you can hold against us as grounds for accusation is that we do not worship the same gods as you.[4]

In this particular text Justin does not go beyond an appeal for fair play. In demanding freedom of worship for the Christians he asks only that they be given freedom of religion equal to others. Other apologists took up this theme and developed it. In 177, Athanagoras the Athenian invoked the same reason, and added that the logic behind the Roman's customary policy of religious freedom was fear of the divinity. To refuse a people freedom of worship was unjust and sacrilegious, and risked bringing down upon the State the ire of the offended god or gods.

> . . . both you and the civil law concede to all that absolutely no one god is wholly evil and wicked; rather, you judge that everyone should worship the god which he feels he should worship,

4. *I Apol.*, 24, ed. L. Pautigny (Paris: 1904), p. 48.

and thus keep from wickedness out of fear of that divine power. Why, therefore, is our name . . . held in contempt?[5]

Naturally neither Justin nor Athanagoras appealed to Christian doctrine as an authority in their plea for freedom. To appeal to the name of Christ would have carried no weight with their hearers. However, they imply clearly that they, as Christians, believed in freedom for all men to follow their religious convictions.

With each succeeding apologist the argument became more and more distinct. The next Christian voice to be raised in favor of religious freedom came from a different corner of the empire. The African, Tertullian, placed the argument on broader and more philosophical foundations. He appealed to a law recognized equally by the Romans and the Christians: the natural law. In the year 212 he addressed the following words to his local civil superior, the Roman proconsul Scapula:

> It is a fundamental human right, a privilege of nature, that every man should worship according to his own convictions; one man's religion neither harms nor helps another man. It is not proper to force religion. It must be undertaken freely, not under pressure. Sacrifices are to be demanded only from a willing soul. And so, though you may compel us to sacrifice, you will, in doing so, be offering nothing at all to your gods.[6]

Here we have, from the most important Latin Father of his day, a clear statement of what was to become the accepted Christian teaching on what was later to be called "freedom of conscience." Not one Christian writer has ever denied it, even during periods where practice could hardly be squared with the principle. Tertullian's language here is not that of later writers, but his thought is clear enough. Religious belief is a

---

5. *Legatio pro Christianis,* 37, P.G., 971.
6. *Ad Scapulam,* P.L., I, 699. See G. Guinebert, *Tertullien* (Paris, 1901), p. 145 ff., and C. Becker, *Tertulliens Apologeticum* (München, 1954), p. 384 ff.

matter of interior conviction. This belief, by its very nature, can in no way be forced. Any outward manifestation, if brought forth either by moral or by physical force, is utterly worthless and abominable. The authority appealed to is human nature itself, and is patently valid for men of all creeds. We see at once how universal and how Christian is this truth, when we see it springing up in various parts of the Christian community. It was the major weapon of the apologists against the cruelties of Roman totalitarianism. Christ's law is essentially one of love and not of force, and this law was made by the same Creator who fashioned human nature.

After the empire became a formally Christian one, those Fathers who defended the forcible restraint of heresy were always at pains to try to show how the force advocated did not go so far as to violate this basic principle of human rights. This we shall see below.

The apologists, like the apostolic fathers, lived in an era when no formal relations existed between the Catholic Church and the State. Therefore they did not greatly concern themselves with the problem. Nevertheless, in developing the concept of freedom of conscience, they gave to Christian tradition one of the most important concepts in its doctrine of church-state relationships. It was the subsequent period which really gave to the Church a formal system of church-state relations.

2. THE GOLDEN AGE

We, Constantinus and Licinius the Emperors, having met in concord at Milan and having set in order everything which pertains to the common good and public security, are of the opinion that among the various things which we perceived would profit men, or which should be set in order first, was to be found the cultivation of religion; we should therefore give both to Christians and to all others free facility to follow the religion which each may desire.[1]

The above Edict of Milan, published June 13, 313 by the then co-reigning emperors Constantine and Licinius, is doubtless one of the most important documents in the history of church-state relations. Its effects in its own day were immense, and throughout subsequent centuries it exercised great weight in the formation of both practical policy and abstract theory. Though the edict is a wholly civil, not a patristic, document, its significance must be noted here because like other civil regulations regarding religion, it literally created the concrete and official civil set of day-to-day relationships with religion. Its influence on the thinking of the Fathers was very great. On the other hand, the influence of previous Fathers on the very coming into existence of the edict is beyond question.

But, immensely important as it was in its own right, the Edict of Milan actually carried much less practical influence during the subsequent millenium than did another edict: that of Thessalonica, published February 27, 380. Following the Edict of Milan by less than a single lifespan, the Edict of Thessalonica was, according to one way of looking at it, a total reversal of the religious policy of its predecessor. In it the Emperors Theodosius and Valentinian decreed:

> It is our will that all the peoples who are ruled by the administration of Our Clemency shall practice that religion which the divine Peter the Apostle transmitted to the Romans.[2]

1. From the Edict of Milan, as contained in *De mortibus persecutorum*, P.L., VII, 267 ff., (Barry, p. 77). See also N. Baynes, "Constantine the Great and the Christian Church," in the *Proceedings of the British Academy*, 1931, and S. Greenslade, *Church and State from Constantine to Theodosius* (London, 1954), pp. 9-36.

2. *Codex Theodosianus*, XVI, I, 2, Mommsen (Berlin, 1905), 833 ff. (Barry, p. 142). This is the first certain establishment of the Church. The laws of Constantine and their exact import are disputed by historians, cf. Augustin Fliche and Victor Martin, (eds.), *Histoire de l'Eglise depuis les Origènes jusqu'a nos jours*, 21 vols. (Paris, 1936-1963), III, pp. 181-182.

By this proclamation the Roman empire formally became a Christian one. Theodosius, who in the meantime had become sole emperor of both East and West, soon made it clear that this was aimed not only at heretics, as the text might lead one to believe, but was intended for all men of whatever previous religious leanings, living anywhere in the vastness of empire. By subsequent edicts he ordered all pagan temples closed and forbade pagan worship under pain of grave punishments.

At first glance, perhaps, this new policy of Theodosius seems to be another about-face in church-state matters: a switch from total religious freedom to a total wedding of the empire to the Christian faith. Actually it is closer to the facts to describe the change as a steady and rapid advancement in a single direction: from paganism to the Christian religion. Since the time of Jesus and his apostles the Christian faith had spread rapidly through the hearts of the empire's peoples. Every weapon in the hands of a totalitarian State was thrown against it in vain. The Roman military and civil force, the force of pagan philosophy, the power of economic persuasion—all were powerless before the mighty advance. A policy of official tolerance was really wrung, in its first instance, from the emperor who had engineered the last of the persecutions. The tone of the edict of the Emperor Galerius (311) sums up well the final overwhelming of the official resistance to the Christians. Its manner is almost pathetic:

> Among the other measures that we frame for the use and profit of the state, it had been our own wish formerly that all things should be set to rights in accordance with the ancient laws and public order of the Romans; and to make provision for this, namely, that the Christians also, such as had abandoned the persuasion of their own ancestors, should return to a sound mind; seeing that through some reasoning they had been possessed of such self-will and seized with such folly that instead of following the institutions of the ancients, which perchance their own forefathers had formerly established, they made for themselves, and were observing, laws merely in accordance with their

own disposition and as each one wishes, and were assembling various multitudes in divers places: Therefore when a command of ours soon followed to the intent that they should betake themselves to the institutions of the ancients, very many indeed were subjected to peril, while very many were harassed and endured all kinds of death; And since the majority held to the same folly, and we perceived that they were neither paying the worship due to the gods of heaven nor honoring the god of the Christians; having regard to our clemency and the invariable custom by which we are wont to accord pardon to all men, we thought it right in this case also to extend most willingly our indulgence: That Christians may exist again and build the houses in which they used to assemble, always provided that they do nothing contrary to order.[3]

Such was the power of Christians in that era. The following year religious tolerance was placed on the more dignified foundation of a right of nature by the Edict of Milan. From the above necessarily long quotation one can appreciate the steady forward thrust of Christianity. Its momentum carried it on until, in the reign of Theodosius, it replaced paganism as the official religion of the State; and the former incumbent of this favored place took its position among the persecuted.

In order that the church-state teaching of the Fathers of this period be appreciated accurately we must describe the civil position a bit more completely. The Roman empire, though it gave ever increasing recognition to Christians, remained the same Roman empire. That magnificent government, well ordered by the sound, well-balanced complex of Roman law, had lost little of its forcefulness as director of the civilized world. Though the empire was already split into East and West, the emperors still had the traditionally firm control over most areas of public life. They considered themselves and were considered

3. As quoted by Lactantius, *De Morte Persecutorum*, P.L., VII, 249-250 (Barry, pp. 76-77).

by everyone as being the personal embodiment of the world State. None other existed.

When Constantine appeared on the scene, the fact that he favored the Christian Church made relatively little difference. Though baptized on his deathbed, he had remained throughout his long reign—officially, if not in practice—the Summus Pontifex of the pagan Roman religion. Even his sons, the emperors Constantine II, Constantius and Constant, remained officially the supreme directors of both civil and religious matters. In all probability the pagan subjects still considered them divine.

They had been reared as Christians. They continued their father's policies respecting State relations to religion in almost every respect. One important exception was the fact that for the greater part of their reign they supported heretical bishops against the orthodox ones. But, though as Christians they "rendered to God the things that were God's," they remained Caesars to the core. Like their father, they did not hesitate to wield the traditional imperial influence on religion. As Christians they recognized the bishops and the popes as supreme in matters of the faith; but they convoked councils, "appointed" bishops and saw that Church laws were obeyed. Nor did they intend anything in these actions other than a conscientious fulfillment of their office.[4]

They gave privileges of judging even civil cases to bishops, similar to the rights of the pagan Roman magistrates. Constantine had already begun to divest paganism of its capacity as the official state religion. He allowed Christians to exercise civil functions without the traditional acts of pagan cult. Roman sol-

---

4. If the emperors remained emperors after their conversion, it is no less true that the Christian leaders—bishops and people—remained Roman citizens. What must not be forgotten is that the finished product of both civil law and patristic and conciliar doctrine was a result of a mutual cross-fertilization of the Caesars and Christians. This truth, sometimes forgotten, is vital for an accurate view of the development of church-state doctrine during its most crucial stage. Cf. for example, Fliche-Martin, III, p. 65.

diers were no longer required to have any connections with paganism.

His sons continued this leveling process. They added favors to the Christians and subtracted privileges from the pagans. But they could not endanger their personal authority by removing all traces of connection between their office and the religion so closely linked to it by hundreds of years of tradition. Though sincere in their Christian faith, it was both psychologically impossible and politically unthinkable to erase immediately the strong lines of unity between the imperial throne and the temples of the empire's gods.[5]

The Emperor Julian (361-365) succeeded the sons of Constantine, and once again united the empire under one ruler. But Julian was a pagan, and from all appearances a sincere and devout one.[6] In order to reestablish paganism he brought back the policy of official freedom of religion, which had begun to wilt under the Constantinian dynasty. His rule however was a short one—scarcely three years.

His successor, Jovian (363-364), ruled less than a year. From his time on there were only Christian emperors, and these resumed the policies of Constantine and his sons. Valentinian I (364-375) and Valens (364-378), while maintaining official freedom of cult, favored their Christian faith. Gratian (375-383 in the West and 378-379 in the East) appears somewhat contradictory in these matters. He was a Christian and at first followed what was becoming the traditional course of Christian emperors: official neutrality accompanied by overt persecution of paganism. But it was he who actually achieved almost total separation of paganism from the Roman State. He took away the State revenues of the pagan priests and the support for their temples and ceremonies—a fatal blow.

5. See K. Voigt, *Staat und Kirche von Konstantin dem grossen bis zum Ende der Karolingerzeit* (Stuttgart, 1936), pp. 34-39.
6. See Fliche-Martin, III, pp. 183-191.

Following Gratian came Theodosius, first in the East (379) and then also in the West. Here a climax was reached, for with Theodosius the empire became a Christian State. A new era opened, that of "Christendom," of a western world which for more than a millenium would have at least one common trait in all its governments: profession of the Christian faith as the official religion. Paganism became a civil offence punishable by severe sanctions:

> If ever the pagans who remain are apprehended in the act of sacrificing to their devils, though they should be subjected to capital punishment, they shall at least suffer conscription of their goods and exile.[7]

The Roman emperor, still very much the master of the world, by such prescriptions transformed his empire into an officially Christian one. Effects on practical relations between empire and the Church were great but paradoxical. During the ensuing era Church and State were, in a sense, united but were more separate than they had ever been in the history of the world. Neither Egypt, nor Greece, nor Israel, nor Babylonia, at the height of their influence, had granted religion such independence from the political regime as the Christian Church enjoyed.

On the other hand, of course, this separation of religion from the State did not leave matters of religion in the hands of the individual. It supported with its might a separate institution which it considered to have been deputed to govern religion by God himself. The result of this arrangement was certainly not complete freedom of religion. However, the removal of religious leadership from the hands of political masters was an advance of incalculable importance for religion in general and for church-state history in particular.

After the Edict of Milan Christian thinkers were able to express themselves freely. Christian schools could integrate thought and

7. Cod. Theod. XVI, 10, 23, June 8, 423: Mommsen, 902.

form the minds of youth to see implications and applications of Christ's divine message. The result of this situation was a series of brilliant thinkers still afire with the zeal of the martyrs and able to give full intellectual account of their convictions. Ambrose and Augustine in the West and John Chrysostom, Athanasius and Gregory of Nyssa in the East are among the most outstanding by almost any standard, and no less so for our subject. We have noted that until this period church-state doctrine was limited to general affirmations of the legitimate authority of the State and its duty to allow freedom to the Church and to religious practice in general.[8] The developments made during the remainder of the patristic age can be divided as follows:

1) The development of a concept of human society as a unified whole wherein the Church and the State exist side by side and collaborate in leading society toward its temporal and eschatological ends.

2) The specification of areas where the two instruments meet and aid one another.

a) The Church aids civil order by achieving public morality and teaching the duty of all men to support the State by administration, taxes and military service.

b) The State aids the Church by guarding her institutions against violence and by using its might in limited measures against heresy, schism and paganism.

3) Attempts at the solution of the problem of freedom of belief occasioned by the use of civil restraint on "unbelievers."

1. *The patristic concept of human society:* Once the Christian faith was recognized civilly as the truth, the Christian concept of what humanity is could be applied to the existing society. In

---

8. By the time of the Golden Age of the Fathers the barbarians had already overrun large portions of the empire, and the civil authority was imperceptibly moving towards the loose, semi-anarchic structure of the early middle ages.

formulating this concept the Fathers used as a foundation the
teaching of Jesus and the Scriptures. This, however, was merely
a beginning. In the infinitely complex task of comprehending
and arranging human society, the more specific (but practically
important) areas must always be built up slowly and painfully,
by using elements which only centuries of experience can guarantee to be genuine. This task, however, is unavoidable in any
society, and the Fathers, the guiding lights in the first Christian
centuries, did have firm truths as a starting point.

Man was created by God and then was commanded to "mul-
tiply and fill the earth and subdue it" (Gen 1:28). God is the
Lord of nations, holding all creatures in his hand and manifesting his glory through them. In such a concept there can be no
airtight partitioning of the sacred from the civil. Both areas are
before all else creatures and humble servants of their Lord and
judge. Christ's "Render to Caesar the things that are Caesar's
and to God the things that are God's" could never be seriously
interpreted as meaning that ultimately even Caesar's things are
not also God's. Caesar's authority comes from God, as Christ
reminded Pilate, and Paul gives its ultimate purpose and end:
"He [the civil authority] is God's minister, an avenger to inflict
punishment on evildoers" (Rom 13:4).

It was this over-all concept of humanity, with its natural and
supernatural ramifications seen together, which the Fathers took
as a starting point. But their final view was also necessarily
influenced by the existing customs and institutions of their age.
Let us examine their writings.

Ambrose was among the first to express a comprehensive view
of Church and State in human society. His background experience made him excellently prepared to do so. The son of a
Roman civil official, he had abandoned a brilliant beginning in
the same field to become, by popular demand, the bishop of
Milan. He was, then, intimately aware of the functioning and
needs of both the societies concerned. That he saw them both

as creatures of God is illustrated by the following significant event. The emperor, calling on his supreme dominion over all things, demanded possession of Ambrose's cathedral. Ambrose responded:

> . . . I am ready to give him whatever is mine. My property, my money and all such things (though everything which I own really belongs to the poor): this I would not deny him. But things which belong to God are not subject to imperial power.

Later in the same document, he repeats:

> It is alleged that anything is permitted to the emperor; that all things belong to him. I answer, do not burden yourself, O emperor, by thinking that you have some sort of right over those things which belong to God. Do not so exalt yourself; rather, if you wish to keep on ruling, be yourself subject to God. For it is written, "Render to Caesar the things that are Caesar's, and to God the things that are God's" (Mt 28:21). Palaces belong to the emperor, churches to the priest.[9]

Here Ambrose's over-all conception of society is clearly visible. It is scriptural in structure. Time and again he repeats the same doctrine in various circumstances. Canon Holmes Dudden, in his *Life and Times of St. Ambrose,* sums up his doctrine as follows:

> Ambrose himself had no desire to exercise political power. He regarded the Church and the State as two independent authorities, each autonomous within its own sphere, but each rendering general support and assistance to the other. The Church offers prayers for the State and the State is the "secular arm" which gives effect to the decisions of the Church. The spiritual and the temporal authorities collaborate.[10]

It was, however, Ambrose's spiritual son, Augustine, who formulated the classic Christian theory of human society. In his *City of God* Augustine elaborated the above idea and integrated

9. Epis. XX. 8, P.L. XVI, 996, 999.
10. Oxford: Clarendon Press, 1935, II, p. 500.

the whole of history with it. Augustine's two cities, the heavenly city and the terrestrial one, do not correspond to the Church and the State. The heavenly city in its fullest sense literally embraces heaven and earth, and is essentially eschatological. Here below the two are inextricably intermingled. The great Father's idea of the State is a wonderful example of the grand simplicity of his thought. There is no exaggerated duality between natural and supernatural, for (like St. Paul) he sees everything through the eyes of faith. The State is God's earthly authority to keep peace and promote prosperity so that man can more easily attain his final divine end:

> Things being as they are, let us attribute to no one the power of giving rule and empire except to the true God, who gives happiness in the kingdom of heaven only to the holy, but who gives the governance of territories to both the pious and the impious, according to his good pleasure, for whom no unjust thing is pleasing.[11]

The both societies, if they serve God in the manner intended by him, will cooperate amicably and peacefully in advancing toward the unique, ultimate goal of human society. The State's immediate function of keeping temporal order must never be seen as an end in itself. It is rather a means. Both Church and State have their proper duties and their proper instruments, and no one has a right to interfere with them. But this should be a cause of unity and peace, because each has need of the other. Only sin, and the blindness and strife which follow from it, can and do wreck this harmony. The fallen condition of man is the unique cause of discord and a common enemy of both.

Augustine did not concern himself with the exact boundaries of Church and State. He simply wrote that the State functions for promoting temporal well-being. If he allowed for a certain

11. *De civitate Dei,* Book V, 1, P.L. XLI, 167. For a balanced description of Augustine's Church-State doctrine see H. X. Arquillière, *L'Augustinism Politique* (Paris, 1934).

intercommunication of authority—as we will see that he did—
he saw no contradiction in doing so. He concerned himself primarily with the common goal of the two societies and not with
their respective frontiers. He took for granted that the State,
being in itself essentially an instrument, would recognize the
supernatural order centered in the Church and cooperate with it.

But, while admitting the greatness of his thesis and its fundamental validity, it is only just to point out an important limita-
tion in this Augustinian masterpiece. The *City of God* is controversy literature: it is apologetical. It undertakes to defend the
status quo, the newly Christianized empire. The unthinkable
had become a reality, and Rome had been sacked by barbarians.
The abandoning of the gods for a thoroughly Christianized
government was the cause alleged by the pagans: a most serious
and damaging charge.

It was under these circumstances that Augustine constructed
his grand theory of government. The object of the work is,
therefore, not primarily the outlining of an ideal Christian State,
or the crystallization of Christ's and the apostles' teachings on
the subject. Rather, the object is first of all to defend what was
actually in existence. True, the ultimate nature of both Church
and State are treated, but these concepts are called up and
marshalled into battle in order to defend the edifice which
Constantine and Theodosius had already constructed. The
weakness of such an approach is exemplified in Augustine's very
negative treatment of the pagan empire.

In Book Nineteen he goes so far as to claim that, because it
lacked true (that is, supernatural) justice, the pagan *respublica*
did not ever really exist. The reason for such a claim is evident.
It was against a return to such a pagan State that his whole tract
was directed. Later, in the same Book, he retracts this claim, and
accepts as more probable the opinion that all the great pagan
States were indeed legitimate. But how great an influence would
the first claim, and similar ones, have on subsequent thinkers!

Such weakness does not, of course, destroy the whole validity
of Augustine's thought. Every thinker, to be sure, is influenced
by circumstances and practical considerations to some degree.
The great merit of the *City of God* is precisely in its author's
demonstrated ability to rise above so great a portion of his circumstantial limitations, and consider institutions in their fundamental aspects.

But political institutions are, more than most, highly change-
able. Augustine's aim was to defend one particular constellation
of relations between the Church and one particular type of
State, the Roman empire. This end could not have but influenced
the course his genius took in conceiving the *City of God*.

The magnificent unity and all-embracing scope of Augustine's
view of human society inspired the minds and hearts of churchmen and statesmen alike during the ensuing centuries. It bound
the interior life of man and his external, social activity together,
making them mesh accurately in a way that they never had
before. Its influence in western political thought has been incalculable. Etienne Gilson, in a foreword written to an English translation of the *City of God*, gives us in a few words an idea of the
importance of this work and of its startling comprehensiveness:

> The historical significance of the *City of God* can hardly be
> exaggerated. From the point of view of St. Augustine himself,
> it was a companion to the *Confessions*, whose final books deal
> with the history of Creation as told in Holy Writ. With Creation
> the history of man began; that is, the centuries-old tale of two
> cities, a tale which will end with the final triumph of the City
> of God, the ultimate end, and final cause of the divine work of
> Creation.[12]

The *City of God* may well be considered the Magna Carta of
Christian church-state relations during the patristic and medieval periods. Its theory of human society is clearly derived from

12. *City of God*, Books I-VII, translated by Demetrius Zeno and Gerald
Walsh (New York, 1950), p. lxxxii.

the scriptural teachings on creation, the original sin, and the distinction of Church and State. It is a work whose major inspiration is indeed from the Old and New Testaments.

But Augustine built a theory which used Scripture only as a starting point for its vast edifice. The superstructure contains stones quarried from many and various sources, not the least of which is, as we will see, the very Roman tradition which he makes his central point of comparison. It is for this reason that the Christian concept of society forged by the Fathers was a rich and solid one: at once original, for its basis was Christ; but at the same time very traditional, for it by no means scorned to re-use all that was most solid in the crumbling pagan empire.

One example of this borrowing from Rome is very important for our study—the intermingling of religious and civil authority. Certainly this is not a scriptural concept. But the Fathers are unanimous in giving the State a rather large authority in matters essentially religious, and in granting to the Church powers which are really political. What better place in which to seek the source of this policy than in the milieu in which the Fathers were born, reared and educated? We have already seen how closely religion and politics were united in the empire.

Both Ambrose and Augustine were outstanding students of the Roman tradition before their conversion. They saw nothing unchristian in a degree of intercommunication of authority between Church and State, and they saw grave dangers from a sudden rupture between the two. So they tailored a time-tested system to meet Christian standards, changing only what they considered contrary to Christ's teachings.

Since Christian revelation said little enough about church-state relations, the Fathers found little to eliminate from the pagan Roman system. By simply putting the Christian faith in the former place of paganism and making minor necessary adjustments, the essential task was done. Much of the authoritarian position as regards religion was kept. It is true, one could not be forced to accept the orthodox Christian faith, but one could—according to the Fathers' view—be forced not to practice anything else. These patristic views on what constituted unchristian force on the religious conscience will be discussed in the last section of this chapter.

Such was the manner in which the patristic theory of human society was formed. But it is necessary to look more carefully at the details of this theory. What were the precise relations between Church and State? In exactly what areas did Church and civil authority meet and intertwine?

2. *Specific areas of contact:* We have seen that under Constantine contacts between Church and State became possible. Since that emperor and most of his successors favored the Christians, they immediately began to make official contacts a reality. Once the Church became the official religion—in itself an outstanding example of an official contact—the areas where the Church and State met took on a definite shape. Besides simple contacts there was a mutual intermingling of civil and religious authority in certain areas. We will first consider the patristic doctrine about the areas where the Church occupied essentially civil terrain.

a) Areas where the Church shared civil authority: The first duty of the Church toward the State, according to the Fathers, was prayer. This, of course, was inherited from the apostolic fathers. By paying taxes, obeying civil laws and upholding public morality, the Church was also making the task of the State lighter and easier to achieve. By lifting her early ban against Christians holding offices of public service, both civil and military, and beginning to insist on the Christian's obligations in these matters, the Church dutifully aligned itself among the friends and supporters of the post-Constantinian State. All these measures received the full support of the Fathers. Augustine says in this regard:

If anyone thinks that because he is a Christian he ought not have to pay taxes, that he ought not have to pay tribute or honor to the officials who look after such matters, such a one is in serious error. After long deliberation we have come to realize that the chief concern which our love of the people has placed upon us is our guardianship of the true religion. If our nation could only hold fast to the worship of God we would be on the road to prosperity in all of our human affairs.[13]

Up to this point there is no question of the Church sharing the State's authority. There is only a single example of such direct civil power exercised by Church officials that is recognized by the Fathers as legitimate. This was a limited judicial power. From Constantine on, bishops were given official power to act as civil judges in certain cases. The people were given the right to have their cases tried by an ecclesiastical court if they so preferred.[14] Along with this direct civil power, churchmen were given a special place in other matters. Bishops could intercede for clemency after a condemnation by civil judges. Criminals were also given certain privileges of asylum when they fled to the bishops. Gratian and Theodosius granted exemption from civil trial to delinquent members of the clergy. This system of civil judiciary power was approved of by patristic writers such as Ambrose. He had the confidence and respect of the emperors Gratian, Valentinian and (in the end) Theodosius: the rulers responsible for most of the original enactments of this nature.[15] Not that Ambrose considered such favors to be a right essentially connected with the office of bishop and priests; we will examine the reasons for these and similar enactments at the end of this chapter.

But patristic teaching allowed religious influence on the State a much broader scope than actual civil authority. There are two important examples of civil influence being exercised by bishops which did not entail any specific civil authority. The first is the

13. *Propositio lxxii*, P.L. XXXV, 2083.
14. Fliche-Martin, III, 519-521.
15. J. Palanque, *Ambroise et l'Empire romain* (Paris, 1933), p. 43 ff.

"right" of bishops to invoke the aid of civil force in religious difficulties such as heresy, schism and the like. This was not incorporated into formal law, but it was successfully used time and again by Church officials. It is again St. Ambrose who first defended the justice of such trading in jurisdictions.[16] The second claim is still broader and more powerful. And while essentially religious in nature, it carried political significance of great magnitude. The bishops, as Christ's representatives, were responsible for preserving Christian morality in the Church. The emperor's edicts and policies were not beyond morality, but must conform to it if they were to claim the title and dignity of Christian legislation. If the representatives of the State act in an immoral fashion they must be judged guilty, as any other man.[17] It is for the bishops to judge. In this way, the religious authority exercised a virtual veto over large areas of political behavior. For instance, when the Emperor Theodosius perpetrated his slaughter of the citizens of Thessalonica he found himself suddenly outside the Church and treated like any other grave sinner. He was readmitted only after having done sufficient penance.[18] Gregory Nazianzus expresses succinctly why the emperor must obey him as a bishop: because the bishop represents the "law of Christ"—"For Christ's law subjects even you to my authority and office."[19]

When these points of religious influence in civil matters are considered objectively, they are seen to rest on very small legal grounds. Had the emperor wished, he could have gone directly contrary to the Church without even violating the existing legislation. The influence was almost entirely a moral one. But,

16. *Epist. xvii*, P.L., XVI, 961.
17. This is a good example of how Christian revelation did, in fact, originate separation between Church and State. Before Christianity it would have been unthinkable for an emperor to accept being judged by another power.
18. H. Dudden, I, pp. 381-392.
19. *Oratio xvii*, P.G., XXXV, 975.

though moral, the power was nevertheless great, for the State was Christian and believed that human society could best be served by close cooperation and mutual assistance between civil and religious authority. The sharp delineations of boundary lines between the two, of which the modern world is so conscious, simply had not yet evolved. The Fathers and their civil rulers were more preoccupied with the whole than with a careful separation of its parts.

> And therefore, neither those who govern the civil realm nor they who govern the spiritual have been able to administer their offices in a successful manner. Let them first govern well their own affairs in a fitting manner and then they will keep each other's laws without any difficulty. For it is true that there exists a double sphere of authority in the public forum, just as two authorities are also within the individual. And in the first as in the second case, the spiritual authority goes before the civil.[20]

b) Areas where the State shared ecclesiastical authority: If the influence of the Church in political matters was very broad in the patristic doctrine, the weight of civil authorities in religious matters was more decisive. This latter influence can best be divided into two sections—civil authority in enforcing orthodoxy, and imperial right to convoke councils.

1) Enforcement of Orthodoxy: Once the emperor declared by the Edict of Thessalonica that the Christian Church was the official State religion, he was committed to enforce his declaration. Though the Fathers unanimously insisted that no one be forced to join the Church, they were—despite what appears to us as somewhat of a contradiction—just as unanimously in favor of forcibly preventing adherence to paganism, schismatic sects and heresy.

The method of constraint for each of the three types differed in severity. As we have seen, paganism was totally forbidden,

20. St. John Chrysostom, *Homilia xv in II Epist. ad Corinthians*, P.G., LXI, 507.

and imperial edict decreed the death penalty for violators. The
Fathers disapproved only of the penalty (but in this disapproval
they were firm and unanimous).[21] Schismatics and heretics were
proscribed, their churches and other property seized, and recal-
citrant individuals subject usually to fines, imprisonment and
the lash. Jews alone, of all non-Christians, were allowed some
freedom of worship, for they believed at least in the one, true
God. They were, however, forbidden to proselytize and were
subject to various limitations in other matters.[22]

This attitude of the Fathers permitting force against unbelievers is difficult for us to understand, much less to approve. It
is intelligible only when we understand fully their concept of
the totality of human society. Some of the Fathers' notion of
the nature of conscience was a contributory factor, as we will
see. Still, these laws were not considered by men in patristic
times as a State entry into the authority of the Church. That is
a modern way of describing the phenomenon. It was the Church
who made the final decision as to what was the true religion.
The emperor, according to patristic thinking, only lent his might
to protect and foster what the Church decided in matters of
religion: "The emperor should watch over religion, and he
should not demand from religious authorities any countenancing
of false religious practices."[23]

Still such policy necessarily involved religious power. The
emperor could make use of his civil power only after deciding
that a purely religious matter—orthodoxy—was also within the
competence of the State. Whatever the precise degree of actual
religious power he exercised, in exercising it, the ruler thereby
wielded a tremendous and direct influence on religion. In the
eyes of the unbelievers it was the State which was to be feared.

21. See Joseph Lecler, *Toleration and the Reformation*, trans. T. L.
Weston, 2 vols. (New York, 1960), I, pp. 59-60.
22. See below, in this chapter, "Freedom of Conscience and the
Fathers."
23. Ambrose, *Epist. xvii*, P.L., XVI, 961.

In the eyes of the orthodox bishops, action or non-action on the part of the State made a great difference in their conception of ecclesiastical authority.

But there is another side to the question. Often, particularly at the beginning, the reason for the emperor's action was largely a civil one. Religious quarrels in those days usually had serious effects on public peace and order. Similarly, from the Fathers' point of view, internal ecclesiastical peace was a primary motive for advocating State force. They were reluctant to use force of any kind in the service of the Gospel. In particular were they loath to call in the secular arm. This measure is always considered exceptional in the Fathers. Augustine and Ambrose were always at pains to explain how circumstances forced them.

The reason for this hesitation is always the same: religious doctrine is, in itself, not the affair of the State. It was not so much a matter of clear principle, allowing this State force, as practical necessity on both sides, since they were unable to find any other effective means. St. Augustine at first limited his calls for assistance to cases of public violence. In the end he speaks out for this State restraint, while in the same breath asking that restraint itself not be considered but rather the reason for it:

> Wherefore, if those people found in the hedges and byways [i.e., heretics and schismatics] are forced to come to the wedding feast, prodded by the power which the Church receives by divine graciousness from the piety and belief of our kings; let them not complain that they are being forced to do so. Rather let them understand *why* they are so forced.[24]

2) The second case of State use of essentially religious authority consists in civil convocation of councils. Such official ecclesiastical assemblies concern only religious problems and they are, so it appears today, in no way the object of civil authority. The emperors of the first Christian centuries did not see it in

---

24. *Epist. clxxxv*, P.L., XXXIII, 804.

this way, however, and began immediately to call bishops together by imperial decree. The Fathers implicitly gave their approval by themselves asking the emperor to use this questionable power.

The great Ecumenical Council of Nicea was convoked by Constantine, at the behest of the Catholic bishops. Augustine not only asked the emperor to use the same power, but defended his right to do so. Against the Donatists, he and his fellow African bishops made use of imperial convocations. He defended the procedure in his famous letter to the heretical bishop, Vincent.[25] During the patristic era, little objection was voiced against this practice. Ambrose accepted it as at least the established mode of procedure.

We see, then, that the State authority in religious matters was small, perhaps, when the number of actual laws allowing it are considered, but quite extensive when viewed in its practical effects.

The linking of Church and State authority which we have described is one of the basic characteristics of the socio-religious thought of the patristic period. It was their legacy to the middle ages. But when the views of both emperors and Fathers are examined carefully on this point, an important fact becomes clear—*neither side had as yet crystallized its idea of how far its own authority extended.* Both admitted a degree of overlapping. Neither attempted to define how far the overlapping could proceed.

As time went on, both began to see the danger involved: encroachment from the other, for the existence of a roughly defined middle ground constituted a temptation to ambitious leaders of either party. Still, the lack of clarity was perfectly natural. Since such matters were not included in revelation, the

25. *Epist. xciii*, P.L., XXXIII, 321-347.

two authorities involved had to work out a system gradually within the framework of mutually accepted principles.

Such an evolutionary process is not the work of pure theory. One does not design church-state relations on a drawing-board. They are the work of the centuries. A Roman empire of new dimensions had just been born—one limited, and even dominated, in religious matters by a newly accepted, divine authority. But what remained was still the Roman empire, with a very traditional mode of procedure. The exact frontiers of imperial power in religion had to be mapped out slowly and painstakingly by years of coexistence.

The same concept is valid for the Church. Only the bare essentials of the structure of the Church are revealed. During the patristic age of which we speak here, the Church was indeed a novice at socio-civil relations. The guide-rules were few. Only time and experience could sound out its limits in relation to the State with any great degree of accuracy. The state of affairs described in this chapter was the "deposit" of the first age of this evolutionary process.

The resulting frontiers were, therefore, understandably vague. The Church is a living thing. It grows and develops. Just as the organs of an embryo, an infant, and a youth evolve and differentiate themselves into ever more defined entities; so do those visible organs of the Church—her hierarchy, her doctrine, and her authority in relation to civil societies—become ever more sharply defined. One cannot expect, already in Augustine's age, to find clear-cut boundaries in church-state relations. Beyond certain necessary features founded on revelation, only time could distinguish the passing from the permanent.

But one final point remains to be clarified in this regard: the question of the exact origin of the areas of union we have just examined. Though patristic writers gave their assent, one cannot conclude that they deduced this system from abstract principles of their faith by a purely syllogistic process. The centuries of religious power in the hands of the Roman emperors surely played an immense role here, for it could not simply have broken off suddenly with the conversion of Constantine.[26] This matter of origin is of utmost importance for our subject. It concerns nothing less than the precise nature and degree of unchangeability of a type of union between Church and State which lasted for more than a thousand years, and which still wields influence today. It is necessary, then, to return to the concrete examples of this union and search for the origin of each one.

What was the actual origin of the judicial powers of bishops that we have described? Did the emperors give these powers because the pagan priesthood and the office of civil magistrate were united traditionally in the pagan empire? Or was it because they were convinced that a spiritual leader had a right to such civil powers? There is little evidence to support the latter possibility. The former, however, is very probable.

Christians, at the time when these laws were enacted, were in great need of acquiring dignity before the public. What better way for a Christian-minded emperor such as Constantine to accomplish this than to raise the Christian bishops to the dignity and trust of public office, making them the equals of the pagan *Flammes* (who were at the same time public magistrates)?[27] It is unlikely that the privileges came from the promptings of the bishops.[28] Ambrose, whose opinions were respected by most of the emperors of his age, and Augustine as well, complained that the privilege was a burden hindering pastoral duties.

26. See R. W. Carlyle and A. J. Carlyle, *A History of Medieval Political Theory in the West*, 6 vols. (London, 1930), I, p. 3.

27. See Fliche-Martin, III, p. 61, and also p. 560.

28. The laws exempting the clergy from being tried in civil courts most probably *did* come from doctrinal and religious motives, for trial by pagan judges would have harmed their apostolate. But the central civil authority considered here is the power given to bishops themselves to judge cases of all kinds, not just erring priests.

It is true that Pope Gelasius was to claim these powers as a right because of the hierarchy's essentially superior authority, but this was at a much later period, and was made within the context of a growing rivalry for power between the papacy and the throne.[29] From all appearances, therefore, the purely civil judiciary power given to the bishops by Constantine had for its major inspiration, not the bishop's right to such power but a common desire on both sides that the Christian religion be placed at least on equal footing with the pagan cult. Hence, this particular bond between Church and State originated from the circumstantial needs of the era which gave it birth.[30]

Now let us consider the origin of the two examples of imperial sharing of religious authority; and first, the imperial right to call councils. Almost as soon as an emperor recognized the right of the Church to exist he began to take a part in its internal affairs. Constantine, without any hesitation or authorization, convoked the Council of Arles less than two years (August 314) after the Edict of Milan.[31] This example was imitated time and again by his successors, until a tradition of imperial influence in councils was established. It is morally certain that Constantine did not consult Pope Sylvester before he called that first council. Rather he seems to have done all he could to limit the pope's influence therein.

However, Constantine's action was not without good reason. The Arian heresy was causing great civil unrest. If a council could resolve the difficulty it would be rendering valuable civil service. The same was true of most of the ensuing councils. The system even offered advantages to the Church. Councils called

29. See W. Ullman, *The Growth of Papal Government in the Middle Ages* (London, 1955), p. 16 ff.
30. Except the laws of exemption of the clergy. See note 28 above.
31. Cf. R. Hernegger, *Macht ohne Auftrag* (Freiburg im B., 1963), p. 159 ff. He shows clearly how much the emperor was influenced by the old pagan ideal of the "divine" quality of his office.

to repel heresy usually met with strong opposition from those bishops who happened to side with the errors. In those times of stormy religious controversy it was quite useful to have a few troops around to encourage bishops to attend and to temper their zeal at times. Still, whatever the needs and circumstantial advantages, the point to be made here is that imperial convocation of councils was inaugurated by the emperors to serve primarily political ends. Only after the custom was well established do we find churchmen asking the emperor to make use of it.[32]

Still more important is the union involved in imperial repression of paganism, heresy, and schism. The origins of this union are more difficult to trace. Again it was Constantine who first used civil authority to curtail non-Christian worship. We have seen how his successors steadily augmented this practice until the Christian faith was the only legal religion. What were the origins of this fact? The measures certainly had the approval of the bishops both East and West, as long as they did not involve torture or death. But were they originated at the demand of the bishops?

The emperors Valentius and Theodosius made such measures official, and in the policy they were encouraged by St. Ambrose.[33] But when we look at the defence given by Ambrose we find among his arguments an appeal to political tradition. He says that it has always been the Roman tradition that citizens follow the religion of their emperor.[34] His main argument was, of course, that truth has a right to prevail against error. When perverse and blind minds resist the true and persist in corrupting others by the practice of falsehood, this scandal must be prevented by whatever force is necessary.

32. As Augustine, after long hesitation, finally did in the Donatist controversy. Cf. Lecler, p. 54.
33. See S. L. Greenslade, *Church and State from Constantine to Theodosius* (London, 1954), p. 24 ff.
34. *Epist. xviii*, P.L., XVI, 833.

However, in order to understand this position, which seems somewhat harsh, we must not neglect to study the context in which it was taken. In making such an appeal Ambrose was not so much a radical as a conservative. His own appeal to tradition proves this. He too was a Roman citizen and, as all his contemporaries, was formed in an empire which professed one religion. He had every reason to fear political as well as religious chaos if the government were to disassociate itself from all religions. That would have been a move unprecedented in all of history. And if the Church officials could reasonably be thought to have been influenced in their judgments by this consideration, what must have been the attitude of the emperor himself?

Until Gratian, the empire had been officially pagan. Christians had been free and even greatly favored for some sixty-five years, but the pagans could take comfort that the emperor was still officially the Pontifex Maximus of their religion. Such a situation was intolerable for both the bishops and the Christian emperors. The only solution which would preserve a unified empire seemed to be to reverse the position of paganism from the persecutor to the persecuted and make Christianity the state religion. This course seems to have been chosen by common consent of the Emperor Gratian and Ambrose. It was that emperor who officially rejected the title of Pontifex, and he acted almost certainly under the influence of Ambrose.[35] But this could be done safely only if the resulting alienation of the pagans could be offset by the balancing support—involving a return guarantee of being supported—of the Christians.

There is no denying the existence of strictly religious motives for the suppression of paganism which accompanied these political motives. Indeed, in reality there is no separating the two, for they were surely intertwined in the minds and consciences of those responsible. To all Christians, paganism was not only false but despicable for its cruelty and its immorality.

35. See Fliche-Martin, III, p. 514.

And it was essential that a Christian emperor acknowledge his faith publicly as well as privately. It is necessary to admit, then, a mixture of religious conviction, imperial tradition, and political necessity as the origin of the laws of repression of paganism.

The reasons for State suppression of heresy and schism seem also to be mixed. Here, too, one can allow for a direct influence on the emperors by the Fathers themselves. The patristic writers' reasons for advocating State suppression of unorthodoxy were basically inspired by faith. They hated this evil as a false seducer of the faithful and a destroyer of the unity of Christ's Church.

As we have already seen, both Ambrose and Augustine invoked the aid of their emperors against heresy. But here, unlike the case of paganism, they were going against the explicit teaching of previous Fathers, such as Athanasius and Chrysostom. They were using an instrument against heresy which had neither scriptural nor traditional approval. And Augustine was contradicting his own earlier position on the matter. In defending the change of opinion he never appeals to the right of the State. He cites, rather, indirect scriptural support and the effectiveness and necessity of the measure.

Again, however, both Ambrose and Augustine were children of their times. Ambrose had himself been a Roman official. Augustine was the son of a pagan public servant, and had been an ardent student of classical Roman civilization and politics. It is hardly possible that the long tradition of close association between religion and civil authority did not influence their attitude towards these matters when they became bishops.[36]

But, though these practical and environmental factors undoubtedly influenced their decision to invoke civil aid, the fact remains that they sincerely believed that to do so was not contradictory to any Christian principle. Hence, it seems that their reasons were mainly practical ones whose nature seemed

36. See H. X. Arguilliére, pp. 6-7.

not contrary either to the rights of the heretics' consciences nor to the limits of State power.

It can be safely concluded therefore, that the origins of church-state doctrine in patristic times were three: 1) traditional union in the Roman empire; 2) practical civil and religious necessity; 3) a scriptural notion of the universal orientation of all elements of creation toward the glory of God.

We have seen how the system approved and partially founded by the Fathers embraced a very close cooperation between Church and State which amounted to what can be termed union —if one understands what kind and degree of "union" is here implied. But it is also now clear that, when considered in its historical perspective, the same system was really a great step towards separation; for, though participating in one another's authority in several important areas, a basic distinctness was constantly affirmed.

In constructing such a system according to the dictates of hard, existential demands, the Fathers remained ever aware of scriptural guide-lines and the scriptural interpretation by earlier holy men. The result was the fusing together of a unique and new conception of human society and its functioning. There was one thorny problem, however, which kept arising. It bothers anyone studying these matters, and it bothered the Fathers themselves. This is the problem of the freedom of conscience of the individual believer. How is it possible to square St. Paul's reverence even for the pagan's conscience with the force countenanced by Augustine and Ambrose? This question is the subject matter of the following section.

3. Freedom of Conscience and the Fathers

We have noted that the Fathers of all periods were in agreement that no one could be forced into the Church. Faith had always been considered as a supernatural and free gift. Further, the apologist fathers claimed a much wider freedom. We have heard Justin Martyr and Tertullian claiming that freedom to follow one's conscience in belief and worship is a sacred and natural right for all men. Throughout our discussion about the Roman State's suppression of paganism and heresy this claim of the early Fathers kept rising in seeming contradiction. How could some of the most inspiring examples of personal holiness and love of neighbor among Christians disregard what was proclaimed by their immediate predecessors? How could they defend and even invoke total restraint of this right of pagans and heretics?

There is a solution to this problem, and it is very illuminating for the understanding of the whole history of Christian church-state doctrine. It is not, however, a simple matter. It deserves much more attention than can be given it here, but a brief treatment is essential. The key to the answer lies in Augustine's exact notion of freedom, of freedom of conscience, and his understanding of conscience itself.

During his first years as bishop, Augustine was opposed to all State force as a weapon against religious deviation. Like Athanasius and Gregory Nazianzus, he believed that the only arms worthy of being used in Christ's interests were those of brotherly love and sincere discussion. In this light he wrote, around the year 388, to Maximus, the Donatist bishop:

> On our part, let the terror cease which is caused by the civil powers; but on your side let the terror cease which is caused by the organizers of the Circumcillians. Let us rather strive to get to the root of this problem; let us use reason to settle our differences; let us use the Holy Scriptures.[1]

Slowly, however, he reversed his opinions and defended State suppression. But the reasons for his change had nothing to do

1. *Epist. xxiii*, P.L., XXXIII, 98.

with his view that religion must be a free act. He continued to uphold his proposition: "No one believes unless he is willing."[2] At the end of his life he stated his reasons for reversing his opinion:

> . . . Because I had not yet seen either how much evil their absence of restraint would cause, or how effective solid discipline would be in changing them for the better.[3]

He changed his course because of practical reasons. His convictions regarding the necessity of freedom in belief remained unchanged. Here we meet the apparent contradiction. How is it possible to assure that belief in the truth will be sincere and free when every other path of belief is closed by armed troops? Doubtless the great doctor was simply applying here what he taught as a general moral principle—that it is a sin to follow one's conscience in approving of what is really (objectively) sinful.

> If anyone were to think something to be good that is in reality evil, and proceeded to do it, he would certainly sin. Thus all actions are sins which are done by someone who thinks what he is doing is good when it is really evil.[4]

If by practicing their religion the pagans and heretics were indulging in even subjectively sinful behavior, then suppressing them is no more damaging to true freedom than to prevent by law sincere perverted minds from indulging in adultery. As a matter of fact Augustine, in all sincerity, appeals to precisely this analogy.

To place religious error on a par with sins of impurity in this manner seems strange to modern minds. So indeed does the

2. P.L., XXXV, 1607.
3. P.L., XXXII, 632.
4. P.L., XXXIII, 186. This doctrine appears in various forms in Augustine's writings. It had a tremendous effect on later theologians, who used the Bishop of Hippo as their chief authority. Thus the opinion remained the common one for hundreds of years. See Eric D'Arcy, *Conscience and its Right to Freedom* (London, 1960), p. 78.

underlying principle that one sins by following an invincibly erroneous conscience. But they seem to be among the main reasons why Augustine permitted force against heresy. These difficulties cannot be totally resolved by appealing to the violence and the suppressionist traditions of the era. What is the source of these views on conscience? How can unconscious error be sinful? The answer to these questions seems surely to lie in Augustine's idea of the nature of the conscience, and of the nature and scope of the natural law.

The great doctor conceived of conscience as a divine light, infallibly—however obscurely at times—pointing to the truth. Heretics and pagans, therefore, if they sincerely examined religious truth, could not fail to see it for what it was. If a knowledge of the natural law and the conscience were infused into the soul by God and needed only sincerity and purification from carnal ways to be discerned, then any rejection of the truth by pagans and heretics might very well be compared to other carnal sins. In this matter it is of utmost importance to seek out Augustine's notion of conscience.

Much light has been thrown on the history of the word conscience *(syneidesis)* by several recent studies.[5] From its first use in a moral sense by Democritus up until its christianization by St. Paul, it was above all the property of the Stoics.[6] Cicero adhered generally in his ethical philosophy to at least the fundamental notions of Stoic thought, especially in his idea of conscience:

> The ancient Stoics conceived of the world as a giant animated being, a living being, completely organized and all comprehensive. It was endowed with an immanent soul which penetrated

5. For example, Spicq, *Les Epitres Pastorales* (Paris, 1947), pp. 29-38; Schnackenburg, *Die Sittliche Botschaft des Neues Testament* (München, 1954), p. 30; Deman, *La Prudence* (Paris, 1949), p. 479 ff.; and Stelzenberg, *Conscientia bei Augustinus,* Studien zur Geschichte der Moraltheologie (Paderborn, 1959).
6. Although the followers of Plato also made wide use of the term.

all its parts with an intelligent and divine energy. This soul was the law of the world, the infallible governor ruling the universe and all its parts with a sovereign necessity. Destiny, providence, the Logos: such was the force or tension which assured the cohesion of the world. It was the guide of history and the law which gave to nature her order. It was in participating in this that the human soul was rational . . . Such was the metaphysical teaching which Cicero inherited from the Stoics.[7]

According to the Stoics the conscience and the universal, natural law go hand in hand. Conscience is nothing other than the presence within man of the divine Logos, perceiving eternal order and testifying to it before the individual. Since, then, man's conscience is part and parcel of this divine Logos, it cannot really err; too great attachment to the material body and its lust obscures this spark but, once seen, it is infallible.[8]

There is no doubt that both Augustine and Ambrose were not only very familiar with this substratum of Stoic ethics, but that they were profoundly influenced by it. Ambrose's own great work on moral matters, *De Officiis Ministrorum,* which was one of the Christian attempts to present morality in a scientific fashion, was modelled in form, vocabulary, and philosophic fundamentals on Cicero's *De Officiis.* Cicero's influence on Augustine—specifically his Stoic morality—is equally well established. Abercrombie writes:

7. M. Valente, *L'Ethique Stoicienne chez Cicero* (Paris, 1956), pp. 103-106. See also Festugière, *La Revelation d'Hermes Trismegiste* (Paris, 1949), II, "Le Dieu Cosmique," and "Le Temoignage de Ciceron sur la religion cosmique," pp. 370-459. Cicero did not follow Stoic doctrine in all its aspects. He began with the general principles, but his moral doctrine as a whole differed considerably from that of the classical Stoics. (Valente, pp. 409-416). Still, as regards the Logos as man's one guide, he remains in accord (cf. Valente, p. 120).

8. Cicero made conscience the proof positive of "honesty" (cf. Valente, p. 136). But for all the Stoics, it seems, conscience is just one facet of the intelligence in general, which is the Logos. The very source of value, and hence of morality, was ascribed to a just evaluation between one's animality (with its desires and pleasures) and one's intelligence (with its connections with divinity). See Valente, p. 108. Hence the necessity to control the passions in order to see better the light of the Logos.

Indeed, the description of the *lex aeterna* given by Augustine
in this work (*De lib. arb.*) is textually identical, in almost every
particular, with the several descriptions to be found among the
works of Cicero. The very fact that the moral law, transcendent
and immanent, appears in this work along with the rules of
proportion and the truths of number, is significant enough; for
it implies already a large similarity of views between Augustine
and the Stoics.[9]

Just as St. Thomas adapted Aristotle's philosophic ideas to
Christian revelation, so Ambrose and Augustine seem to have
interpreted Paul's doctrine on conscience according to the epistemology of the Stoics.[10] When one reads Augustine's account
of his own search for the truth—in an appeal protesting force
against the Manichaeans—the Stoic epistemology behind his
thought is unmistakable:

> Those men vent their rage against you who do not know how
> rare and difficult it is to overcome carnal imaginings by the
> serenity of a devout mind. They rage against you who do not
> know with how much difficulty the eye of the interior man is
> made sound so that it can look securely within itself. I myself
> am quite unable to rage against you. I must be patient with you
> now and deal kindly with you, just as those friends of mine in
> past days dealt with me when I, raving and blind, strayed into
> your beliefs.[11]

But Augustine's ideas on conscience can justly be said to be
primarily Pauline in origin and character, and only secondarily
Stoic. For the great bishop, as for the apostle, conscience was
an essentially religious power. The overly philosophic character

9. N. Abercrombie, *Saint Augustine and French Classical Thought*
(Oxford, 1938), p. 29, as quoted in Deman, *Le traitement scientifique de
la morale chrétienne selon Saint Augustin* (Paris, 1957), p. 73, n. 2.

10. Jerome too seems to be similarly influenced. Cf. E. D'Arcy, *op. cit.*,
p. 16. See also the Carlyles, I, p. 104, n. 4.

11. P.L., LXII, 174-175. It is important to note also how Augustine's
Christianized Stoicism seems here to have included within the powers of
conscience the light necessary to see supernatural, revealed truth in its true
perspective, i.e., separate truth from falsehood.

which it had among the pagans is gone. It is man's point of contact with the Person of a transcendent and loving and self-revealing God. God's Spirit dwells there, and through conscience inspires, illumines and directs man toward the truth and the moral law.[12] Conscience in both Augustine and Paul contains all the richness of the Hebrew concept of "heart" (the Hebrew "leb"). The term, or at least the concept, is found in almost every book of both Old and New Testaments. *"Conscientia"* and "heart" are often used interchangeably by both men. There is God's dwelling place and the arbiter of man's moral life. They have their power because they are in close union with the Maker of truth and morals:

> Augustine very often understands by *conscientia* the inner part, or the heart of man, in so far as this is the organ of man's religious and moral life. By this term he refers to that part of man which enters into a contact with the sphere of the divine. More precisely, it is the recognition or the power to take up, to feel and to realize something bordering on the supernatural and eternal. Often *conscientia* is identical with "heart" *(cor)*. The two words are used as synonyms.[13]

Conscience in Augustine as in Paul has a close connection to the natural law. Paul declares in his epistle to the Romans that what the Jewish Law commanded was also written in the pagans' hearts, so that "their consciences will testify for them" (Rom 2:15). Here Paul's doctrine coincides with Stoic thought. There is little wonder then that Augustine, who had already admired Cicero's Stoic thought so much before his conversion, saw a natural parallel in divine revelation. It is true enough that Pauline and Stoic thought in this passage are in agreement; but Paul's ideas themselves are not of Stoic origin.[14] In other pas-

12. Stelzenberger says: "A characteristic of Augustine's idea of conscience is its essential dependence on God. It is the organ and bearer of man's connection with the eternal and supernatural," *op. cit.*, p. 26.
13. *Ibid.*, p. 47.
14. See Spicq, *Les Epitres Pastorales*, p. 30.

sages Paul clearly does not think in Stoic categories. He allows for an erroneous conscience (1 Cor 7:10-12), a thing unheard of in all Stoic literature. Indeed, such a phenomenon would be contrary to Stoicism since, as a divine thing, the true conscience is not subject to error.

The significance of this fact lies in Augustine's thought. He agrees, naturally, with Paul that an erroneous conscience positing an *indifferent* act—the eating of meat offered to idols (1 Cor 7:10 f.)—should be followed. But when a case arises which has no parallel in revelation—that of an invincibly erroneous conscience demanding an objectively illicit act—he reverts back to the Stoic line of reasoning and denies its liceity. The Stoic origin is clear:

> Value and merit are not conferred on an act according to the subjective intention of the doer, but rather according to the objective conformity of that act with a given order of things: that is to say, according to its *rapport* with the sovereign good, with a *Logos,* and it is that which the Stoics, and Cicero after them, called the *homologomenous zen*.[15]

Paul's doctrine, as we have noted, is founded not on Stoicism but on the Old and New Testament concept of "heart." This, though subject to divine grace and light, remains a human—and therefore a fallible—instrument. Augustine's idea of conscience is, then, occasionally at variance with Paul's, seemingly because he interpreted Paul in too Stoic a fashion. It was this Stoicism and not Paul which caused Augustine to deny that the individual can always follow the dictates of his conscience.

The above digression was necessary in order to appreciate more accurately why force vs. freedom in matters of conscience appeared to Augustine in a different light than they appear to the contemporary mind. Since St. Thomas Aquinas proposed the then startlingly new "theory" that one *must* follow an invincibly erroneous conscience, there has been a gradual but complete

15. Cf. Valente, *op. cit.,* p. 108.

revolution on the point.[16] For Augustine and Ambrose, paganism and heresy were never seen as simple errors. It is easier now—having seen at least a partial explanation of what lay behind this presumption—to take Augustine seriously when he equates heresy with adultery. (Of course, this was a simplification even for Augustine—and not without some psychological and theological truth and depth. Purity of heart is surely always an aid to purity of faith, as St. Paul also teaches.) Further, St. Augustine, in his defenses of force, usually spoke of heretics who had *personally* fallen from the truth, and often for reasons other than sincere differences of belief.

It is not my intention to claim that Augustine and Ambrose's Stoic concept of conscience, by itself, explains why they were instrumental in the formation of repression of religious freedom. It would be extremely difficult, if not impossible, to untangle and arrange logically the complex social, traditional, philosophical and theological motives which inspired these men and the rulers with whom they cooperated. Still, an insight into Augustine's psychological *Weltanschauung* on conscience, so vastly different from our own, seems to me to be absolutely necessary if his ideas on State suppression of unorthodoxy are to be properly understood. Only recent investigation into the history of the development and usage of *conscientia* has made this possible. Now we must get an integral look at Augustine's "theology of force" as revealed in some of his most characteristic writings on the subject.

In the chapter on scriptural foundations of church-state doctrine we saw St. Paul's concept of freedom. Augustinian freedom, like conscience, is based solidly on the thought of that great apostle. This means that, for St. Augustine, freedom was never an end in itself. Personal freedom was a necessary means and spiritual freedom—the freedom of the sons of God—was a

16. E. D'Arcy, *op. cit.*, pp. 113-141. This matter will be treated more fully below, in Chapter Three, "The Nature and Dignity of Conscience."

concomitant result of the putting on of Christ. To place a means in contradiction to its end seemed unnatural. God could not have meant that freedom should block the passage to the truth. The real block was confusion and error caused by sin. The truth could better be seen in some cases only after a certain degree of force, after which the soul would freely come to its mother. A certain degree of force did not seem to him really to damage freedom; but this "certain degree" included imprisonment and confiscation.

Both Augustine and Ambrose were vehemently opposed to total force. The type of force they allowed they thought of as that loving severity administered by a father or mother to an erring child. The child sees the laborious search after truth as an evil; but after it has benefited by going to school, it is grateful for the stripes of the parent who led it, unwilling, along the way. The child's free will, in this view, is not abused. It is merely bent, and even strengthened and exercised by the persuasion. If the child remains utterly incorrigible, and refuses to be led, then it deserves the misery which results. But abuse of the child's will can never be allowed. Thus, what the age of Augustine considered real abuse—torture or death—was always prohibited as a method of religious persuasion. When used, such action was always condemned.

That this was Augustine's real frame of mind in the matter is unquestionable. The logic, making "discipline" the servant of freedom, is evident in each of his letters to the Donatist bishops. Let us take one of the most famous of these and see how unmistakably clear is that Father's conviction that force and freedom could go hand in hand in "leading" erring believers to the truth. If we remember his convictions that the real voice of conscience is practically infallible when brought face to face with truth, it ceases to appear so strange.

The bishop of Hippo wrote Epistle Ninety-three to the Donatist bishop, Vincent, in answer to his protests that civil force was

an unchristian and immoral weapon to use in achieving religious
unity. Vincent protested that it was using evil against evil,
which Christ had expressly forbidden. The holy doctor's first
reply was that, actually, not to use force would be rendering
evil for evil:

> If anyone saw his enemy, overcome by a fever, hastening head-
> long over a precipice, would he not then render evil for evil
> more if he should permit him to proceed than if he should see
> to it that he be seized and bound up?[17]

This correction, however, must always be done out of love and
not out of hatred or vengeance. Freedom would truly be abused
if the object were merely to terrorize into subjection and not
teach, sternly if necessary:

> However I think that it was out of love, not hatred, that they
> had been put to the lash. And you ought also to take note of the
> great multitude in whose salvation we are now rejoicing. For if
> they were merely terrorized and not instructed our mastery over
> them would seem indeed to be evil. Likewise, if they were
> instructed and not terrified then, hardened by bad habits,
> they would more slowly be moved to lay hold of the way of
> salvation.[18]

Immediately afterwards he adds that compulsion, if used with
love, is in accord with a father's love for his child.

Although Augustine constantly insisted that no one could
believe unwillingly, yet he refused to admit this principle was
apropos in the case of the bishop Vincent:

> And you think that no force ought to be applied to a man in
> order to free him from his insidious errors. But you see that God
> himself, than whom no one loves more effectively, tells us to do
> this by very clear examples. For you hear Christ saying, "No
> one comes to me unless the Father draws him." This drawing

17. P.L., XXXIII, 321-347.
18. *Ibid.*, 322.

occurs in the hearts of all who turn themselves to Him out of fear of divine wrath.[19]

It is not necessary to believe the holy doctor to be merely avoiding the point here when we understand his opinion of how unlikely it was that invincible error could be involved.

Another passage of the same letter demonstrates very clearly that he did not consider measures such as confiscation (of which he had just spoken) to constitute real force:

> Not that anyone can be good unwillingly, but still, by fearing what he does not will, either he leaves behind the pride that is hindering him or he is compelled to learn what he does not know. Thus by being afraid he either rejects the falsehood for which he was fighting, or he seeks the truth which he did not know, and comes to hold willingly what he was earlier unwilling to hold.[20]

Such is the great African's idea of force in matters of religious belief—very Christian in inspiration and intention, but inevitably doomed to be abused and thus to cause scandal after scandal in the name of Christ. Since this idea was the common property of the Fathers of the era of the first Christian emperors, it was incorporated firmly into the system of church-state relations then being formed. Few other ideas exercised greater influence on the history of either Christianity or of the Western State.

In order better to fix the bounds of this influence, it will be good to compare the patristic view of these matters with the typical modern attitude, and to trace very briefly the transition from the one to the other.

Imprisonment, flogging and confiscation as means of persuasion seem to us poor methods of achieving real agreement. But let us see just exactly where and to what extent modern conceptions differ from those of Augustine and his age. Is the difference essential—or is it a matter of degree?

19. *Ibid.*, 323.
20. *Ibid.*, 329.

First of all, consider the modern, Christian conception of conscience. Where does it agree with Augustine and where does it differ? We agree that conscience is an instrument created by God to lead man to the truth. We agree that a conscience directing one to follow error is an unnatural state of affairs. We agree that utterly to over-ride this conscience with force and fear, forcing outward concurrence, is an abomination. Torture and death are commonly condemned. Further, Augustine's principle of persuasion of consciences by argumentation encounters no objection. Therefore the broad outlines of our convictions coincide with the bishop of Hippo. The differences are chiefly two. They result not so much from basic disagreement as from a different state of development.

The first real point of contention is the concept of force. We have today a clear idea of the difference between moral and physical force as applied to the human will. All men today know that imprisonment and similar punishments constitute such a pressure that the victim's psychology may well be upset. Indeed, this truth has been so thoroughly investigated that some have turned it into a highly developed science, popularly called "brainwashing." One's power to say "no" may not be completely removed, but certainly any consent given will be less than wholehearted. Even when done with good intention and with love—a thing that was rare even in Augustine's day—it more often than not stirs up new depths of inner resistance and hatred.

But the concept of moral force was not developed in patristic times. They were heirs to a long history of quite complete totalitarianism, where brute physical force by the State made unnecessary a precise knowledge of the limits of moral persuasion. The vast difference between a father's loving discipline and that of a State prison cell was evidently not sufficiently appreciated. Moreover, the results of such tactics in the field of religious belief had not yet presented themselves clearly.

Secondly, Augustine's optimistic view of the sincere conscience's power to know truth is different from our own. We know that a sincere soul can search vainly but sincerely for the truth, and blamelessly reject it as false when presented. Similarly, modern men disagree with Augustine's refusal to admit that one can follow a conscience erroneously but sincerely in permitting what is evil. But here, too, the change was effected by gradual development. Augustine's Stoic-founded opinion remained the generally accepted one among Christian theologians for almost a thousand years.

The early scholastics debated and investigated the nature of conscience *per longum et latum* during the century before Albert and Thomas. The former was the first to propose that one could, without sin, follow a conscience sincerely ordering what was evil. Thomas declared that one must do so. This was the logical conclusion to be drawn from the Aristotelian concept of the nature and origin of man's power to know truth. The acceptance of this principle as a universal moral rule by all theologians took several hundred more years. Its logical application to the various recurring moral cases has been even longer in gaining affirmation.

Today we stand at the end of what amounts to a complete reversal of the Augustinian position on this matter. What was then more or less universally affirmed is now equally universally denied. That is to say, we see conscience as a human power (though open, of course, to divine influence and inspiration), and not a divine thing. We believe that since it is man's inward norm, it must be followed in its subjectively certain decisions even when those decisions are objectively wrong or sinful.

The consequences of these developments for freedom of conscience in church-state relations are truly immense. And they go a long way in relieving the horrified unbelief of the modern mentality when first faced with the fact that the great St. Augustine was really the greatest single apologist for State suppression of religious error.

But—and this is a fact of great importance—the reversal

wrought between patristic and modern times has more the nature of a steady development than of simply a gradual decision to reverse Augustine's opinion. The unraveling of the history of the term *conscientia* is a very recent development. In fact, it is still incomplete. Only slowly did the scholastics evolve their complicated concept of conscience as a purely human thing giving the final decision on a proposed act. Thomas' contention that an erroneous conscience must be followed was a logical next step. Simultaneously, the idea of what constitutes moral force was developing.

Modern men, then, differ from Augustine and his contemporaries in two areas: 1) as to the point at which force becomes a violation of man's nature; 2) as to the relative facility of the conscience's ability to discern religious truth. In other respects, Augustinian and modern Christian ideas on such matters are generally in accord.

We have examined chiefly Augustine's ideas on freedom of erroneous consciences. They are representative of the era which originated the policy of Christian restraint of religious error by State force. Do they constitute a contradiction of the "natural rights" proclaimed by the earlier apologists? It is evident that Augustine did not think so. He was convinced that freedom when one believed—when one entered the Christian Church— was the freedom to be loved and protected. Freedom to believe error was, in his way of thinking, sheer slavery.

But when Justin Martyr and Tertullian appealed to Caesar they appealed to a subjective right—the right to follow what they believed to be true. They ceded the same subjective right to those whom they believed in error: "However, it is of *human law* and *natural power* for each one to worship whatever he believes in."[21] It is difficult to see how one can absolve Augustine from commanding practices which went contrary to the

21. Tertullian, P.L., I, 699. Italics mine.

doctrine of the apologists. What we can do, however, is to reaffirm that Augustine and Ambrose, according to their own convictions and in relation to previous civil practice, were still proponents of freedom of conscience. While they deny as complete a freedom as the apologists held, they at least refused to accept anything but sincere belief, and urged mercy and love toward dissenters:

> Let us also consider these words: "Lest perhaps gathering up the cockle the root of the wheat also gather with it." Thereby Christ seems to say: If you take up arms to kill heretics, you risk exterminating the just men at the same time . . . Thus Christ does not prevent us from repressing heretics, shutting their mouths, depriving them of freedom of speech, reunion or association, but he forbids us to put them to death.[22]

This is a far cry from wholesale slaughter of opposition to the State religion which had been the tradition before. The appreciation of this fact is, it seems, indispensable for an accurate understanding of the historical development of church-state relations. Whenever force was applied in the name of the Church it was usually done in accordance with the *then current* concept of the limits of freedom of conscience.[23]

This truth is the only adequate answer to a grave accusation often repeated by enemies of traditional Christianity. Such modern thinkers as Friedrich Nietzsche, Adolph Harnack and Karl Jaspers charge that persecution and suppression are the ineluctable consequences of any religion which claims to possess a body of divinely revealed truth.[24] Without attempting to deny

22. Augustine, *De Sacerdotio,* II, 3, P.G., LVIII, 634-635, trs. Joseph Lecler, in *Toleration and the Reformation,* I, p. 60.

23. See A. Bea, *op. cit.,* p. 326.

24. K. Jaspers, *Der Philosophische Glaube* as translated and quoted in *Unité Chrétienne et tolérance religieuse,* by J. Cadier, *et al.* Max Pribilla also quotes it in his article in *Intolérance dogmatique et tolérance civile* (Paris, 1950), 159: "The pretension of dogmatic exclusiveness is always ready to resume the butchery of heretics. This is embedded in the very nature of dogmatism."

numerous examples of utter abuse of human rights in the name of religion which were clearly contrary to any standard of freedom, one can nevertheless say in all honesty that the patristic age, which founded the Christian system of governmental restraint, included in the notion of restraint a recognition and respect for what it considered to be the limits set by the sacredness of the human person.

Having seen how much tradition, political motives and philosophical theory demanded the restrictions placed on freedom of religion, it is difficult to see how the Fathers could have taken any course other than the one they chose. It is always a temptation to think that they originated the policy. The exact opposite is closer to the truth. What they really originated—or rather, what the Christian faith originated—is the beginning of the era of freedom of conscience.

Governmental constraint in religious matters, adopted under patristic influence, was infinitely less extensive and severe than that of previous centuries. Religion for the first time in all of history was separated from the absolute control of the State. Its separateness, in essence, was recognized once and for all. It should surprise no one that the process of differentiation, begun at this time, continued to refine itself over the centuries. Neither should it be a surprise that in subsequent centuries the process of individuation—at work in both Church and State—witnessed periods both of retrogression and of excess. Neither the divine Church nor the human State is a static being; rather, they are dynamic. They develop and take more precise form. The relations which exist between them advance by the same dynamism. This is clearly what has happened in every age since the patristic period, and what will surely be the case in the future.

The patristic period saw a great flowering in Christian church-state doctrine. The respective concepts of Church and of State became clearer. For the first time a specifically Christian theory of the State appeared. The great view of human society as a

whole, of creation as a whole, was conceived, wherein the
Church and State were allotted positions according to their
nature and activity. They were both seen as separate entities
with separate authorities; both necessary and both serving
according to their capacity the same final end. So all-embracing
and so fundamentally biblical was this view, that it will surely
remain in its broad outlines as *the* Christian concept of society.
Whatever way the doctrine on church-state relations develops
in the future, it will not affect this concept of two entities, one
divine and one human, leading man according to his respective
capacities to the goal for which he was created.

Chapter Three

The Middle Ages

In modern times the term "Middle Ages" has come to denote that period in Western European history between the end of the old Roman civilization and the renaissance of Roman classical culture. Such an outlook places the epoch from the fifth to the fifteenth century "between" something that was and that came again, thus missing the continuity and the dynamic, natural development that actually took place in European civilization.[1]

For our subject this statement is especially true—for two reasons: 1) The period between the fifth and the fifteenth centuries, while seeming to form a natural whole, is an equally natural continuation and progression of what went before. 2) This period is not a dead and inactive space of time, but one of slow, evolutive generation. The understanding of this is vital for an accurate appreciation of modern realities. Although the chief ecclesiastical figures of the first stage of this era are numbered among the Fathers of the Church, still, from our point of view at least, the age has all the characteristics of a new period.

The age of Augustine, Ambrose and Theodosius had given the Christian religion a definite pattern of relations between the civil and spiritual authorities. The empire was solidly welded to the Christian religion, and the initial turmoil of rebellion by the pagans was rapidly and effectively controlled. Affairs having reached this state of equilibrium, both Church and State began to turn away from what had occupied them both so thoroughly and had welded them into one. Each turned to its own urgent

1. C. Barry, *Readings in Church History*, I, p. 223.

affairs: the emperor to the pressing barbarian armies and to his divided empire, the Church to missionary and monastic activity. And so a new phase of church-state development dawned. It began in the second half of the fifth century, and its first stage was to last until the founding of the Carolingian empire.

Both parties were inspired by Augustine's magnificent vision of society and both continued, each in its own way, the work of making it a reality. There was little change or development in the overall framework itself. The framework of the *City of God* was quite sufficient and satisfying to both. The normal activity of the next few centuries, activity both harmonious and strife-ridden, both constructive and destructive, was to forge important new developments within this framework.

Unfortunately, the relations in these centuries were to prove very painful and full of friction. Beyond any doubt, they were in their broad outlines the cooperative labor of partners, but they appear to us as a continuous battle. Still, the end result included something positive: a somewhat clearer notion of just what an emperor's influence should be regarding the spiritual problems of his realm, and what the pope's should be regarding politics. The struggle was possible only because in the system embracing both there existed an area of "free maneuver" where spiritual and civil authority overlapped and intertwined.

The parties involved began this era under the great handicap of being separated from one another's seat of operation by a vast distance. Even after Constantinople became the imperial city, rulers up to Theodosius were in constant contact with the Roman See from their residences at Ravenna and Rome. At the opening of the new period, however, Theodosius II (408-550) was prevented from this important contact by the presence of Italy's barbarian invaders.

Added to this handicap of space was the advent of new doctrinal disturbances in the East. Since the new rash of heresies were eastern, and since tradition gave him great influence in religious matters, the emperor thought himself more qualified to handle them than the distant pope, especially since Theodosius' trouble, Monophysitism, was by no means purely religious but had heavy political overtones and consequences. The pope, separated by distance, culture, and office, was in no position to consent to the emperor's high-handedness, nor even to understand clearly the highly complex issues involved. A clash was inevitable.

The really tragic part is that clash followed clash—not for a generation or a century, but for a thousand years and more. The issues at stake came and went; the scene changed from Byzantium to Rome to Avignon; one empire followed another and a whole new civilization arose. But the struggles continued. Let us make no mistake. The medieval church-state system was not totally bad. This union actually built a truly great civilization. Emperor and pope collaborated in this great achievement. But the friendship between the two turned time and again into enmity, strife, and bloodshed.

During the whole of the greater middle ages, from the fifth to the fifteenth century, Peter and Caesar worked together in directing and constructing the destinies of the western world. Their accomplishments were, in many areas at least, monumental. But their unique partnership itself occasioned more strife than any other single factor during the whole "middle half" of the Christian era. The church-state system inaugurated by Constantine and confirmed by Augustine contained one particularly glaring weakness. It was over-optimistic.

Kings sighed for the conservation or the return of the Roman peace and order; popes longed for the ideal of the "one fold and one shepherd." In avid pursuit of this common ideal they were both impatient of the depths of human weakness. When men's blindness prevented them from following the Good Shepherd, the pope was impatient for the emperor to give them the needed civil prod. And when his empire refused to hold together at its seams, the emperor was angry that the pope would quibble over doctrinal or canonical objections to reinforcements which his majesty thought politically useful.

The big weakness, therefore, was the same over-optimism from which the primitive Christian community suffered. It was the conviction that the "kingdom of God" should really not be too hard to achieve nor be too long in coming. And both king and pope were too prone to opt for the shortcut of brute force and repression in their eagerness to achieve their goal. In other words, this excessive optimism stemmed from too much impatience and too dim a grasp of man's dignity and inviolable right to freedom. King and pope did, at least dimly, recognize one another's rights. But neither were very strongly impressed with the dignity, freedom, and inviolable rights of their subjects. As we examine briefly the concrete events which were the actual, existential, church-state relations of the middle ages, this truth will time and again reassert itself. When we come in turn to study the expressions of church-state theory given by the medieval theologians and canonists, the same truth will constantly emerge.

1. THE MEDIEVAL REALITY

The scope of this study does not permit us to delve deeply into the details of what actually took place between medieval ecclesiastical and political leaders.[1] Nevertheless, concrete events are the actual stuff out of which any relationship is made. Although God himself has furnished us with some broad church-state principles, the development of doctrine is always powerfully influenced by the experiences of men as they go about trying to put these principles into practice. Hence, to understand

1. For a concise, reliable account of this and subsequent Caesaro-papal conflict up to the end of Justinian's reign, see P. Hughes, *A Popular History of the Catholic Church* (Garden City, 1954), pp. 35-46. For a more complete account see Fliche-Martin, *Histoire de l'Eglise*, IV, pp. 271-476.

Catholic church-state doctrine, it is necessary to review briefly what historical research has revealed about actual church-state experience.

1. *The Pope and the Eastern Emperors:* After Constantine and Theodosius had succeeded in setting up a Christian Roman empire, and their successors had been forced to make it into an eastern, Grecian empire, friction mounted steadily between the pope in Rome and the emperor in Byzantium. Open hostility broke out with the renewal of the great doctrinal controversies concerning the nature of Christ. By the year 449, when Theodosius II convoked a council at Ephesus, both physical distance and cultural-lingual differences had made cooperation between pope and emperor extremely difficult. The question at hand was the alleged heretical teachings of Eutyches. During the embroilment, Theodosius II, Marcion and Zeno succeeded one another as emperor, and they all conducted the doctrinal debates of the Church in such a manner as to virtually ignore Pope St. Leo I (the Great). But Leo's firmness in fighting for his ultimate authority in matters of doctrine established an important precedent. Thereafter, at roughly thirty-year intervals, other famous popes were to fight doggedly for, and slowly make more explicit, their rights over the emperor in matters of faith and morals.

Pope Gelasius (492-496) clarified what had been Pope Leo's position. Even before he was pope, as secretary to Pope Felix II, he was responsible for a papal letter sent to Emperor Zeno telling him that his place in religious affairs was one of submission, not domination: "It is certainly salutary then, when court cases are being heard involving the things of God, that you, according to the law of God, seek to submit your own opinion of the matter to that of Christ's priests."[2] He proceeded to make the matter even more clear: "There are indeed, most august

2. *Epist. ad Athanasium,* A. Thiel (ed.), in *Epistolae Romanorum Pontificium* (Brunsberg, 1868), I, pp. 350-351.

Emperor, two powers by which this world is ruled: the sacred authority of the popes and the royal power. Of these the priestly power is much more important, because it has to render account for the kings . . . at the Divine Tribunal."[3] This statement of a fifth century pope is one of the clearest ever uttered on the Christian church-state position.

Another thirty years brought the great Justinian I (527-565) to the imperial throne. History has acknowledged him to be one of the most able of all the Roman emperors. Because he continued and expanded the caesaro-papism of his predecessors, he serves admirably as a representative of the throne in this long battle. Justinian was a most devout and learned Christian, and was intensely concerned in healing the bitter divisions which the monophysite heresy had wrought among his people. The methods he employed were typical. By simple edict he condemned the teachings of three dead theologians as heretical. With armed might he forced the pope, Virgilius, to come to Constantinople, and he tried by jailings and various ill treatment to force him to approve his doctrinal viewpoints. But the pope and those siding with him resisted manfully, year after year. The results, at the end of Justinian's forty-year reign, were nil; the empire was more divided than ever, both politically and religiously. Justinian did not, however, follow such a course simply out of pride. He was a Roman emperor. And as such he was deeply convinced that ordering Christianity in the empire was his sacred right and duty.

Such unabated domineering policies in doctrinal matters inevitably brought about a strong reaction on the part of the popes. It was not long before they began a series of slow but deliberate maneuvers to protect themselves against the strangling pressure of their distant political masters.

Thirty-five years after the death of Justinian, Pope Gregory the Great (590-604) began his reign. He used his political

3. *Ad Anastasium Augustum*, 2, *loc. cit.*

influence and skill to come to terms with the barbarian Lombard masters of the areas surrounding Rome. He likewise strengthened ties with the English and especially the Frankish kingdoms to the north. His motives are clearly reflected in his writings:

> This man [the emperor], going far beyond the rights of royal power, is attempting to make his handmaid that Church which our Saviour intended to make free by the price of His Blood . . . So great is the extent of his temerity that he has subjected to himself the head of all the Roman Churches.[4]

Thus, the fifth and sixth centuries were an era where the pope-emperor alliance was sorely strained by increasing imperial domination in religion. The battle continued for another century and a half. No permanent break occurred. Justinian, for example, solemnly affirmed his acceptance of the pope's leadership in religion. Likewise Pope Gregory, for example, affirmed his political submission to the emperor. But in this, the first round of the battle, one sees how dimly defined were boundaries between the spiritual and the temporal authorities. Even with both parties acting in good faith, neither knew where his legitimate authority ended and that of his partner began. One sees also how undeveloped was the appreciation of both pope and emperor concerning the ordinary man's right to make up his own mind about religious matters.

2. *The Beginning of the Papal States and the Holy Roman Empire:* The religion which Christ founded he called an *"ekklesia,"* a "sheepfold," and a "body." Hence it was, and still is, a society, an *organized* society. Three hundred years of being slapped this way and that by wave after wave of barbarians and schismatic emperors left the popes eager to steer Peter's battered bark into the nearest politically calm port. This is not to

4. *In Psal.* V., P.L., 79, 661.

be wondered at, for without a reasonably calm milieu, which only stable political order can give, Christ's society finds normal growth impossible. It was little wonder then that in the year 750, when the Lombards around Rome could no longer be held at bay by respect for the tombs of the apostles, Pope Stephen II steered for the only port in sight and asked help from the would-be usurper of the Frankish throne, Pepin.

The whole political mechanism of the middle ages was pieced together in the ensuing latter half of the eighth century. This period is of fundamental import for an understanding of Catholic church-state relations.

A chain of events had begun with the conversion of Clovis (*ca.* 498) and his subsequent successful formation of a kingdom. Clovis' line ruled the Franks for over two hundred years. But the Franks' great eighth century general, Charles Martel, was not of this dynasty. Nevertheless, it was he who saved the Franks from the Islamic threat at the battle of Poitiers (732), reunited the kingdom, and enlarged it. Martel's son was Pepin. He proved himself as capable as his father, while Childeric, the pretender to the line of Clovis was incapable of effective rule.

Pepin was the *de facto* ruler of a powerful and Catholic kingdom with a tradition of strong loyalty to the papacy, but he needed to be confirmed in his position as king of the Franks. The papacy, in turn, needed Pepin's protection desperately, and already had the admiration and obedience of the Frankish nation. It was under these conditions that Pope Stephen II set out for Gaul to beg help. He and Pepin were able to work out a most important pragmatic solution: Stephen would first declare and consecrate Pepin king of the Franks; in return Pepin "gave" the pope the area around Rome as his temporal domain, guaranteed him protection from the Lombards, and accepted the title of "protector of the Romans." Pepin had his crown and the pope finally had political independence and protection.

What Pepin began, his son Charlemagne continued to grand completion. In 768 the latter began his historic reign of forty-six years. During the first thirty, as king of the Franks, he worked near miracles of military, civil, educational and religious restoration and consolidation. The happy alliance between the papacy and the Franks was the solution to the main problems of western Europe, or so it appeared for a time.

Charlemagne was well aware that he had created a new empire. He united, in potent combinations, the rather totalitarian notions of his own Germanic heritage and that of ancient Rome. He informed Pope Leo III in 799 that he had in mind to build a "new Rome" in Aix as the new "center of the world."[5] Papal reaction to such a plan could scarcely have been favorable. Already the king had asserted a domination over the affairs of bishops, abbeys, and even of the papacy. This domination brought back unsavory memories of Byzantium. It was becoming clearer and clearer that the religious center of Christendom could not avoid paying a dear price in liberty for the lavish temporal support and security which it had so readily accepted. The unity of Church and State was fast obliterating the spiritual and religious freedom of action which Pope Stephen thought he had obtained from Pepin. One need only glance at some of the letters and capitularies of Charlemagne to see this. He seemed to want to be both priest and king, and to leave the priest a merely passive role:

> It is our part, with the help of divine holiness, to defend by armed strength the holy Church of Christ everywhere from the outward onslaught of the pagans and the ravages of infidels, and to strengthen within it the knowledge of the Catholic Faith. It is your part, most holy Father, to help our armies with your hands lifted up to God like Moses.[6]

5. Cf. Fliche-Martin VI, pp. 71-106. The papacy staved off this growing royal imitation of eastern domination as best it could—for example, at the election of Leo III (see Fliche-Martin, p. 154). On the other hand, Charlemagne's immense power, even over the supposedly independent papal states, was shown by the fact that Leo III, after his election, felt obliged to recognize his civil fealty to Charlemagne (cf. Hughes, p. 86).

6. *Epist. ad. Leonem III, Papam,* as quoted in G. Pilati, *Chiesa e Stato nei primi quindici secoli* (Rome, 1962), p. 86, n. 48.

Even more clear is a terse sentence from the capitularies: "We wish . . . to regulate our Churches according to the authority of the canons, and to govern the behaviour of our clerics."[7]

Beyond a doubt Charlemagne had a sincere concern for the uprightness and literacy of clerics and monks. Beyond a doubt, too, his laws did much toward reforming their morals and guarding them. On the other hand, this very power in the hands of a civil ruler could, and usually did, lead eventually to corruption rather than a reform of morals. Charlemagne himself, by doling out bishoprics and abbacies (the nomination and investiture of these leaders of the spiritual were in his hands) as rewards or tokens to his favorite lieutenants, undermined hopelessly his own reform legislation.

In spite of these clear dangers, Pope Leo III realized that civil as well as religious order and government was an absolute necessity for normal Christian life, and that Charlemagne had given him both in almost incredible abundance. Further, he himself was firmly committed to the ideal of a certain union of the Church and State. After all, the papacy had given to Charlemagne and to the Frankish kingdom as much as it had received. It was the unity of faith and the learning of the clerics which had made the new empire possible. A new world capital to the north would weaken and divide the alliance as well as increase Charlemagne's predominance in the Church.

It can therefore be called a stroke of genius when Pope Leo hit upon the "perfect" solution. He could crown Charlemagne the new "Emperor of the Romans." In this way Charlemagne would receive all the tremendous prestige connected with that magic phrase. He would have his empire and his capital, yet he would still be united to the papacy. Indeed, since he would receive his crown from the pope and would be emperor of the city wherein the pope was undisputed master, he would not be able to impinge upon either the political or the spiritual inde-

7. *Capit Mant.*, as quoted in Pilati, p. 85, n. 44.

pendence of the papacy. Finally, the eastern emperor would, in effect, be unseated from the Roman throne.

Charlemagne was crowned Emperor of the Romans on Christmas day in the year 800 in a ceremony which came as a complete surprise to him. He later swore that if he knew what was being offered him, he would never have accepted it. But he never repudiated either the crown or the title. A new Europe had been born.

This deed was one of momentous significance for Christian church-state relations. Charlemagne was showing his own genius in being loath to accept his new honor. But conditions being what they were, he must also have seen the need for the move, for it made him beholden to the pope. The exact circumstances and motives on both sides of this great event are lost in history. Historians continue to debate exactly what happened and why they happened.

One of the documents which sheds more light than any other is, as a matter of fact, a forgery. The "False Donation of Constantine," which was supposed to have attested that the first Christian emperor in history had given Rome and the surrounding territory to the papacy, is certainly inauthentic.[8] But it was believed to be authentic by Charlemagne and his successors for hundreds of years. Thus, it gave powerful "foundation" to the pope's claims to the right to crown kings and emperors, and his right to political independence. Though forged, it was based on a real oral tradition widely accepted as true. It was intended to "authenticate" a legend that Constantine had even offered Pope Sylvester his imperial crown.[9] The forgery was almost certainly the work of either the papal court or papal forces in Gaul. However unworthy of the Holy See such a ruse may have been, its

8. For a good evaluation see Carlyle and Carlyle, *op. cit.*, I, p. 287 ff., and G. Laher, *Die Konstantinische Schenkung in der abenländischen Literatur des Mittelalters bis zum Mitte des 14. Jahrhunderts* (Berlin, 1926).

9. As found in Gratian's *Decretales*, in *Corpus iuris canonici* (Freiberg, 1879), I, pp. 342-345.

purpose was not an entirely selfish one. It aimed at a long needed reorganization of the political-religious structure of the day, and at stabilizing an already existing system of church-state relations.

It is useless to try to assign theological reasons for the pope's power to create an emperor. If he possessed any such power, it did not come from his petrine powers but from political ones which his office acquired along the course of the years. Rather we must see this event for precisely what it was: a purely political, sociological occurrence. Charlemagne was in fact the monarch of all the West and, whatever the circumstances, he accepted the pope's action and became an emperor. This action shattered definitively the eastern empire's last pretentions to western sovereignty and formalized Charlemagne's own actual status as ruler of the West. Had any method other than a papal act been used to accomplish this, the results would have been little different.

Charlemagne respected and loved the papacy and the Faith which it led. The Roman See in turn recognized both the legitimacy and the effectiveness of Charlemagne's rule. It was to be expected that a Christian body politic such as western Europe in 800 would choose a Christian way to consolidate a working agreement between its spiritual and its civil authorities. The duress under which the papacy found itself may not excuse the unchristian methods which helped it to free itself; but at the same time Charlemagne could have easily weakened or nullified the agreement at any time during his subsequent eighteen years as emperor. He chose rather to confirm it tacitly. His successors likewise found it more help than hindrance to be crowned by the popes. And so it was that by plain political expediency the papal right to crown slowly was etched into medieval tradition. Its favorable effects were reaped immediately; the lamentable consequences appeared more slowly, but lasted much longer.

Upon the death of Charlemagne his empire fell rapidly into ruin and the darkest of the dark ages got underway. But that great figure, together with his father, Pepin, and the popes of the times, had done more to establish the pattern of medieval church-state relations than any other group of men. They had established the pope as a political power in his own right and had given him the power to crown both kings and emperors. They also cast the die of eventual schism with the East.

3. *The High Middle Ages:* After a century and a half, three successors to Charlemagne's imperial crown were able to bring order out of chaos. Otto I, II, and III, father, son and grandson, worked hard for the better part of a century (936-1002) to re-establish Charlemagne's empire. Their key technique in so doing was reforming, aiding and cooperating with the Holy See. The great civilization which was the high middle ages began to take shape. Monasteries and cathedrals flourished and became centers of piety, learning and culture. Pope and bishop worked hand in hand with emperor, king, and prince to create the loosely organized society which was the feudal system. This process had, of course, begun with Pepin and Charlemagne.

But again, the close intertwining of spiritual and temporal authorities and structures soon proved to have its liabilities as well as its advantages. When kings and emperors began to appoint bishops, and even to manipulate papal elections, the men they selected were rarely chosen primarily for their pastoral qualifications. Further, as episcopal, abbatial, and papal thrones began to carry with them considerable wealth and temporal power, they did not even need the power of kings to corrupt them. Though many very holy bishops and popes found their way to positions of ecclesiastical power from the ninth to the thirteenth century, the abuses began slowly to become more and more widespread.

Inevitably a reaction against this corruption began to gain ground. There arose a mounting ground swell of reform. Under the aegis of the three Ottos and the great reforming abbeys such as Cluny, the drive towards general reform gradually acquired a definite form. It soon accurately located the root of the widespread corruption among the leaders of the Church. That root was the selection and investiture of bishops and abbots by kings and emperors. When even popes began to take steps to uproot this practice, the emperor and the kings soon turned from friends into enemies. For here was one of the king's most secure sources of power and rule.

Pope Leo IX (1049-1054) first brought organization and leadership into the reform movement. He legislated against lay investiture, and toured throughout Europe holding synods and councils, deposing unworthy bishops. He surrounded himself with zealous reformers, and it was one of these who would eventually bring the matter to a head. His name was Hildebrand.

When Leo died, Hildebrand became Pope Gregory VII. This man possessed both zeal and genius in abundance. His continuation of Leo's drive soon brought him into a head-on collision with another man of genius and determination, the emperor, Henry IV. Gregory forbade him in the strongest language to continue his practice of selecting his henchmen to be bishops and abbots within his realm. When Henry responded with a bold attempt to remove Gregory from the papal throne, Gregory answered in kind. He excommunicated Henry, declared him deposed, and commanded all the German bishops to forsake their allegiance to him.

Much to the emperor's surprise, the movement worked. He found himself alone and forced to beg forgiveness and reinstatement. After those famous three days of waiting barefoot in the snow at the papal camp at Canossa, Hildebrand relented and Henry was again emperor. But no sooner had he regained his native land than the emperor began his lay investiture practices all over again. Another decree of deposition followed, but this time his bishops chose to side with their emperor. Soon it was Gregory who found himself "deposed" with a pretender pope now on the throne in Rome and himself forced into exile.

Gregory VII died without regaining his throne. But his reform drive had been mounted so firmly that it could not be stopped. After further wars and turmoil, Henry finally abdicated the throne in favor of his son in 1105. Though Henry V continued the strong-arm tactics of his father the strength of the reform movement eventually became too strong for him, and the matter of lay investiture was settled by the famous Concordat of Worms. The emperor foreswore all right to elect bishops and invest them with the ring and crosier:

> I, Henry, do surrender to God, to the Holy Apostles of God, Peter and Paul, and to the Holy Roman Church all investiture through ring and staff; and do agree in all churches throughout my kingdom and empire there shall be canonical election and free consecration.[10]

Still, the arrangement was a real compromise and one based solidly in reality. The king, by reserving the right to invest bishops with temporal administrative power, retained control over material and political affairs:

> I, Bishop Calixtus, concede to you, beloved son Henry . . . that the election of those Bishops and Abbots in the German kingdom who belong to the kingdom shall take place in your presence without simony and without any violence . . . the candidate elected may receive the [civil] regalia from you through the sceptre and he shall perform his lawful duties to you for them.[11]

Considering the times, a happier solution would be difficult to imagine. The concordat marked the greatest advance in Christian church-state relations in hundreds of years. At last a foundation was laid for the beginnings of a realistic division of power between the Church and civil government. (If such a solution could have been found in the age of Justinian how hap-

---

10. *Pax Wormatiensis, Monumenta Germaniae Historica* (Berlin, 1926), I, p. 159.

11. *Ibid.,* I, p. 161.

pily different might Christian history have been.) A major phase
in the growth-process of Christian society is to be noted here.
Since ancient Rome, the border lines between the respective
jurisdictions of religion and the State had been dim, and often
indistinguishable. They would remain blurred, and future kings
and emperors would renege on their agreement. But the Concordat of Worms would remain a milestone in Christian church-
state relations.

But in the bitter struggle to obtain this perfectly just conces-
sion, the papacy had established still another precedent of papal
interference in civil power: it had declared its power to depose
kings. For over a hundred years before Hildebrand's *coup*,
ecclesiastical forces had been again building up their claims
against lay investiture. The rudiments of canon law had been
laid whereby the papal court marshalled the power and prestige of ancient Roman law behind its claims to spiritual power
and independence. Incorporated into this was the power to
crown kings and emperors, and therefore to depose them also
if they proved themselves unworthy of ruling a Christian people.
This was the famous "indirect power theory." If king or emperor
by their sins became unfit to rule, the pope, because of his power
of binding and loosing sins, had the power of deposition.

This was the beginning of the so-called "hieratic theory"
which held that the pope was, by divine ordinance, at the apex
of power, both civil and spiritual. Did Gregory VII actually
believe he possessed such power? This is another problem which
still leaves historians divided. Certainly Gregory knew he had
the raw power to depose.

But did he believe it came from the powers granted by Christ
to Peter? A careful study of his writings will show that the pope
had only a vague notion of the exact nature of his power in this
regard.[12] He was not a theoretician but a man of action. Still,

12. See F. Kempf, "Die Papstliche Gewalt in der Mittelalterlichen," in
Miscellanea Historiae Pontificii, XXI (Rome, 1959), p. 149 ff. Here Kempf

there seems to be little doubt that he did espouse the "indirect power theory" in one form or another. Further, he certainly helped lay the rudiments of the hieratic theory and practice. His many writings on the point leave little room for doubt: "Let us all humbly obey those whom the Holy Church calls by her own free choice to be king, or those whom, by very deliberate counsel, she calls to be emperor."[13] But there is no real evidence of a "direct power" theory in Gregory's writings.

In spite of the insistence of some historians,[14] Gregory made no claim to be absolute ruler over both temporal and spiritual. But both his writings and his actions did give powerful impetus to the growth of medieval papal power. More important, it gave the kings and emperors even more cause to fear for their legitimate authority and to fight desperately for their own independence. It caused them to answer papal hieratic tendencies with a theory of their own: the old claim of the Roman emperors to be supreme in both civil and religious matters. Soon they had their own lawyers and ancient canons, and eventually would use them even more successfully than the popes. This new fear soon undermined the great gains made in the Concordat of Worms. New battles were in the making.

In 1150 Barbarossa crossed the Alps to aid the pope against his enemies and to be crowned emperor in return by Pope Adrian IV. But the collaboration ended shortly. The emperor soon made evident his intent to make Italy and the pope his vassals. Adrian IV died in 1158 and the college of cardinals elected Alexander III to succeed him. Frederick Barbarossa,

---

expresses the well founded conviction that, 1) Gregory's theory was to a great extent untraditional; 2) that it was itself only rudimentary and was to become a full-fledged "hieratic theory" only after being added to and developed by succeeding popes and theologians.

13. Gregory VII, Reg. VIII, XXI as quoted in Ullman, p. 284.

14. See Leo XIII, *Immortale Dei*, and Pius XII, Address to the historians, 1953; and also Lo Grasso, p. 34; Y. Congar, "The Historical Development of Authority in the Church," in *Problems of Authority* (Baltimore and London, 1962), p. 119 ff.

however, set up an anti-pope, Victor IV. There followed a period
of almost twenty years filled with war and intrigue, with the
future of Europe and the Church hanging in the balance.
Finally, in 1176, the papal forces completely routed those of the
emperor at the battle of Legnano. Frederick then recognized
Alexander as pope. Before he died, the great pope called the
Third Lateran Council, which consolidated the reforms and
enhanced the independence of the papacy.

The very next emperor, Henry VI, also attempted to subju-
gate the papacy, but died before his plans could be effected.
The initiative swung to the side of the papacy with the election
in 1197 of Innocent III. This was one of the ablest of the medieval popes. He was a scholar, a brilliant canonist, an excellent
administrator and a good man. It was he who did more than
anyone to bring the hieratic theory to completion. During his
long reign he contributed, both by his actions and by his theory
and legislation, towards maintaining the papacy as the powerful
unifying force of Europe.

His influence was felt everywhere: by the Albigensians in
France, by the Islamic forces in the Middle East, and by the
imperial forces in Germany. When a fierce contention for the
throne arose between Philip of Swabia and Otto of Brunswick,
the pope declared it his right to decide the issue: "The leaders
ought both to recognize, and certainly do recognize, the fact
that the right and authority of examining the person elected to
the kingship and of advancing him to supreme dominion
belongs to us."[15]

It took twelve years of war for the pope to enforce his "right,"
but eventually he won the day. Even when his choice was murdered by a personal enemy and the alternative, Otto, was
crowned and began an invasion of Italy and Sicily, Innocent
still was able to win out. He deposed Otto and placed young
Frederick II on the imperial throne.

Thus Innocent III did, in fact, rule Europe. His successor,

15. *Decr. de iure Pontif.*, M.G.H., II, pp. 505-507.

Innocent IV, made even stronger claims to "fullness of power." These two Innocents mark the apex of actual papal power in the middle ages. Yet neither of them came out unambiguously in favor of the theory of "direct power" over kings. Though they deliberately left many of their statements capable of being so interpreted, and though many of the canonists and theologians of that time *were* espousing such direct power, neither went beyond claiming civil power indirectly, and power to depose "by reason of sin."

Many positive results can be claimed for the papal predominance of this period. Through the popes, Europe achieved more unity, order, and perhaps even more peace, than it had seen since the rule of ancient Rome. Even up to our present age, this has never been equalled. But there is also a debit side to the ledger. The Crusades and the Inquisition must both ultimately be attributed to the papacy. These two phenomena could simply be written off as unfortunate necessities, if one judged them by purely political criteria. But they were carried out in the name of Christ by his representative. Both were religious repressions wherein bloodshed and torture were sanctioned by the bishop of Rome as a means of religious as well as political unity. They were the extreme but logical consequences of a papacy shackled to the thrones of both Peter and Caesar.

4. *The Decline of Medieval Papal Power:* The next confrontation between spiritual and temporal rulers revealed that the tide of papal power was beginning to run out. Thirty years after Innocent IV's death, Boniface VIII came to the throne of Peter and soon was embroiled in a life and death struggle with King Philip the Fair of France. He had levied a tax on the French clergy, and they had appealed the case to Rome. The papacy was already on the defensive politically. It needed the tax money from French clerics almost as badly as Philip, because of its own war in Sicily. So Boniface forbade the payment of taxes to Philip and fortified his prohibition with copious penal-

ties of excommunication. The tax question was only the beginning. The feud soon involved the whole of Europe. It was to
end in a complete victory for Philip, climaxed by the shameless
physical mistreatment of Boniface at the hands of Philip's troops
at Anagni.

Again, the details of the struggle are not within the scope of
this work. Our interest lies in the development of church-state
ideology which this bitter conflict produced. This development
is not so clear and incontrovertible as many historians and theologians lead one to believe. Boniface was one of the middle
age's best canonists, and knew the position of his predecessors
perfectly. He was well aware that none of them had officially
and unambiguously defended direct political power over kings
in the temporal realm. But, by the time of his reign, not only
most canonists but also the best theologians[16] were arguing in
favor of the pope's direct temporal power. Though the pope
"deposed" Philip, he never, in the vast number of letters and
bulls aimed at his adversary, directly denied the king's claims
to supreme political power. He even protested his recognition
of this, and limited his claim to cases where the king's spiritual
delicts forced him to interfere:

> He has accused us of commanding that the king acknowledge
> that his kingdom comes from us. For forty years we have been
> expert in the law, and we know that two authorities have been
> arranged by God. Therefore, who ought to believe or can
> believe that such folly, such foolishness, is or has been the juris-
> diction of the king; however, our brother Portuensis did say:
> "It cannot be denied that that king is indeed subject to us by
> reason of sin."[17]

The truth of the matter seems to be that in theory Boniface was
content with an "indirect power," but in practice he always
found a moral or doctrinal ground on which to interfere when-

16. These will be discussed below in this chapter, "Theologians and
Canonists."
17. See Pilati, p. 281, n. 50.

ever vital interests were at stake. This policy was not done with cynical insincerity. He was convinced of the pope's right to the summit of power in Christendom, and was equally convinced that indirect power over kings was the manner by which God intended the pope to maintain this power.

However, in his less official, more private, writings one finds frequent unqualified affirmations of direct power. For example, while the imperial throne was vacant, Boniface nominated a protector for that part of Tuscany ruled by the emperor, alleging that the imperial authority returns to the pope while the throne is vacant. Even the pope's most solemn documents contain essentially the same teachings, though they are always worded so as to allow a double interpretation. This is especially true of his most famous bulls aimed at King Philip: the *Ausculta Fili* (1301) and *Unam Sanctam* (1302):

> [We are] the vicar of Christ . . . and have been given the keys of the Kingdom of Heaven . . . [to us] it belongs to destroy all evil according to our own insights . . . For God established us over Kings and Kingdoms so that, in feeding the Lord's flock we may strengthen the weak and heal the sick.[18]

> We are urged to believe in and to fear the One, Holy, and Catholic Church . . . Therefore, in this One and only Church there is one body and one head and two heads, as if it were a monster, namely, Christ and Peter the vicar of Christ, and the successor of Peter. . . . We are taught by the words of the Gospel that in this Church and in its power there are two swords, a spiritual to wit, and a temporal . . . one indeed is wielded for the Church, the other by the Church.[19]

These, however, were extremely polemical documents. One wonders if he himself did not realize that the theology on which he based his theory was extremely tenuous. Why else would he have made them so ambiguous?

Pope Boniface, like many of his immediate predecessors and

18. *Ausculta Fili,* as cited by Pilati, p. 280, n. 47.
19. *Unam Sanctam,* in Denzinger-Bannwarts, 468.

successors, mistook his naturally acquired political supremacy to be divinely given. Their teachings on this point were not infallible.[20] They never declared them unambiguously, much less in an *ex cathedra* fashion. There was always a great percentage of Christians and theologians who disagreed with them and sided with the imperial position. One conclusion alone, then, is admissible: Boniface VIII and those popes who taught as he did simply erred. Their particular political circumstances led them to attribute far too much political power to the Christ-given office of Peter. Subsequent pronouncements, especially the declaration on religious liberty of the Second Vatican Council, make this quite clear.

After the humiliation of Boniface VIII at the hands of Philip, the prestige and power of the papacy began a long and steady decline. The famous "Babylonian Captivity" of the popes at Avignon was the first step. When Boniface died shortly after being manhandled by Philip's troops, his successor, Clement V (1305-1314), capitulated abjectly to Philip's pressures. The fact that he was a Frenchman shows the power Philip was wielding in the Church at the time; the fact that he remained in France during his whole reign underlines his weakness. For seventy-three years Avignon remained the residence of the popes. During practically the entire period they felt the heavy hand of the king of France, and lost irrevocably any semblance of leading the Christian world. Even worse was the steady loss of the healthy reforms so laboriously built up over centuries. Lay manipulation of clerical offices again became the order of the day.

20. Theologians agree that such statements have been rare. See C. Journet, *The Church of the Word Incarnate*, I, p. 446. Other types of papal teachings, to be sure, enjoy the special guidance of the Holy Spirit in proportion as they are vital to the well-being of Christ's Church. But the very care of papal infallibility as proposed by the Church tends to emphasize that the pope can err in his teachings. It would indeed be remarkable if occasionally during the two-thousand-year history of the office he had not done so. See Journet, pp. 420-447.

Pope Gregory XI finally was able to effect a return of the popes to their See city. But no sooner was one evil rectified than another of equal virulence arose. Gregory died within a year of his return to Rome and the French cardinal electors assembled in Rome to elect a successor. They found themselves surrounded by an angry mob demanding that they elect an Italian or die. They elected the Italian Urban VI. But when they found their new pope not to their liking, they slipped away from Rome and declared the election void. With the backing of the French king they elected a rival pope, Clement VII. Thus began the "Great Western Schism." For thirty years the whole Church would be in confusion, not knowing who was really its leader.

After a decade or so of unbelievable chaos and intrigue between pope and anti-pope, the remains of Christendom began to take matters into its own hands. The emperor called a council at Pisa which "deposed" both contenders and elected a third. This, of course, only added to the confusion. It was the first concrete appearance of the "conciliar theory" according to which a general council was believed to be the ultimate ruling power in the Church, with the pope considered to be a merely human institution.

Almost unbelievably, it was just such a council which settled, to the satisfaction of all, the great western schism. Upon request from the council, Urban III, the successor to the legitimate pope, first "convoked" the council and then tendered it his resignation, leaving it the right to elect his successor. This successor was Martin VI. During his fourteen-year reign, his major work was doing battle against the conciliar theory. His successor saw this cause succeed when, in 1439, the Council of Florence itself solemnly admitted that the papacy was divinely established as head of the Church.

In the century and a quarter between Boniface VIII and the Council of Florence the medieval church-state system had been wrecked beyond repair. Indeed, the whole Church had been shaken to its very roots. The papacy managed to regain some of its lost prestige as spiritual head of the Church. But, already at the beginning of its sojourn at Avignon, the papacy had lost forever its privilege of crowning emperors. In 1356 Charles of Bohemia had issued his "Golden Bull" proclaiming that his successors were to be chosen by seven princes of his realm. Though pope after pope tried in various ways to recapture the independence and power of the thirteenth century, their efforts were completely unsuccessful. During the seventy-odd years which separated the Council of Florence from the Protestant Revolution, the compromises and intrigues of the papacy succeeded only in further blackening their reputation. Added to these intrigues were the immoral personal lives of the "Renaissance popes." By the beginning of the sixteenth century, the Church was, indeed, in bad need of a reformation.

The existential relations between the religious and the political authorities during the middle ages have now become simply history. They seem, in some of their manifestations, strikingly unchristian to the modern observer. This is partially because one tends to contrast it with the system of our own day, which has learned by the mistakes made then. It was Augustine's great vision that served as a model for the inter-relations between the spiritual and the political in those medieval days. The system formed a framework wherein the West achieved very significant progress. Under the mutual guidance of ecclesiastical and political leadership, the barbarian hordes who overran the empire were slowly Christianized. They were also civilized, Romanized and enabled to erect their own civilization. What may have happened to Europe had not Pepin and Charlemagne linked arms with the popes is an interesting subject for speculation. But one thing is too evident to question: the Church and the civil power needed one another desperately in those troubled times. And in spite of their continual in-fighting, their union helped them to accomplish many great things.

In recounting the existential church-state relations of the middle ages we have tended, perhaps, to overemphasize the weaknesses of the system and the lamentable results. But what better way to illuminate the fact, first, that there *were* weaknesses, and secondly, that these weaknesses gradually became so evident that in subsequent eras improvements were inevitable. In fact, the great medieval minds themselves were constantly engaged in observing the existential functionings of their Augustinian ideal and, through the influence of their thought, making necessary adjustments. These great theoreticians played almost as great a role in the outcome as did the actual experiences. We must study briefly what their observations were.

2. Theologians and Canonists

Throughout the early middle ages the great inspiration in church-state theory had been St. Augustine. His great apology for the Christian monarchy, involving unity based on a primacy of the spiritual without subjugation for the emperor, inspired king, pope and theologian alike. But history is dynamic, and constant flux of actual church-state relations caused Augustine's thought to be re-interpreted time and again in the light of current events. Justinian, Gregory, Isidore and Charlemagne; Stephen, Henry IV and Hildebrand, added layer after layer of experience and interpretation to the thought complex of the great African doctor.

He became inseparable from the deposit of tradition. Seven hundred years had passed and the Christian Roman empire still endured with roughly its original outlines—until thinkers no longer dreamed that such a constellation was not as essential and unchanging a part of Christian society as its two component parts: the Church and the State. Such, in brief, had become the substructure underlying the thought of the period which we are now examining. Taking these things more or less for granted, one attacked the old spiritual-temporal problems in their then current form.

When the great reform movement developed, however, it brought a new element with it into the dialectic: a renewed concept of law. Knowledge of law presupposes a high degree of education and, in that age, erudition was the domain of the cleric. The result was naturally that, until the universities could educate lay experts, law was ecclesiastical law. But ecclesiastical law was, by nature, concerned with the Church's rights and duties.

Therefore when the eleventh and twelfth century reformers added legal science to their arguments for the rights of the papacy in relation to the crown, the imperialists had no ready defense. Presented with this vast and venerable array of immemorial customs, laws and theory, marshalled in the name of moral and social reform, the whole western society was won over in both heart and mind. The reform was a success and its chief result was an immeasurable advance in prestige and power for the papacy.

The two leading originators of this new science were Cardinal Humbert and Gratian. With the establishment of the University of Bologna, it went forward uninterruptedly for the next several centuries. It was on the basis of this new science that Hildebrand made the first claims to papal temporal supremacy—and was accommodated in his demands by society.[1]

With the appearance of such canonical collections as Gratian's *Decretals* a whole new *Weltanschauung* began to spread

1. But, as we have seen already, the claims which this new science made respecting papal temporal power was based to a large extent on false documents. This fact must never be forgotten in the evaluation of the actual theological soundness of the church-state argumentation presented by the medieval canonists.

throughout Christendom. Any complete collection of law has order and justice as its essential ends. All of society is ordered in its various components so that justice can be administered according to a well-designed plan. The particular conception of the canonists regarding the hierarchy of authority, plus the canonists' own particular idea of the nature of justice, were perhaps the two greatest formative principles of the medieval *Weltanschauung*. The canonists who forged concepts into a unity were, by definition, lawyers and not administrators. They were a step removed from existential governing, and so theoretic perfection of order was their goal. But these pioneers were also clerics and were involved in the general enthusiasm for reform.

As good clerics and good lawyers, the structure of authority which they envisioned was thoroughly Christian; and the type of justice to be administered was also essentially Christian. Their justice was that of St. Augustine. Their notion of a graduated order of authority they derived from Roman law and from the documents of the papal archives, both authentic and spurious. Out of the efforts of the successors of Gratian there gradually emerged a well-ordered system of law which was as unique as it was excellent. It was not only law but *canon* law. It was a fearful weapon when wielded against rulers such as Henry IV for, as a Christian monarch, he was powerless before it. It was also an excellent tool for ordering and directing the internal, spiritual affairs of the Church.

But the canonistic conception of church-state relations was centuries in the making. It too had its evolution, though, being unfettered by the bitter reality of every-day politics, it matured much faster than did the concrete teaching and policy of either king or pope. Once the great compendia of canon law were composed and their content diffused, a new type of thinker, the juristic theologian, arose. A hundred years after Gratian we find two men, Hugh of St. Victor (died 1141) and John of Salisbury (died 1180), drawing ever clearer outlines of the hieratic theory. This was the goal toward which ecclesiastical canonists had tended from the first.

Hugh was not a canonist so much as theologian, but he embodied the arguments of the canonists and fitted them in nicely with Augustine's thought. His doctrine was not fully hieratic, but it prepared the ground by envisioning an ordered society—he calls it simply the "Church"—in which temporal and spiritual power form one whole in a manner comparable to the whole constituted by body and soul.[2] He makes no claim that the pope himself possesses temporal power, which he gives to the king. Rather, the pope is the instrument by which the king receives his power and—if the king abuses it—the tribunal before which he is to be judged:

> Those things which belong to the earth, and pertain to earthly life, pertain to the authority of a king. Those things which are spiritual, and all things assigned to the spiritual life, pertain to the authority of the supreme Pontiff . . . For spiritual power was instituted by God first, and if it should err, it can be judged by God alone, as is written: "the spiritual authority judges all things, and itself is judged by the divine will" (1 Cor 2:15). . . . wherefore the priestly dignity still consecrates the regal power and sanctifies it to a blessing; it forms and institutes it. If therefore the Apostle says, He who blesses is greater, and he who is blessed is lesser (Heb 7:7), it is true without any doubt that the earthly authority, which receives its blessing from the spiritual authority, is rightly regarded the lower of the two.[3]

The hieratic *Weltanschauung* is already present; but the king's basic independence is still intact.

A few decades later, in England, John of Salisbury, an even greater proponent of juristic theology, wrote his *Policraticus*. He was the secretary to Thomas à Becket, the archbishop of Canterbury who was murdered by the king's henchmen for clinging

2. See Ullman, pp. 437-440.
3. *De sacramentis christianae fidei*, P.L., 176, 418.

to the practices and principles which John wrote about and defended. He too combined Augustinian and canonical influences. He was probably the first theologian of note to state unambiguously the pure hieratic theory. He did not argue the point. He simply presumed it to be a fact:

> The prince therefore, as very many assert, is the public authority, and a certain image of the divine majesty on earth . . . Therefore, the prince receives this sword from the head of the Church, since She herself would never wield the sword of force. However she has it and she uses it through the hand of the ruler on whom she confers the power of keeping persons within limits, though keeping for herself the authority of spiritual things in her Pontiffs. Wherefore it is that the chief authority seems unsuited for the hand of a priest . . . Certainly, as is witnessed by the testimony of the Teacher of the Gentiles, he who blesses is greater than he who is blessed; and the authority with which the dignity has been conferred distinguishes the spiritual power insofar as it has been placed under it by God, namely, in those things which pertain to the salvation of the soul; and therefore in these things the spiritual power must be obeyed rather than the secular power. In those things which pertain to the civil welfare the secular authority must be obeyed rather than the spiritual authority, in accordance with Matthew 22: "Render to Caesar the things that are Caesar's, etc." unless perhaps the secular power is joined to the spiritual power, as in the Pope, who holds the summit of each power, namely spiritual and secular.[4]

Here, a hundred years before Innocent IV and Boniface VIII, we find a finely organized, universalist theory of society based solidly on canonical reasonings and placing the pope at the pinnacle of both spiritual and temporal power. The *Policraticus* had great influence, not only among the clerics but among the royal theorists, both during the lifetime of its author and in subsequent centuries.[5]

4. *Polycraticus*, 1. IV, P.L., 119, 516.
5. See N. Curtis, *The Great Political Theories*, I, "From Plato and Aristotle to Locke and Montesquieu" (New York, 1961), p. 152.

The great proponent of papal supremacy during the same period was St. Bernard of Clairvaux (died 1153). Though a monk and mystic and by no means a canonist, nevertheless he propounded the supremacy of the pope with a fiery evangelical zeal which made fine canonical arguments pale by comparison. He was a learned man, a diplomat, a preacher of crusades and a friend of popes; but above all he was a saint. For him papal supremacy was a necessary premise for Church reform. If Hildebrand had wielded "both swords," then they were his to wield. The spirit of universalism inspired by the canonists pervaded the whole atmosphere of his time. Bernard based his arguments chiefly on the allegorical type of biblical exegesis popular in his day. He was reflecting a general, almost limitless, esteem of the papacy which the canonists were instrumental in arousing.

By the thirteenth century the canonists began to occupy the papal throne itself, and slowly they translated their theories into policy. The voices of Gratian, Bernard, and John of Salisbury had demanded attention, but they remained more or less private opinion while official policy had remained more conservative. But the combination of explosive relations with the monarchs and the presence of brilliant canonists among Peter's successors brought actual papal policy ever closer toward the opinions of the legal theorists. By the end of the century, the gap had been more or less closed. The more cautious, traditional demand for only a primacy of dignity had been supplanted by the doctrine of *plenitudo potestasis*.

During the second half of the thirteenth century two more important elements began to take their place beside the Augustinian outlook and canon law as fundamental influences in the formation of church-state doctrine. The first was the appearance in the royal courts of educated laymen to fill the breach made by canon law in the imperial defences. The science of civil law, based on a resurrected Roman law, slowly took form.[6] By the time of Philip the Fair this new science had advanced far enough to answer papal universalists' claims with a cogently thought out universalism of its own. This was manifested by the appearance of such anonymous tracts as *Rex Pacificus* and *A Dialogue between a Cleric and a Knight*. Appearing as they did after the papal prestige was already on the wane, they did much to build up the whole new outlook of the lay state, and to further discredit papal "interference" in politics.

The other great element to make its appearance was that of Aristotelianism. St. Albert the Great made preliminary attempts to wed the thought of the great Greek philosopher to Christianity at the University of Paris. Thomas Aquinas brought Albert's efforts to grand, definitive conclusion. The repercussions on church-state theory of this crowning of the scholastic movement were to be immense. Aristotle's theory of the State places its origin in the natural law. Man is a social animal and the State is the natural termination of this social instinct. Though Augustine had, in some passages, rather hesitatingly supported a similar theory,[7] this fact had long since been in the shadows and the State had come to be considered the result of sin. Thomas placed the State once again in a favorable light.

This contribution alone makes St. Thomas one of the greatest of the medieval developers of church-state theory. The distinction between the natural and the supernatural which Thomas so skillfully drew was surely abused during the subsequent decline of Scholasticism. It is, however, not only valid but necessary if properly understood. Thomas' dictum, "grace builds on nature," does not mean that nature itself is not also a creature of God and sanctified by its place in the providential scheme of salva-

6. J. Rivière, "Le Probleme de L'Eglise et L'Etat au Temps de Phillipe le Bel," *Specilegium Sacrum Lovaniense* (Louvain, 1926), 252 ff.

7. See above, p. 45 ff.

tion. Both the gospels and St. Paul are full of references to the
"old" and the "new" man. Thomas' teaching of the natural origin
of the State had the effect of gradually clearing away much of
the confusion which at times had all but destroyed the Christian
church-state dualism and caused it to slide back toward the
ancient Jewish and pagan theocracies.

Though Aquinas himself did not carry his distinction to its
full logical conclusion, his Aristotelian doctrine was to serve
as one of the king's most powerful arguments against papal
supremacy. Thomas, in his earliest major work,[8] upheld the then
general opinion that God bestowed temporal power through the
pope in such a way that the pontiff retained the height of the
spiritual and temporal power.

But it is interesting to note that this opinion is nowhere
repeated in Aquinas' more representative work, the *Summa
Theologiae*. In fact, the opposite opinion (the rulers do not
receive their power from the pope) seems to be implied when,
explaining how an apostate prince loses his power, he says that
the right to rule is a *human* (i.e., a natural) right. And, although
he goes on to allow that the pope can, by a condemning sentence, take away this dominion from a Christian prince, nevertheless the implication seems to remain that the dominion comes
not from the pope but from natural sources:

> I answer by saying that . . . infidelity in itself is not contrary to
> civil rule because ruling was introduced by the natural civil law,
> which is human law, but the distinction between the natural and
> the supernatural is the divine law, which does not take away
> human law. But one can lose the right to rule through a court
> sentence by sinning against the Faith.[9]

When he states, "Ownership is something from the law of
nations and so it is a human right," he makes an absolute state-

8. *Commentary on the Sentences of Peter Lombard*, Dist. xliv, q. II,
art. 3, *Opera Omnia* (Roma, 1570), VI, fol. 147. This work was written
before Thomas had worked out his consensus with Aristotelian philosophy.
9. *Summa Theologiae*, II-II, q. 12, art. 2.

ment which Thomas seems to apply to both Christian and non-
Christian rulers. What he adds subsequently does not modify
this statement. The absence of the opinion expressed in his
earlier work, and the existence of this positive evidence for a
change in the theory that the pope has only spiritual power,
both indicate a change of stance by Thomas. But, as St. Robert
Bellarmine was to write several centuries later concerning
Thomas' opinion on papal temporal power: "What St. Thomas
thinks on this subject is not very clear."[10]

Thomas deserves special attention here for another, indirect,
contribution to church-state doctrine. He developed almost
without assistance the first cogent argument in favor of the
necessity of following an erroneous conscience. But the development of this doctrine is both complicated and very important. We will discuss it below.

Aristotelian-thomistic theology and method spread rapidly
throughout the Christian world through the influence of its center, the great University of Paris. By the beginning of the thirteenth century it had taken a firm place along with Augustine,
canon law, and Roman law, as a major weapon in the hands of
church-state theorists and polemicists. The first half of this century was to see the maturation of both papal and royal absolutist
theory, as well as the beginnings of a *via media*.

On the papal side we find Giles of Rome and James of Viterbo.
These two thinkers can be treated together since, in the final
analysis, their doctrine is the same. Giles was James' teacher,
and his work, *De ecclesiastica potestate,* served as source for the
latter. Giles took a more canonical approach to the problem,
while James' work was more theological and speculative.[11]

Both these men lived during the reign of Boniface VIII. Giles
was probably a source for the pope, and James used both Giles
and Boniface as authorities. The ideas of the three are very

10. *De Summo Pontifice,* V, 1.
11. See Rivière, pp. 191-251.

similar, except that Boniface, because of his position as official
teacher of the Church, was more reserved in his presentation.
In Giles and James we see exposed the hieratic theory in all its
glory. The picture painted of Christendom and its constitutive
authority is magnificent in its ordered simplicity. Over all reigns
Christ—Priest and King. On earth, Christ's vicar, the pope,
enjoys *plenitudo potestatis* over both the temporal and the
spiritual:

> . . . as the inferior bodies are ruled by the higher, and the whole
> substance of the body is ruled by the spiritual, which itself is
> ruled by God, thus also in the Church the temporal and inferior
> rulers are governed by the higher, and the whole temporal
> power is ruled by the spiritual, principally by the Supreme
> Pontiff.[12]

Here, then, the question is not merely the origin of temporal
power. The pope had direct power over the internal affairs of
the kingdom:

> The art of ruling in the political sphere, as well as political power
> itself, ought to be subjected to ecclesiastical power in such a
> manner that that order itself, and all its organs and instruments,
> be in accord with the good pleasure and the will of the spiritual
> power.[13]

There still remains a theoretic distinction between the pope's
spiritual and temporal powers, but it has dwindled to the vanish-
ing point. James of Viterbo gives the theory a fine scholastic
finish and precision:

> The institution of temporal powers naturally comes into exist-
> ence in its most fundamental form from a natural tendency of
> men. Hence it comes from God, the author of nature. But in its
> final and perfected form, it takes its being from the Spiritual

---

12. Giles of Rome, *De Ecclesiastica Potestate,* I, 4, as quoted by Rivière,
p. 199.
13. *Ibid.,* p. 203.

Power . . . Indeed, every human power is imperfect and form-
less unless it is formed and completed by the spiritual realm.[14]

Such a doctrine was to remain more or less generally accepted
in ecclesiastical circles until the Reformation.

But the aristotelian, scholastic method was used likewise by
those supporting the royal and imperial side. Following close
behind the papal defenders, Dante, Marsiglio of Padua, and
William of Ockham argue forcefully for the independence of
royal power in origin and in essence. Dante is the best representative of this group both because of the moderateness and
cogency of his arguments and because of their great influence.
Marsiglio's writings are of a later period and are highly colored
by a controversial and partisan—even vindictive—stand against
the papacy.

Dante was a poet and a layman. In the first part of his
only political work—*De monarchia*—he defended the German-
centered empire. This was not because he particularly loved
the Germans, but because he generally kept his argumentation
on a strictly philosophic, deductive plane. Favoring a monarchical empire, he had nowhere to turn except to the holy Roman
empire. The Roman empire is set up as in every way the ideal
form of government. He deplores nationalism which has ruined
the empire:

> I am deeply saddened over the fact that Kings and Princes are
> united in this fault [nationalism] so that they resist their one
> and only Roman ruler. . . . I can declare with him who cried
> out to the ruler of Heaven: (Ps 2:1) "Why have the nations
> raged and the people devised vain things?"[15]

After this philosophical praise of the monarchy he sets out to
defend its independence theologically. First he answers the
arguments in favor of papal universalism, denying that the sun-

14. *De Regimine Principum*, II, 7, as quoted by Rivière, p. 234.
15. *De Monarchia*, I, 16, as cited in Rivière, p. 334.

moon allegory, or that of the two swords (or even Peter's power
of the keys, or the Donation of Constantine) could prove the
dependence of king upon pope. Then he brings in the new
aristotelian reasoning about the natural origin of the State, to
show how civil power is independent of the pope and rests on
a different basis—the natural law: "The authority of a temporal
monarch descends without any mediation from the source of all
authority."[16] But the typical medieval unity of view is preserved.
Dante gives the pope his rightful place as spiritual—and therefore ultimate—head of Christendom as such:

> The temporal kingdom does not receive its being from the
> spiritual power, and neither does it receive from that source its
> power nor simply its power to operate. However, it does receive
> from the spiritual power the means whereby it can work more
> virtuously by means of the light which the blessing of the
> Supreme Pontiff graciously imparts to it in heaven and on
> earth.[17]

Thinkers such as Dante slowly turned the medieval mind
away from papal absolutism. Dante was the forerunner of a
whole new class: the educated layman, whose outlook, though
still wholly Christian, was slowly turning away from the spirit-
ualist world of his fathers. The clerical world failed to see any
good in this, and clung (at least in church-state theory) to an
attitude which disparaged the claims of civil authority as
unchristian.

We have seen how church-state theorists of the high middle
ages tended toward either one universalist position or the
other. While always keeping a certain dualism, they were so
much men of their times that they saw the answer to the government of Christendom to be one of two opposing unistic ideals.

There is one exception to this, however: John of Paris. He
was the most far-seeing of them all, as a great theorist of another

16. *Ibid.*, Rivière, p. 335.
17. *Ibid.*, p. 336.

age—Robert Bellarmine—was to indicate.[18] This successor of St. Thomas at the University of Paris took a middle-of-the-road approach from the beginning. He lived in the high tide of the controversy (died 1306). Though a Dominican he did not side with his former confrere, Boniface VIII; and though a Frenchman he did not take the part of Philip. He was a teacher, not a polemicist.

His approach to the church-state problem as outlined in *De potestate regali et papali,* is thoroughly Thomistic. The "kingdom" and its authority arises from man's natural instinct, and is necessary in order that man fulfill his natural end. But man has also a higher, supernatural, end which requires a different authority for guidance. What is to be the rapport between these two? The fact that one power comes before, or springs from, another does not make it dependent on the other. And though one may be superior in dignity, it is not necessarily superior in all other things. The two powers in question are both supreme in their respective spheres and coordinant with each other:

> . . . And therefore, in certain things the secular authority is greater than the spiritual authority, namely in temporal affairs. Nor is the secular authority subject to it in anything that does not spring from the spiritual authority, but both spring immediately from the one supreme power, namely, the divine. Because of this the lower has not been subjected entirely to the higher . . .[19]

Next, John denies that the pope received power from Christ which would in fact place him over kings. Christ's power as King of kings pertained to his divinity, and there is no indication that he wished to unite it to the spiritual power which he left to his Church. Indeed, the indications of Scripture are to the contrary. If the pope, then, ever had any temporal power at all, it was he who received it from the king and not vice-versa.

18. See Hughes, *A History* . . ., III, p. 112.
19. *De potestate regali et papali,* in Rivière, p. 286.

"The lord pope does not have either sword, nor jurisdiction in temporal affairs, unless the prince has conceded it to him through outward devotion."[20]

The pope's powers, then, are purely spiritual, and even his punishments must be limited to spiritual excommunications and the like. This does not mean that king and pope are to be separated in their functions; nor even that they are equal. The pope should direct the king, but in his conscience and not in his politics. Finally, he allowed for an indirect power over the king when, "because of sin," the pope's spiritual excommunication shows the king unfit to rule a Christian nation.

John of Paris, in seeking the middle way, hit in fact upon the right way—as subsequent centuries have amply demonstrated.

After John of Paris' time, medieval theologians continued to seek the truth about the pope's authority over kings and the temporal. They employed all the subtilities of a Scholasticism already beginning to decay. Endless distinctions and sub-distinctions were formed concerning the exact degree and nature of the indirect power.[21] It would avail little to explore here these multiple and hair-breadth ratiocinations, for the end result was rather sterile. The main outlines of the problem had already been proposed, and it was to be long centuries before any one of the three basic positions (the "imperialist," the hieratic, and the "middle way") was to prevail. The remainder of the middle ages was taken up with continuing claim and counter-claim from royal and papal quarters, while theologians swung ever more solidly towards the *via media*.

This trend towards the center was ably represented by Cardinal Turrecremata (1388-1468):

Having examined closely many various treatments of the subject, we have found that among the others there are two outstanding theories on the matter. First, many declare that the

20. *Ibid.*, Rivière, p. 290.
21. See Pilati, *op. cit.*, pp. 376-381.

Roman Pontiff, by reason of his own pre-eminence, has authority only in spiritual things, and thus in no manner may he by the power of the papacy extend his say into temporal affairs. They admit, along with other thinkers, that by the right of the papacy he can have some jurisdiction in temporal affairs, mainly in those matters that have been added to the Church by the confession of the faithful, or of the rulers. The second opinion is the exact opposite, namely, the Roman Pontiff, or if you will the Vicar of Christ, has by the right of his pre-eminence full jurisdiction in the whole world, not only in spiritual things but also in temporal affairs, adding that the power of jurisdiction enjoyed by all secular rulers has been given to them from the Pope. But we rejecting . . . the aforesaid ways which seem to us less probable . . . turn rather to the happy medium . . .[22]

The arguments of this new generation of theologians, while they remained a dead letter to the popes of their own age, were to furnish direction to popes during and after the Reformation.

Having seen the church-state thought of the great medieval theoreticians, we have now a clearer understanding of the idea patterns which shaped the general medieval *Weltanschauung*. The rising universities were the nodes of popular thought. Great canonists like Humbert and Gratian and theologians like John of Salisbury and Thomas distilled the prevailing concepts, orientated and developed them, and gave them definite legal or theological form. It was not these men, however, who molded official policy and created lasting institutions—at least not directly. They were the great "middle men." That is, they absorbed the whole (then current) complex of culture, piety, and civilizational level, and incorporated it into a doctrine which mirrored the essence of medievalism. This product of the universities and the scholars became in turn the source material on which both king and pope came to depend for creating institutions.

22. *Summa de Ecclesia*, II, cxiii (Venetiis, 1561), p. 262 ff.

We have seen how several characteristics of this source material stand out. It was first of all universalist and unistic in nature, spanning heaven and earth, and ordering carefully in a hierarchic fashion both the natural and the supernatural spheres of human activity. Secondly, it was sacral, attributing to even the most mundane affairs of serf and king alike their proper relationship with the eternal end of all things. Neither of these two qualities were negative; indeed, from them sprang the greatnesses of the era.

Their defects sprang chiefly from their being carried too far, for theoreticians are always tempted to impose more order on the object of their analysis than the Lord saw fit to place there, when he created that object. This defect is most evident in their attempt to establish the limits of authority between Church and State. Because they persisted in putting either one party or the other at the absolute summit of human authority, the natural autonomy of both had to suffer. It seems today that God himself would have served well enough as a universalist coordinator and unifier. But such was just not the spirit of the times.

The absolute hieratic doctrine, which was so prominent on both sides, never managed, for any length of time at least, to become fully official doctrine with either king or pope. Since the theologians and canonists were a step removed from those officials who formed concrete policy, their dreams were never completely realized. But their influence was immense. When one wonders today how Boniface VIII or Frederick II could have been so bold in their campaigns for total power, it is in the contemporary streams of university opinions that one will find the answer. The rulers were forced by bitter reality to temper their demands and actions to meet the restraints imposed by their opposition. Canonists and theologians were not troubled by these limitations. By working the general sentiments of the times into abstract universal theory, they presented a doctrine which served as a constant spur to emperor and pope.

In one area, however, theorists were so far ahead of administrators that their doctrine appeared to run directly contrary to policy. This "premature" advance was the scholastic doctrine on conscience. Because conscience and its dignity is so important in church-state doctrine, this advance must be examined next.

3. The Nature and Dignity of Conscience

It would be a grave mistake to think that the evolution of church-state doctrine took place only as a result of concrete interaction between the two societies. We have already seen how philosophies and abstract social theory influenced this evolution in very decisive ways. But it is safe to say that no single idea so affected the long-range development of church-state doctrine as did that of the conscience and its dignity and rights.

In Chapter Two, Augustine's idea of conscience was investigated and its influence noted in the formation of his attitude towards the State's persecution of heretics. His notions on the binding force of an erroneous conscience were particularly stressed. We saw how his conceptions of both conscience and repression—which he shared with Ambrose and others—set the tone for the entire middle ages. So inspiring was the grand design of the *City of God,* and so completely involved therein were his ideas countenancing State protection of religion, that both were universally accepted almost without question until the eleventh century. At this time the notion of conscience and its binding force became the subject of constant thought and fierce argumentation. The new trends had little effect at the level of church-state relations during the middle ages, but they were destined in the future to exercise a truly decisive practical influence.

Peter Abelard stirred up the controversy about the binding force of an erroneous conscience.[1] In his work *Scito Teipsum,* he presented the outlines of a purely subjective morality. All

1. See Lottin, "Les éléments de la moralité des actes dans l'écoles avant Saint Thomas," *Revue Neo-scolastique,* XXIV, no. 93, 1922, 23-65.

exterior actions are in themselves indifferent, even homicide. The morality of an act, then, proceeds from the intention of the agent. It was from this principle that Abelard concluded to the goodness of an act commanded by an erroneous conscience. If no objective morality exists, then even an act against God's law, if done with a good intention, is good. Abelard's conclusion as to the propriety of following a conscience demanding evil was condemned by the Council of Sens in 1140. Being based on the premise of a purely subjective morality, it is little wonder.

But the question, once raised, furnished material for specula-tion during several centuries of schoolmen.[2] Peter Lombard reverted back to the Augustinian position. Alexander of Hales (or one of his students who wrote the treatise ascribed to him) treated the same question and came up with a rather perplex-ing answer. Yes, he says, an erring conscience must be followed, providing it commands what is good or indifferent, but when it commands what is evil the authority of God takes precedence over that of conscience and so the bad conscience must be "put away." He does not suggest how this might be done.

Nevertheless, this solution was the commonly accepted one until the time of Albert the Great.[3] This instructor of Thomas first enunciated the position which his student was to take up and develop: A sincere conscience binds always, because ultimately

2. A few of the best works on medieval theologians and canonists and church-state doctrine are: Fournier, and Le Bras, *Histoire des collections canoniques en Occident*, 2 vols. (Paris, 1931); C. Erdmann, *Forschungen zur politischen Ideenwelt des Frühmittelalters* (Berlin, 1951); R. Hönig, *Beiträge zur Entwicklung des Kirchenrechts* (Gottingen, 1954); J. Dicken-son, *The Statesman's Book of John of Salisbury* (New York, 1927); J. Hull, *Medieval Theories of the Papacy* (London, 1934); J. Rolbiecki, *The political theory of Dante Alighieri* (Washington, 1921); C. Davis, *Dante and the Idea of Rome* (Oxford, 1957); A. Gewirth, *Marsilius of Padua* (New York, 1951); A. Mannan, *La doctrine de l'Eglise et l'Etat chez Occam* (Paris, 1942); Roland-Gosselin, *La doctrine politique de Saint Thomas d'Aquin* (Paris, 1928); J. Eschmann, "Saint Thomas Aquinas on the Two Powers," in *Medieval Studies*, 1958, 154 ff.

3. See D'Arcy, *op. cit.*, pp. 84-86.

it is man's only source of information concerning morality.[4] But Thomas was the real master in the question. His elaboration was complete and finely integrated.

Aquinas, like Augustine, went first to St. Paul for an answer. In his commentary on the epistle to the Romans (14:14) he treats the question at length.[5] In the epistle, it will be recalled, the question was whether newly converted Jews sin in eating food which they still believed (erroneously) to be prohibited to them. Paul decides that they do sin because they violate their conscience. Thomas clarified Paul's decision by appealing to a parallel case. But in his case the individual considers good what is objectively evil; not—as in Paul's case—what is objectively indifferent:

> If anyone thinks that he is sinning mortally if he does not steal or commit fornication, does such a conscience bind him so that he clearly sins mortally if he acts against his conscience?[6]

He treats the case in the manner of a *questio* in his purely theological works, first listing objections to what will be his position. The first objection is precisely that which troubled Alexander of Hales: "This seems to be false . . . because the law of God which prohibits fornication binds one even more strongly than does one's conscience." But Thomas holds firm. His reason is based on Paul first, but also on his whole Aristotelian conception of conscience:

> As has been said, even an erroneous conscience binds things which are morally evil by their very nature. For, as has been stated, it would follow that, to the extent one acts against his conscience, he would have the intention of sinning . . . and does in this regard, as the Apostle says . . . if anyone have a conscience bidding him to make exception as to some foods, that is,

---

4. Lottin, *op. cit.*, pp. 44-55.
5. *Comment. in Epist. ad Rom.*, in *Omnia Opera*, ed. S. Fretté (Paris, 1876), p. 579 ff.
6. *Loc. cit.* The next three quotations can also be found here.

if he thinks that something is unclean, and he does not refuse them, then by abstaining from them, he sins just as if he were really eating something unclean. And so an erroneous conscience binds even in things which are wrong by their very nature.

Next he answers the objection by saying that, for the individual, conscience is the same as God's law because it is by conscience that one discerns the divine will:

> Nor does the first objection about the law of God change the conclusion, because the binding force of conscience is the same as that of the law of God. For conscience does not declare that something ought to be done or avoided unless it believes that this is contrary to or in accordance with the law of God.

In his theological writings the great doctor took the same stand, supporting scriptural arguments by psychological ones. In the *Summa* he poses the same question: Would it be evil to go against an erring conscience? The reason for his affirmative answer is enlightening: ". . . conscience is a certain dictate of reason, for it is an application of knowledge to an act." When he deals with the conscience erroneously commanding *what is evil*, he again rejects Hales' position:

> But this is unreasonable. For in matters of indifference, the will that is at variance with erring reason or conscience is evil in some way because of the object on which the goodness or malice of the will depends; not indeed because of the object according as it is in its own nature, but according as it is accidentally apprehended by reason as something evil to do or to avoid. And since the object of the will is that which is proposed by reason, as we have stated above, from the very fact that a thing is proposed by the reason as being evil, the will by tending thereto becomes evil. And this is the case not only in indifferent matters that can receive the character of goodness or malice accidentally; but likewise that which is good can receive the character of evil, or that which is evil can receive the character of goodness, because of the reason apprehending it as such.[7]

7. I-II, q. 19, art. 5.

Thomas' explanation of the Pauline doctrine is, in its essence, a quite simple one. Conscience is but an application of one's knowledge: "a certain application of knowledge to an act." It furnishes the will the material with which to command an action. The will has no other source from which to draw the knowledge about the goodness or badness of a particular action. It is the will which, being free, has the power of sinning, and it sins in not conforming itself to the verdict of the conscience, as this text points out. If the conscience happens to err in its judgment, this does not vitiate the whole action. The act takes on its moral character from the will's adherence or non-adherence to the verdict of the conscience. Thomas differentiates the binding power of the erroneous conscience from that of the correct conscience only in the *manner* in which they bind, not in the *degree* in which they bind. The former binds *per accidens:* that is, because of the error envolved. But the principle remains clear and unaffected.

Thomas was, nevertheless, a man of his times. He could not have failed to see the great discrepancy lying between this doctrine and the teachings and practices around him. He therefore softened this clash, not by sacrificing principles, but by refusing to admit that a sane man could innocently be ignorant of the natural law or of the divine law. In the article following the one just quoted he says:

> For instance, if erring reason says that a man is bound to approach the wife of another, the will agreeing with this erring reason is bad; because that error comes forth from an ignorance of the law of God, which everyone is bound to know.

Joseph Lecler explains this hedging, and brings it into direct connection with our subject:

> Thomas stretches this point so far that he sees a fault in the violation of a pontifical constitution which someone does not know of: "All are held to know in their own way such a con-

stitution of the Pope."[8] . . . There is no reason to be astonished at this. Like all theologians of his day he understood literally the words of the Psalmist: "Their sound hath gone forth into all the earth: and their words unto the ends of the world" (Ps 18:5).[9]

Still, the general principle was stated, not once but many times, and with a clarity and logic and scriptural foundation which were hard to refute. The importance of this position for the dignity and inviolability it attributed to the human person is very great indeed. As it developed more and more—especially under the pressures of the Reformation era—it helped greatly to change the outlook of the Church toward the individual in a most fundamental manner.

But what is the precise philosophic and psychological basis on which Thomas based his epoch-making break with the Augustinian tradition? What is his exact notion of conscience, and how does it differ from the notion it eventually replaced? The clue to the answer to these questions is given in the passage of the *Summa* we have just seen. Thomas calls the conscience a "dictate of reason" and a "certain application of knowledge to an act." It is not itself a *power*. It is an *application* of a power (reason) and of a *habitus* (knowledge) to an act. In other words, it is man's natural reason using its knowledge of good and evil to arrive at a practical conclusion as to the morality of a given proposed act. Dom Lottin's several studies on this facet of Thomistic doctrine are illuminating.[10] On the nature of conscience he says:

> Before studying the obligatory force of the conscience it is well first to look into its nature. Is the conscience a faculty, a habitual disposition, or simply an act? Some thinkers have been led to consider it a faculty, or in any event, they saw it as a habitual

8. *Quodlibet*, I, art. 19.
9. Lecler, *op. cit.*, I, p. 99.
10. See "Les éléments . . .," and "L'Ordre moral et l'ordre logique d'après S. Thomas d'Aquin," *Annales de l'institute superior de philosophie*, V, 1924, 303-399. See also *Psychologie et Morale . . .*, II, p. 356 ff.

disposition [*habitus*], which however is always in action, for all who have reached the use of reason. In his Commentary on the Sentences, St. Thomas opposes such unprecise use. To make conscience a faculty[11] is to wander too far from the proper meaning of these terms. The conscience is an act; the word itself supposes this: is it not said that it (conscience) commits, or aggravates sin? But no one is bound to perform an act except after he has realized that he should perform it. Who speaks of conscience, therefore, implies an actual consideration made by the reason concerning a given act.[12]

Once it has been determined that conscience is an act of the reason, we must investigate *what type* of an act of reason Thomas considered it to be. This will bring us to the heart of the matter. The reason proceeds, here as elsewhere, he says, in a syllogistic fashion. The major of the syllogism is furnished by an inborn general knowledge of right and wrong which he calls "synderesis." The minor is given by the reason, which examines the facts and circumstances of a given case and examines them in the light of the general norm of synderesis. The conclusion is conscience's judgment.[13]

But since this whole idea rests on the mysterious thing called synderesis, we must get a more accurate knowledge of the nature of the mystery. It occurs often in the writings of Thomas.[14] Thomas describes it thus:

> Synderesis is distinguished from practical reason not by the substance of the potency, but by a *habitus* which is somehow innate in our mind and springs from the very light of the agent intellect, as does also the *habitus* of speculative principles.[15]

Synderesis is, then, analogous to our knowledge of first principles in the intellectual field, such as, "a thing cannot be and not

11. This seems to have been Augustine's notion. See above, p. 72.
12. "Les éléments . . .," p. 45.
13. In *II Lib. Sent.*, dist. 24, q. 2, art. 4.
14. *De Veritate*, q. 16, art. 1; *In Sent. II*, dist. 24, art. 3; *Summa, I*, q. 79, art. 12 and *II-II*, q. 47, art. 6.
15. In *II Sent.*, dist. 24, q. 2, art. 3.

be at the same time." But its object is not *knowable* things but
"*do-able*" things, and hence moral things. Thus, "good is desirable and evil to be avoided" is a basic insight of synderesis. It is
up to the conscience to decide if *this act* is good. Both these
faculties, synderesis and the possession of first intellectual principles, are inborn naturally in all men. They form the substrata
on which all knowledge and all morality are based. Without
them all the contents of sense-gained impressions would be
chaos:

> Just as it belongs to the natural power [*habitus*] of the human
> mind that it knows the principles of the speculative sciences,
> there belongs also to the mind a certain natural grasp (*habitus*)
> of the first principles of practical things (*operabilium*) and these
> are the natural principles of the natural law. This natural grasp
> of practical things belongs to Synderesis.[16]

As such, synderesis forms the solid foundation of morality. It
is, as far as it goes, basically infallible.[17] But error can readily
creep in when reason either errs as to its facts or applies the
facts in an erroneous fashion. Lottin sums up the concept of
synderesis in a grand manner:

> Synderesis is then the primary norm of moral activity. It is, like
> the *habitus* of first principles, not able to be lost. Its decrees are
> above all question. They are a faithful and indefectible echo of
> nature's own fundamental exigencies; they always decree what
> is good and incline towards it, and they always repudiate what
> is evil. Synderesis is the point of departure for every judgment
> of the conscience, since every particular judgment derives from
> a universal major of the syllogism. Synderesis is also the point
> of arrival at which all conscience information concerning the
> morality of a proposed action arrives. No certitude and no recti-
> tude is really authentic if they do not stem from the immobility
> and indefectibility of these primary principles.[18]

16. *De Veritate*, q. 16, art. 1.
17. But only as to universal principles. In the concrete act of conscience,
error is quite possible.
18. Lottin, "L'Ordre morale . . .," 335.

Synderesis is, then, the foundation of conscience. Such is Thomas' conception of conscience. It is an act of the reason judging as to the rectitude of a proposed act. It arrives at this judgment by comparing the purpose of the act with the inborn general mirror of good and evil called synderesis. The *act* of making this comparison, thus drawing a conclusion, is conscience.

It was this psychological substructure which bore up Thomas in his interpretation of St. Paul. It led him to conclude that Scripture itself teaches the following proposition: even an erroneous conscience demanding objective evil is *always* to be followed; provided it is not erroneous through its own fault.

Now we must compare this notion to Augustine's. Two main differences are important here. First of all, for Augustine conscience seemed to be in itself infallible. He allowed erroneous consciences, but always attached to them the stigma of some guilt. Conscience's voice, once heard, spoke the truth. Thomas stood against him. For him only synderesis was infallible.

The second point of divergence is the fact that for Augustine conscience seemed bound up essentially with the supernatural. For Thomas, on the other hand, it was in structure purely natural.[19] It was in no real sense a "spark of the divine," as was Augustine's.

The norm of moral action is human nature itself, or if you wish, the substantial form of man. Without a doubt, because of its contingent character, human nature postulates, in the thought of St. Thomas, the existence of God, archetype and providence of the universe; it [human nature] finds its supreme norm of morality in the eternal law. But this law is not an impulse foreign to human nature; it imprints itself in man under the form of natural tendencies. It will suffice then for man to consult his own nature in order to come to know the fundamental exigencies of the natural moral law. The human positive law is

19. True, it is raised to a new level—along with all man's natural powers —by supernatural grace.

related to this other law, and has normative value only if it rests
on the natural law.[20]

This naturalness of man's conscience is of utmost importance
for us. For because conscience is in no essential way tied up
with the infallible voice of God, future ages would be able more
readily to forgive invincible error in regard to religious truth.
And if heretics—at least those who grew up in heresy—could be
innocently convinced of their position, then they would be
bound to follow their beliefs. Any physical force used to make
them act otherwise would be unworthy of Christ's Church, since
it would be abusing the very guide which Christ himself created
inviolable.

Because of these two fundamental differences, Thomas himself was able—indeed, was logically forced—to conclude against
Augustine that man must follow even a conscience demanding
an objectively sinful act. Again, he found himself in perfectly
natural agreement with St. Paul's strict insistence on the importance and dignity of man's moral guide. This facet of Aquinas'
teaching fitted in perfectly with his over-all conception of the
great dignity and essential inviolability of the human person in
general. Man was so constructed that his own natural faculties
were considered by his Creator as a sufficient guide to morality
when enlightened and elevated. He is indeed created "little less
than the angels" and made in the image of his Creator.

The spirit and institutions of his times made it inevitable that
Thomas should temper these teachings with caution. Hence his
denial of the possibility of an inculpable ignorance of the ecclesiastical and divine laws. Thomas' teaching was already in evident contradiction to the accepted tradition and the common
opinion. To admit the invincible ignorance of the divine and
Church law would be equivalent to absolving certain heretics
from blame and hence from being deserving of death. And such

20. Lottin, "L'Ordre morale . . .," 397.

a position was unthinkable to a thirteenth century churchman.

But the underlying thesis which originally helped lead Augustine to defend the persecution of heretics had been refuted. Erroneous consciences could no longer be necessarily connected to a depraved will. Clear principles had been laid down and ably defended. As Thomas' grand theological synthesis gradually became generally accepted, and as times and experience brought new facets of theology to the fore, his doctrine on conscience was slowly developed. It was a seed which was slow enough in sprouting and growing, but its fruits were eventually bountiful. Gradually the possibility of sincere errors of conscience was admitted, and the stigma attached for a thousand years to the erring conscience began to be lifted. The benefit of the doubt began to be accorded to people erring in the faith. Eventually, especially in our own age,[21] this development was to have most profound repercussions on the Catholic doctrine of church-state relations.

4. The Permanent Medieval Legacy

The middle ages contain, in a word, the story of the rise and fall of papal predominance in European politics. They are much more than that, of course. But hardly any other single fact of that complex era comes as close to solving the mystery of what made it great and what made it die. It is not accurate simply to say that it was the age of the faith. The faith had been practically universal in the western world for the better part of a millennium before what is called the high middle ages arrived. What really made this era unique was the fact that politics as well as religion was to so great an extent guided by one man at the head of one institution. Only this explains well why its most characteristic achievements became possible. Neither the great

21. See Pope John, *Pacem in terris*, and below, Chapter Seven, "Universalism Achieved."

universities, nor the crusades, nor the inquisition could have been set in motion in an era so lacking in communication, were it not for a supra-national, unifying, politico-religious authority acting as patron and catalyst.

But this political power of the popes contained the germs of its own destruction. We have seen how the fundamental popular support for the papacy lasted only until it had bested its most dangerous rivals. As soon as popes like Innocent III proclaimed themselves not only free from political subordination but, in some way, masters of the political world, the popular support ebbed away. The great ground swell of prestige had been generated by the Hildebrandine reform movement. But its chief goal was to take away royal control of spiritual affairs. The tide turned when both of the Fredericks were bested, and the papacy openly began both to practice and to preach its own political supremacy.[1] It would seem that Christians sensed the necessity of a real duality of governance.

The significance of the growth and decline of medieval papal political might is almost invariably studied in too narrow a fashion.[2] The interpretations, whether by Catholics or not, are too often distorted by merely trying to balance this medieval papacy against the political significance of the twentieth century popes. The defect in such an approach (which almost invariably leads to the conclusion that today's popes are not really sincere in these matters) is not the presumption that popes should be essentially the same in every age. They should and must be this. Rather, the defect lies in not being thorough enough in the task of comparison. Medieval papal power must not become *the* historical papal position; it must be taken for

1. If not in clear and unmistakable terms, at least in an obscure fashion.
2. The study of the actual events of the middle ages which made history has, in recent decades, been accomplished with admirable objectivity, accuracy and depth. Here, however, we are using these objective studies in an attempt to gain an insight into the *significance* of the events for the doctrine under study.

what it is. It is, in reality, only one step in the steady progression of a living doctrine which began in the New Testament, grew through apostolic and patristic times, overreached itself in medieval times, and continued its evolution into modern times, by no means reaching any final end even today. Any other mentality than this tends to "canonize" the medieval papal power constellation and thereby distorts its true significance.

Therefore, in summing up the study of medieval church-state doctrine, it is necessary to recall the basically speculative *theological* nature of that doctrine. Christ's revelation is indeed a *lux magna* given to light man's path through life. It is also the dynamic "Word" (2 Tim 4:1) which lives and gives life. It is not a "letter which kills" (2 Cor 3:6). Catholic church-state doctrine in its medieval "incarnation" must, then, be considered as an authentic part of this dynamic "Word." Like every other part, it must live in order to enliven. And life means growth and change, if not *essential* change. The real significance of the foregoing chapters on medieval church-state theory and practice can only be accurately appreciated when considered in this light.

And those sections not dealing directly with the papal power, especially the section on conscience, become clearly a necessary part of the same doctrinal evolution when seen in this long-range, theological manner. The "deposit" of faith is essentially one, and its parts influence each other intimately. A growth in one means ultimately enrichment and growth in others. Since our subject is not "papal power" but religious freedom and church-state relations, the growth of the doctrine of conscience is, as will be seen even more clearly in the final part, as important as the history of papal quarrels with kings.

Looked at from this theological viewpoint, the hieratic theory and practice of the middle ages was more of a negative than a positive thing. Even the whole concept of papal power, which was far wider and longer-lived during the middle ages than the hieratic theory, takes on something of the appearance of an excessive growth in the living tree of church-state doctrine. But this would not come as too great a surprise. The kingdom of God and its doctrines were planted by God's own will in a weak, sinful and free human nature and society. Even with the constant guidance and cultivation of the Holy Spirit, such a doctrine, rooted as it was in human soil, must be expected to have produced some "limbs" which would need pruning. Seen in the beautiful light of Cardinal Newman's conception of the growth process, such a phenomenon appears quite natural:

> But whatever be the risk of corruption from intercourse with the world around, such a risk must be encountered if a great idea is duly to be understood, and much more if it is to be fully exhibited. It is elicited and expanded by trial, and battles into perfection and supremacy . . . Its vital element needs disengaging from what is foreign and temporary, and is employed in efforts after freedom which become more vigorous and hopeful as its years increase. Its beginnings are no measure of its capabilities, nor of its scope. . . . From time to time it makes essays which fail, and are in consequence abandoned. It seems in suspense which way to go; it wavers, and at length strikes out in one definite direction. In time it enters upon strange territory; points of controversy alter their bearings; parties rise and fall around it; dangers and hopes appear in new relations and old principles reappear under new forms. It changes with them in order to remain the same. In a higher world it is otherwise, but here below to live is to change, and to be perfect is to have changed often.[3]

This concept will appear more and more apropos as our subject unrolls in Part Two. For the wide political influence and raw power of the Church during the medieval period cannot accurately be said to have disappeared as soon as the sociological structure which created and demanded it had disappeared. Indeed, it did not even disappear when the arguments

3. *Essay on the Development of Christian Doctrine* (Garden City, 1960), p. 63.

of Boniface VIII and Innocent III were discarded.[4] In other words, the hieratic theory was simply the most cogent rationalization of a vast structure of *de facto* church-state fusion, at least to a very large extent. This vast and complex structure *was* the medieval system. And the medieval system was the only system with ecclesiastical approval until the reign of Leo XIII.

There is no intermediate church-state system between John of Paris and the twentieth century. Except for minor changes, both the doctrine and the practice which we have just finished studying remained the only ideal concretely proposed by the Church. And yet, as we will see, political and sociological advances made this ideal impractical hundreds of years before another began to emerge. How can this be accounted for? It is merely a strikingly good example of the functioning of Newman's principle: the idea of church-state distinction-in-cooperation, which Christ launched into the stream of history, wavered at the beginning of the middle ages, and then struck out in one direction.

Eventually it "entered on strange territory" and wavered; and, though long delayed by circumstances, the medieval structure fell. But the idea remained. It changed "in order to remain the same."

The medieval system was, then, more than the hieratic ideas of a few generations; it was a way of life which stretched, in one way or another, back to the days of Augustine. But the main point is that it remained a *system*. As such it remained subject to the dynamics of development wherein *ideas* acquire and abandon forms according to the exigencies of time and circumstances.

But there is a positive side also in the church-state experiences of the middle ages. Behind the tapestry of hieratic uni-

4. We have seen how the theories of these men were largely abandoned before the end of the Middle Ages. But the church-state structure (especially papal political power) continued to exist.

versalism were molded several important, positive ideas which were not at all bound up essentially with hieratic theory. These developments, once the cruel realities of a post-medieval world had wrecked any pretension to political universalism, remained as permanent, positive additions to Christian church-state doctrine. In fact, they are so important that it is not an exaggeration to say that they formed already the essential outlines of church-state doctrine as it would take shape in modern times. These developments may be listed as four:

1) The endless struggle for freedom from State domination left with the Church a clear, hardened realization that this independence was of necessity a part of its very nature as Christ's mystical body.[5] The temporary success of the hieratic theory itself served to clarify and solidify this realization. It is a truth which must not be underestimated. The eastern Church had seemingly resigned itself to the inevitability of a large degree of State domination. The pressures of post-medieval times to accept a similar yoke were to be at least as great as those which caused the hierarchy in the East to yield. But the memory of the spiritual fruits of Hildebrand's struggle, and of the general blessings of an independent hierarchy, led western Christians to fight stubbornly and endlessly against subservience to any civil governor.

2) The second permanent medieval contribution was a refined sense of the Church's right and obligation to interpret and define public Christian morality. From the beginnings of the Church, popes had exercised their duties of forming and guiding public morality after the spirit of Christ. Since Constantine they had tried with varying success to assert and to exercise this right before temporal sovereigns. But too often before the age of universalism they had been satisfied with a *de facto* acceptance of imperial poaching in this field. We have seen how Justinian

5. Perhaps the best concrete proof of this realization was the Church's victory over investiture at the Concordat of Worms; see above, p. 99 ff.

and Charlemagne, to name but the two most outstanding representatives, had taken into their own hands the surveillance and direction of morality, even to the extent of legislating for the daily lives of priests, monks and nuns. The great medieval reforms led by popes slowly won them a great degree of independence in this vital field of morals.

The era of the hieratic popes consolidated this gain.[6] It made more solid and credible the pope's claim to be Christ's representative in interpreting his moral law for king and peasant alike. For, in the spiritual realm, "papal universalism" had firm foundations. It was justly claimed to rest on the scriptural power of the keys. This spiritual consolidation was effective enough so that, in the future, Catholic sovereigns would never successfully lay claim to the position of general moral guide.[7]

3) An even greater advance in church-state doctrine was made by the development of the Aristotelian-thomistic concept of the natural origin of political authority. No one single factor had greater ultimate impact on Catholic doctrine than this simple truth. Thomas himself left it undeveloped, and its chief medieval exponent, John of Paris, had no great following. Still, it was a medieval discovery, and destined in the end to replace the hieratic theory. It is important to see clearly that these two theories are in basic, mutual contradiction to one another. Civil authority comes either from the Church or from nature. As soon as the latter is admitted the whole hieratic theory falls to the ground.[8] If the State receives its power from God through the people, it is by that very fact autonomous in its proper sphere of authority. No more revolutionary political idea had

6. True, they abused it by using it as an opening into political matters; but this was the hieratic overtone of the age, which passed.

7. Henry VIII of England and Louis XIV of France attempted it. The former ended in schism, and eventually, heresy. The latter met so much opposition from his subjects that he found it to his advantage to relent.

8. Thomas' own attempt to reconcile them depended on the gratuitous assumption of the validity of the hieratic theory.

been injected into Christian thought since the *City of God*.[9] The revolution, once accomplished, was to take a solid place in Catholic church-state theory.[10]

Thomas' other revolutionary idea, his notion of the conscience, might be listed as of equal importance for the future of church-state relations. But since it bore no medieval fruits, and since even Thomas himself did not apply it to this field, it can hardly be called a genuinely medieval development in church-state doctrine.

4) Finally, it was the middle ages which gave the Church her canon law. Throughout the tortuous history of Christian church-state relations, a constant stone in the way of progress had been undefined frontiers between the spiritual and civil jurisdictions. By forging and institutionalizing a precise system of law, courts, and procedures, medieval canonists made an immeasurable advance in the work of surveying and marking this frontier. Not that any legislation could solve this problem completely. By its nature, the frontier will remain forever a source of friction and difficulty.[11] Nor can canon law, even today, be said to be entirely free from the hieratic overtones of the period which gave it birth. Nevertheless, the political world of today knows with a fair amount of accuracy what limits the Church sets to her authority, and it knows this through the medium of canon law. Hence one great source of strife was removed by this achievement of the middle ages.

These four points constitute the medieval legacy to the doctrines under study here. Even the negative "deposit" mentioned serves positively as a useful guidepost. When one carefully scrutinizes the whole of this medieval legacy, a rather startling truth emerges. Until recent times, not a great deal was added to

9. This is not to say that the two ideas are contradictory to one another, although this was generally believed at the time. See Arquillière, *L'Augustinism Politique*, p. 151 ff.

10. See Leo XIII, *Immortale Dei*, as cited in Lo Grasso, *op. cit.*, p. 311.

11. See Journet, *The Church of the Word Incarnate*, pp. 196-220.

this deposit. The end of the middle ages marked the end of a church-state epoch. The centuries dividing the beginning of Luther's revolution from the twentieth century are, in a very real sense, one long preparation for a fundamentally new orientation in Christian church-state relations. A new world began to be constructed. It would be centuries in the building. But until it was firmly established, there was no new orientation in the Church since it did not forsake those traditionally orientated Christian States in favor of a new order (which was as yet untried and unproven).

At the end of the middle ages the Church's position might be summed up briefly in the following manner. The pope is the supreme head of Christendom with the right and power even to unseat kings if the good of the spiritual demands it. The king's exclusive power over purely secular matters is rather freely admitted, but moral reasons justifying interference by the pope are wide in scope and vague in nature. Secondly, the Church must be free of the prince in her spiritual activities.[12] She is, then, supreme and free in the spiritual realm and the prince must listen to her voice.

As we shall see in the following Chapter, the three hundred and fifty-year period between Luther and Leo XIII neither added nor subtracted anything from this position. The evolution in politics was immense. The intellectual and sociological changes were equally great. But aside from the gradual shedding of most of the hieratic theory, and some rather accidental developments by theologians, the medieval church-state constellation and outlook remained the form and system espoused by the Church up until the beginning of the twentieth century. The church-state part of Christian doctrine might, then, be considered to have been forced into a kind of hibernation while the

12. This was always an important part of Church doctrine in the period under discussion even though, *de facto,* the Church was certainly not free, in her spiritual activities, from State oppression.

life-forces of society and of the Church refurbished themselves for a new season of growth.

Because of the relatively small amount of church-state activity in the period, we will content ourselves in the next Section with a very general survey of the lines of development which led up to the contemporary scene. They are, in essence, nothing other than a long, slow prelude to the relatively swift developments made by the modern popes. As such, then, they should be studied: for they form a kind of introduction to the doctrine of the modern popes, and Vatican Council II, which is the subject of Part Two.

PART II

The Modern Age

Chapter Four

Three Hundred Years

The period between the Reformation and Pope Leo XIII was one of immense change in western thought, politics and religion. Humanism matured in both its Christian and pagan forms. The political unit evolved first from a feudal conglomeration to an absolutist, centralized monarchy and from there to a parliamentary and democratic republic. Christianity was first fragmented, and then largely rejected in favor of Deism and Agnosticism. The Catholic Church fell from a position of the universally accepted authority in religion and life, to that of a minority voice largely ignored in the public forums of science and politics. In the eyes of both scientists and statesmen, church-state relations shrank, along with religion in general, from a status of greatest theoretic and practical importance to that of a relatively insignificant domestic issue.

In the face of all this change the Church changed very little. In her church-state doctrine she changed less, perhaps, than in other areas.[1] This well-known fact of the Church's frozen position in the face of rapidly moving currents all about her has

1. For a few of the important books on this period of church-state development see the following: J. Lecler, *Toleration and the Reformation* (New York, 1960); J. Leclerq, *La Liberté d'opinion et les Catholiques* (Paris, 1963); J. Guiraud, *L'Eglise Romaine et les origines de la Renaissance,* 5th ed. (Paris, 1927); G. Knight, *The Christian Renaissance* (London, 1933); G. Wals, *Medieval Humanism* (New York, 1942); A. Weiss, *Humanism in England* (Oxford, 1957); V. Green, *Renaissance and Reformation* (London, 1952); R. Chambers, *Thomas More,* 2nd ed. (London, 1948); W. Lecky, *History of the rise and fall of rationalism in Europe,* 2 vols. (London, 1882).

occasioned a great deal of adverse criticism. Not all of it is undeserved.[2] To fall behind in its task of rephrasing Christ's message to meet the needs of changing times is both possible and lamentable. Though the guidance of the Holy Spirit is unfailingly present, it does not preclude failure, even on the part of popes, in this delicate task of keeping abreast.

Nevertheless, the kingdom of God which Christ inaugurated in time is not subject to revolution. It changes, but its change always turns out to be in the nature of a growth or an evolution.[3] For this reason (which popes and theologians of post-medieval times understood very well) the Church did not follow the headlong revolutionary stream of the times. Indeed, precisely because of such precipitous disasters as the Protestant Reformation in religion, and the French Revolution in politics, the Church took on a conservative, defensive attitude. The moral reforms did, certainly, demand attention, and they were effected by such measures as the Council of Trent. But other progression in the Church, though also badly needed, was impeded, as we shall see, by ecclesiastical reaction to (and fear of) the revolutionary spirit of the times.

For this and other reasons, there is relatively little Catholic church-state activity to chronicle during this period. Since our subject is *Catholic* church-state teaching and its historical evolution, the era at hand takes on the nature of a "go-between" or "transitional" period.[4] But since it is also a period of intense constructive activity in political matters, as well as in science and sociology, it must also be considered a period of preparation.

2. If the Church is, of necessity, unchanging in essence, it must, of equal necessity, change in its accidentals, as Pope John XXIII so clearly pointed out. See his address to the Fathers of the Second Vatican Council, October 11, 1962.

3. Cf. Newman, *Essay on the Development of Christian Doctrine* (Garden City: Image, 1960), pp. 77-94.

4. Indeed, even from the viewpoint of a general historian the age is one of transition: "Modern history tells how the last four hundred years have modified the medieval conditions of life and thought," (Lord Acton, *Renaissance to Revolution*, 3rd ed. [New York, 1961], p. 31).

For, once this new world had shown itself a durable and positive one, the Church would begin to overhaul her church-state machinery in order the better to deal with it.[5]

In fact, when one considers the great activity and progress made by the popes of the twentieth century, this intermediate period takes on the appearance, in many respects, of a preparation. Considered from the point of view of specifically Christian church-state relations, the interlude between the medieval and the modern eras was a time of gradual sloughing-off of growths no longer functional, in preparation for a new season's development. Slowly the hieratic shoots withered and died, and the whole external system was pruned back. The result was a church-state system looking bleak and strange in a changed world, but ready for the renewal which God would, in his own good time, send to it.

In order to understand the rather cruel life-process by which the old medieval tendencies and institutions were worn away, we must take a brief look at the vigorous developments which conditioned this change. First, we will consider the intellectual revolution, and then the political one. These two mammoth shifts in the whole fabric of western society were themselves the force which wore away the medieval church-state system. The terminus of their development furnished the matrix within which a new system (not a new doctrine) was to be developed.

1. THE INTELLECTUAL BACKGROUND

The Renaissance and Humanism are at the root of the intellectual revolution leading into modern times. They are inextricably interlaced one with the other. The Renaissance saw the rebirth of interest in ancient learning and culture. Humanism was the

5. Naturally, it is to a large extent arbitrary whether one should call this period one of decline, transition, or preparation. It was surely each of these things, and more. But because it does cover that era in which the new world was built which the twentieth century popes used as the basis for their political teaching, we prefer to call it a period of preparation.

acceptance of the anthropocentric outlook discovered in those ancient sources:

> A new type of men began with Petrarca, men accustomed to introspection, who selected their own ideals, and moulded their minds to them. The medieval system could prepare him for death; but, seeing the vicissitudes of fortune and the difficulties of life, he depended on the intellectual treasure of the ancient world, on the whole mass of accessible wisdom, to develop him all round . . . For men craving for self-help and the complete training of the faculties, eager to escape from the fixed types of medieval manhood, minted by authority, and taught to distrust conscience, when it was their own, and to trust it only in others, Seneca was an oracle.[1]

What began with an interest in classical, pagan forms of art and literature gradually expanded into an interest in the human, and a more critical attitude toward medieval thought. Petrarch's pioneering efforts led to such discoveries as Lorenzo Valla's exposure of the falsity of the Donation of Constantine. And Valla led straight to Erasmus. The decay of the scholastic method brought on a reaction against abstract, over-logical ratiocinations and a steadily growing appreciation for the developing science of literary criticism. A general renaissance of learning in all fields advanced with the rise of an urban culture, of the new social class of commercial men, and of the universities. The invention of printing gave tremendous impulse and scope to the general spread of literacy and learning.

In theology the trend throughout was away from the scholastic method through a return to Scripture and the Fathers. Men like Nicholas of Cusa led this trend. Erasmus brought it to maturity. Already popular spirituality had, since the early fifteenth century, embodied the same reaction. The human side of Christ and the Virgin was extolled. The birth of our Lord, the Passion and the Crucifixion were described in all their humanity, and fostered a genuine revival of Christianity and a desire for reform.

1. Acton, *op. cit.*, pp. 71-73.

Paralleling the intellectual and devotional trend, the artists turned to the beauties of the human body and human emotions. Realism and imitation of classical models replaced the stylized stress of the supernatural in religious art. Raphael, Michelangelo and Peruzzi's masterpieces show how Christian was this maturing of humanism. But at the same time they show an emphasis on materiality alarmingly close to the pagan masters which they idealized.

Italy was the center where humanism was born and grew. But shortly after, it appeared in France, Germany, Spain and the Low Countries. It was a *Zeitgeist* which knew no bounds. It pervaded every area of human thought and endeavor. We have already seen how the renaissance popes patronized this movement. This is the era of the founding of the vatican library, the painting of the Sistine Chapel and of the Salle delle Borgie. It also marked an absolute nadir in public and private papal morals.

An emphasis on the human and an idealization of classical paganism naturally presented the temptation to explore human pleasure to its limits and pagan literature and art furnished excellent examples. Once initiated, this chain of responses formed a vicious circle, because sensual pleasures led the humanists further away from a Christian balance between the corporal and the spiritual. But men like Thomas More and (to a less extent) Erasmus proved that one can be a thorough humanist without sacrificing this Christian equilibrium. There were, in fact, any number of strains in the humanist movement. They ranged from unabashed paganism to the highest degrees of sanctity.[2]

The Protestant Reformation appeared on the scene just as the humanist phenomenon was coming to maturity. To say that

2. The spirituality of John of the Cross and Teresa of Avila mirrors strikingly this general interest in the human side of the spiritual life. They were thoroughly Christian, and will remain immortal masterpieces of the spirit of Christ.

there was a causal relationship between the two would be an overstatement. But to deny any connection between them would be inaccurate, too. Luther and his followers were, by and large, not humanists. Nevertheless, several facets of humanism were nailed into the reformer's platform.

Luther denounced loudly the decayed scholasticism and declared the Scriptures to be the only real source of light and truth for Christians. He condemned papal authority and extolled a subjectivistic spirituality which, at least in effect, placed man at the axis of the spiritual life. Though the spirit was to be the guide, it was always the spirit speaking through the individual ego. Without doubt, Luther struck (among other things) the humanistic susceptibilities of his hearers.

But in its essence, the Protestant Revolution was quite separate from humanism. It was a parallel movement. Humanism actually permeated Catholicism to a greater degree than it did Protestantism. (One indication of this is the fact that the "prince of humanists," Erasmus, remained solidly Catholic although he had deep sympathy with some of the reforming goals of the Protestants.) But the papacy, itself the center of the first literary and artistic triumphs of humanism, espoused anti-humanism in many respects, because of its position as guardian of the faith and because of its political position.

A century of strife and turmoil in religious, intellectual and political arenas saw Protestantism of one kind or another firmly planted in every country of northern Europe. This chronic split, plus endless division and subdivision of Protestant sects, had a profound effect on the direction of the intellectual currents of the times. The individual—Catholic, Protestant and waverer—experienced profound disillusionment and confusion affecting every area of thought.

The first shock had come with the discovery of the New World. No longer could the European rest in the tranquil certainty that he was the center of the world. Soon the Copernican system in astronomy proved this fact in an even more startling manner. Now the deep security afforded by a universally accepted faith and *Weltanschauung* had also been shattered. A century of religious warfare had left whole nations devastated. Objective reality itself was soon to be called into question on the philosophical plane by Descartes' unsolvable problem of knowledge. Everywhere uncertainty and nervous apprehension led one to turn ever more inward toward the ego, which even Descartes could not doubt.

An era of subjectivism began which, in the religious field, took the form of Deism. Vast segments of the population simply could no longer be convinced by the arguments of either Protestant or Catholic. They turned a sympathetic ear to the propagators of vague, unorganized, purely private brands of religion. Certainly, it was not the whole of Europe which embarked on this road to secularism. A large minority, both Protestant and Catholic, retained a genuinely Christian orientation and evolved their own form of humanism. Christian humanism may even be said to have proved itself the only genuine type. For it alone did not destroy its own substance by eviscerating itself of that transcendental element which even the pagans knew to be essential.

In the intellectual world a new preoccupation began to supplant religion. Galileo and Copernicus had opened new vistas for thought. Isaac Newton had propounded his laws in physics. Descartes added his brilliance to the new science of mathematics. Anatomy and biology led to vast new discoveries. The age of science began. After the torments of religious frustration, here at least was an area of certainty. Here one could get one's hands on palpable truth.

Natural science and mathematics were the humanists' paradise. In the rash of new faculties at the universities and academies of science which sprang up in the seventeenth century, religion was largely forgotten. The lay world grew steadily in size and influence. Scientific and naturalistic humanism was rapidly changing Europe from a theocentric to an anthropocentric civilization. Subjectivistic trends in philosophy and literature were forming which would carry it a step further, making it an egocentric world.

Along with Christian religion went Christian morals. Diderot and Voltaire became apostles of the new humanist morality. They preached *bonheur* to the world and mocked as medieval the morality preached by the representatives of the Church. A widespread anticlericalism made their task easy. Nothing was more out of style than traditional Christianity and its moral teachings. Louis XIV and his court supplied an excellent example of the new *môde* to his people and the whole European world.

With the development of natural sciences a new rationalism, vastly different from that of the scholastics, began to take shape. Mathematics and the scientific method led to a new awakening of the philosopher. Locke and Hume brought idealism into vogue. The main current of western thought had finally achieved a complete break with the past. It had built itself a new house in which religion had little place at all. It was a structure where humanity was self-sufficient to itself. Art, science, metaphysics, and perhaps a dash of Deism, supplied all the ingredients necessary for the new generation whose goddess was reason. This was the world of the enlightenment.[3]

Slowly developing throughout the age of humanism was a laudable though ill-directed respect for the individual. As the bourgeois class developed and education became more general, the dignity and rights of man as man came to be stressed. The aristocracy was envied for its privileges and condemned for its

3. See C. Becker, *The Heavenly City of the 18th Century Philosophers* (New Haven, 1932) and E. Cassirer, *The Philosophy of the Enlightenment* (Princeton, 1951).

absolutism. Humanism, in the hands of the middle class, became the instrument by which the awakening masses began to recognize their rights and demand them. Reaction against the excesses of the court manifested itself in general by a demand for liberty from the court's repression. Voltaire had stirred a nation against the "oppression" of the Church. Once stirred, it logically became impatient with the other portion of the ruling-class: the aristocracy. The new humanism, or "Enlightenment," was the main intellectual force behind the French Revolution. The enlightened virtues of freedom and equality overturned the last institution of the medieval world when, in 1789, the monarchy was overwhelmed and Louis XVI beheaded.

France was but the first nation of Europe to arrive at this ultimate goal of a centuries-old ferment. Within another century republicanism as a political institution was to cover an area almost as vast as the intellectual spirit which carried it forth.

At the dawn of the twentieth century the European intellectual revolution was complete. It had created the modern age: the lay age, a fairly complete reversal of intellectual trends of the medieval period. It was not a beautiful thing from the traditional Christian point of view. But it was inexorably a part of the modern world; and it has its good points even from that Christian viewpoint.

But we have seen only one facet of the humanist revolution, the secularist one. During these same three centuries organized Christianity had been encountering the same movement and patiently assimilating those elements in accord with the teachings of Christ. Granted, it was not able to so influence the times as to give them a really Christian orientation. The reason is that the main stream of thought and action was running in the other direction. Also, too much of Christianity's energies were being absorbed in endless and largely futile polemics within its own ranks.

The tide may have escaped any real Christian direction, but Christianity itself did not remain static. Its own intellectual currents persisted in a course parallel with the main stream. Christian philosophers and theologians also absorbed a deepened respect for the individual. Erasmian principles, largely neglected during the sixteenth century, acquired an ever-growing respect and development. Though Rome remained steadfast in its old royalist aristocratic coolness toward popular liberty and power, the intellectual element embraced an ever purer strain of Christian respect for the human and for human rights. Individualism was reflected, in different manners, in the spirituality of both Catholic and Protestant. Natural science was accorded an ever greater place in the schools of all Christian sects, and genuinely Christian men like Pasteur and Mendel took their share of scientific honors.

To Rome fell the unhappy task of assuring the purity of the new generation's doctrine. That it often may have been too rigorous a censor is understandable. In the face of continual crisis, normal advance on all fronts was really not to be expected. The success with which the Catholic Church weathered the storm of Reformation and Enlightenment is in many ways remarkable. In the end it could still claim the respectful adherence of a cosmopolitan soul like Cardinal Newman, and produce saints like the Curé of Ars.

2. The Political and Sociological Situation

The political world underwent as great a change during the period of transition as did the intellectual; as always the two went hand in hand. The feudal world was already being welded together into tightly knit nations at the time of the Reformation:

> Towards 1500, European nations, having been fashioned and composed out of simple elements during the thousand years between the fall of the Roman Empire and that of its successor

in the East, had reached full measure of differentiation. They were estranged from each other, and were inclined to treat the foreigner as the foe. Ancient links were loosened, the Pope was no longer an accepted peacemaker. . . .[1]

America had been discovered, trade expanded rapidly, and colonization begun. Machiavelli's *The Prince* (1532) was published only a few years after Luther's ninety-five theses. The religious explosion had even more repercussions in politics than in intellectual matters. The political entity which was Christendom fragmented very rapidly. The papacy ceased to be a uniting force. Religion itself, both on intra-national and international levels, became more divisive than unitive as a political force.

The empire was first to be affected. The emperor, Charles V (1519-1556), also king of Spain, ruler of Naples and the Low Countries, saw his German realm marred by a rash of hostilities between his vassal princes. Charles was a loyal Catholic but he was before all else an emperor. He desired religious unity and the civil peace which it would bring; but, like so many of his imperial predecessors, he felt that religious unity was a matter within his own jurisdiction.

He refused to attempt to solve the problem by military means alone and decided instead on a course of conciliation and discussion. Finally, when discussion proved fruitless, he simply accepted religious division in order to conserve the empire's unity. Or, rather, he saw that religious unity was impossible at the moment and so sought to halt further warfare and conserve national unity by a compromise. The solution—the Peace of Augsburg (1555)—was to allow the individual princes to decide what was to be the official religion in each of their territories. The Holy See denounced the measure forcibly. It had not even been consulted in the matter.

This unheard-of solution was, at best, a very poor instrument

1. Acton, *op. cit.*, p. 34.

for relations between religion and government. But it was never intended to be a permanent thing. It was, however, the beginning of two important developments which would alter profoundly church-state relations in the whole of Europe. First, the pope had become excluded once and for all as an influential voice in even the religiously orientated actions of the Catholic State. Secondly, for the first time in history it had been decided that a State need not rely on religious unity for survival. During the next hundred years both these principles were implanted in all the states of northern Europe.

In 1648 the Treaty of Westphalia clarified and solidified Augsburg's beginnings: *cuius regio, eius religio*. This was indeed the only formula to be found which could halt the terrible devastation of the Thirty Years' War. True, it admitted for the first time some small degree of religious freedom into the European political scheme. But it was itself almost as tyrannical as the former arrangement for the individual, who was always in practice the subject of an individual prince. One still was forced to adjust his religion to that of his political superior. And now that superior was even closer than before to the individual's threshold. But it was the beginning of the separation of the State from an official religion. It was a very tenuous beginning because it received only condemnation from the Church, and even the State looked on it simply as an emergency measure.

The French monarch, Francis I (1515-1547), was spared any great molestation from the first wave of reformers. The few carriers of Luther's ideas who trickled into France were simply suppressed by old and tried methods. His successors, however, saw Calvinism gradually come alive, and with it came political turmoil. Alternating efforts at toleration, suppression and discussion made the crisis less acute than it had been in Germany. Still, civil war raged, off and on, for forty years before Henry IV's Edict of Nantes (1598) brought pacification:

> We allow all those of the so-called reformed religion to live and to dwell in all the towns and localities of our kingdom and the

countries subject to our authority, without being investigated, vexed, molested or forced to do anything religious against their conscience, and without having to suffer for that reason a search of their houses or other places where they choose to dwell.[2]

It was an edict of toleration modelled on the previous unenforced Edict of Poitiers (1517) of Henry III. Here again, the chief reason behind the move was not a belief in the principle of freedom of conscience. Its main motive was simple civil necessity. Something had to stop Frenchmen from killing one another and this was the best solution at hand. It was better than the German method from every point of view. It brought from Rome a withering condemnation of the principle of liberty of conscience,[3] but in the end even Pope Clement VIII agreed that it was necessary. It was clearly better than continued war, for Catholics as well as Protestants.

In this manner northern European nations, one after another, began to lose their character as Catholic States in the traditional sense of the term. They emerged from the crisis more independent of Rome and of one another. They were now more tightly centralized and more aware of (and proud of) those manifold individual characteristics which make a nation one. They had survived the mortal threat to national unity posed by internal religious strife. The experience made them more determined to resist any outside interference, either from Rome or from other nations, which might endanger this hard-won solidarity. Europe had become a group of States and was no longer a Christendom. What had once bound them together, the Roman pontiff's voice, was no longer heard in national councils north of the Alps:

In this respect the Treaties of 1648 really mark the end of an epoch, or rather they are a definite sign that the ages in which the Catholic Church, through its head the pope, was a recognized force in the public life of Europe, had finally come to an

2. The Edict of Nantes, art. 6, as cited by J. Lecler, *op. cit.*, II, p. 142.
3. *Ibid.*, p. 145: "The pope could not find terms hard enough to condemn the royal decision."

end. After more than a thousand years the State was once more to transact its business as though the Church did not exist.[4]

The king, the symbol and creator of national unity, slowly gained more and more power. The long reign of Louis XIV (1643-1715) marked the high tide of this monarchical absolutism. Machiavelli's ideas finally found almost full practical realization. In fact, neither pope nor the moral law could exercise any great force over the new Caesars which Louis XIV epitomized.

Another important political development grew out of the ferment of humanism and warring religions. It was directly inimical to the absolutism of the kings, and was to a large extent a reaction against it. Increasing recognition of individual right, the debunking of the hieratic theory, and the influence of Luther's theories of private interpretation of the Scriptures—all these elements worked together to undermine the king's claim to absolute authority. Resistance to authority had been questioned in most other fields. Now the king's right to unquestioning obedience also came under attack.

Resistance to an unjust monarch, and even his expulsion or death, came to be condoned by many. Political power had its origin in the people, it was widely believed, and so the people could retract this power from a monarch who abused it.[5] The Huguenots in France were, understandably, the leading proponents of this theory. Stephen Brutus wrote, in 1579, his *Vindiciae contra Tyrannos,* in which he more or less transferred to the citizen what had once been a papal claim: the right of deposition. The king's rule was really by contract, formal or informal, with the people. When he failed in upholding either the divine or the natural law, the contract could be voided.

4. See Hughes, *A Popular History,* p. 192.
5. Actually the medieval origin of this doctrine goes back to Thomas. He, of course, got it from Aristotle.

Though it was the Protestants in France and England who first championed these ideas, they were soon echoed by Catholic theologians.[6] Royal absolutism, however, was still very much in the ascendancy. Claims for the ultimate sovereignty of the people were met, in the sixteenth and seventeenth centuries, by counter claims to the "divine right of kings." The king receives his authority, it was argued, neither from people nor pope but directly from God. He is, therefore, absolutely supreme. His will is law and he answers only to God. This was the stand of the largely Catholic group in France called the *Politiques.* James I of England took the same view in his work, *The True Law of Free Monarchies* (1598).[7]

The two opposing theories battled in France and England during two centuries. Gradually the people won the day, after royal absolutism discredited itself by immoral living and crass disregard of human dignity. This popular superiority was gradually institutionalized by establishment of parliamentary systems.[8]

Cromwell sent Charles I to the gallows (1649) and gave England the rudiments of a representative government. It was the beginning of great things for Europe. When Charles II was invited back as monarch he had to accept two important restrictions: the Parliament and a promise of a degree of freedom of religion for the populace.

In France the going was much more difficult. Louis XIV came to the throne after the Thirty Years' War had exhausted his rival in Germany. Since France was Europe's first power, the times were propitious for Louis' absolutist ambitions. He preserved and enhanced France's international position and secured a

6. In this we see the rise of the democratic ideal largely unattained by agnostic or deistic tendencies. Indeed it was based squarely on truly Christian principles. This tradition was never completely overwhelmed by the anti-Christian democratic ideals which the Enlightenment brought with it.

7. See Curtiss, *The Great Political Theories* (New York, 1961), pp. 269-271.

8. See J. Leclerq, *La Liberté d'opinion et les Catholiques* (Paris, 1963), pp. 161-173.

growing overseas empire. But his absolutist methods were too much for his subjects. The disgusting license of the king and his court added fuel to the fire. So did the enormous financial burdens of his wars.

His successor, Louis XV (1715-1774), failed to see the writing on the wall, and continued the same policy. Like Louis XIV, he ignored the Estates General which had been France's only relief from tyranny. During this period the French democratic movement soured.[9] Disgusted with the Bourbons, and with the Church for supporting them, and inebriated with the conquests of science, the intellectuals rallied behind new prophets.

Locke and Hume constructed theories of State which were purely man-centered. Voltaire and Diderot succeeded in lending them a positively anti-Christian direction. The result was a political movement of vast proportions for which man was his own end, and law and freedom from all authority other than his own will was the great cause. General unrest grew steadily.

Louis XVI saw the storm break, and was guillotined in the anarchy of the French Revolution. Not only the monarchy was thrown down in this storm. The fury of a long repressed and abused populace destroyed every institution on which national order could be based. It ended by destroying even the very liberty it championed, for the Reign of Terror and the subsequent Jacobin intolerance was as totalitarian as the monarchy it destroyed. The Church had made the grave mistake of supporting so blindly the corrupt Bourbon rule. It suffered in the persons of its loyal ministers and laymen the same fate as its ally. Whatever restraining and guiding force it may have offered to the new movement had been irrevocably replaced by democratic principles much less sound than those it had discarded in the previous century.

9. Up until the time of the absolutist kings the French democratic movement had been thought quite compatible with Christianity, and was supported even by Catholic theologians.

In the end the Revolution destroyed itself along with the rest. Napoleon took over the reins and soon was an emperor. He set himself up as a champion of individual freedom. Though actually a dictator, he did serve the cause of the new revolutionary liberalism remarkably. His crash through Europe broke up the lingering medieval structures of Germany and Italy. The almost innumerable principalities of the old empire were reduced to a realistic number under new heads.

Though he sowed seeds of a godless liberalism everywhere, the evil was not without a positive side. The scandal of the prince-bishop, and the prince-abbot disappeared forever. Even the papal states disappeared for a time, and Italy was given a glimpse of the dream of national unity and statehood. Finally, a new method of church-state relations was inaugurated: the concordats.[10]

A new method was really necessary. In the past the Holy See had been accustomed to dealing only with rulers who retained some semblance of the old concept of the Catholic monarch. Napoleon made no such pretence. Nevertheless it was absolutely necessary to come to terms with him for the benefit of the prostrate French Church in northeastern Europe. Therefore the concordat was invented. It was basically a question of *quid pro quo.* "What will you [the State] give to me in terms of religious benefits, if I [the Church] give you my *limited* political recognition?" Though not as desirable as genuine unity of outlook about the nature and ends of the Church, still it was more realistic and honest than her dealings with the Bourbons.

Now that the Catholic monarchy was no more, the concordat fulfilled a real need. It furnished a medium whereby the spiritual ruler of the Catholic citizens of a liberalist State might come to terms with the State without giving full approval to its princi-

10. After Napoleon seized Rome and the pope, he was excommunicated. The first modern concordat was signed (1801) only after the emperor agreed to re-establish the Church in France.

ples. Under a concordat, neither party was forced to sacrifice the principles for which it stood. There were real advantages to be gained by both parties.

Napoleon, without really intending to, prepared the ground for the work of a new generation. He himself was soon out of the political picture. But the Congress of Vienna, and the Congress of Mainz constructed new edifices on the ruins which Napoleon left. Germany became a united republic. The Risorgimento in Italy was eventually to produce the same thing for that country. By the middle of the nineteenth century Europe was, for all practical purposes, northern Europe. And northern Europe was a collection of constitutional republics. Elected officials governed nations wherein liberty for the individual was coming to be the most powerful force in politics. Freedom of religion was considered an essential.[11]

The culmination of the political revolution of the modern era was first achieved outside of Europe. The United States of America showed parent Europe the way in two most important areas.

1) In 1789 it became the first genuine constitutional democracy. The Constitution approved in that year erected the first thoroughly democratic government in over two thousand years. The republics on the continent were as yet only partially democratic. In the United States, however, the head of State was elected by popular vote[12] along with all the members of Congress. The individual's rights to freedom of speech, press, assembly and religion had never in all of history been so carefully provided for.

2) The second completely new institution (in its first amend-

11. In the mid-nineteenth century, the ideology behind this liberalism remained largely pagan, but a revived Christian liberalism was progressing rapidly.

12. Though, technically, the President is elected by an "Electoral College," practically he can be said to be elected by the people.

ment) was the absolute prohibition that any religion be "established," that is, declared official:

> Congress shall make no law respecting an establishment of religion or prohibiting the free exercise thereof.

America was little affected in her evolution to democracy by the naturalistic, unchristian liberalism of France. Firmly and explicitly founded on Christian principles, and holding religion in highest honor, the new country nevertheless had already learned from her own experience that a nation of many religions can best serve and protect religion itself by guaranteeing all faiths equality before the law. Equality, it was realized, is impossible with an established religion. The only answer lay midway between establishment and scorn of religion. The young American nation possessed the genius to incorporate this "golden mean" into its governmental structure,[13] without compromising in the least its religious foundations.

With the establishment of "separation of Church and State," the primary political church-state principle of three thousand years' standing was reversed. From the very beginning of recorded history it has been believed that a single, universally imposed religion was necessary for the well-being of any political system. The United States proved by its subsequent phenomenal prosperity and progress that, in modern times and conditions at least, the opposite is true. Equal protection and freedom for all religions proved to be a nation's best guarantee to internal peace and stability. Historians in future ages will no doubt place this discovery among the greatest contributions of the United States to world political development. Our founding fathers were indeed wiser and greater than even we Americans credit them to be.

One after another the European nations followed America's

13. See John Courtney Murray, *We Hold These Truths* (New York, 1960), pp. 48-78.

example in whole or in part. By the beginning of Pope Leo XIII's reign the political revolution of Europe had been largely accomplished. The Industrial Revolution had also been realized and the modern papacy was faced with a new world and with the new task of presenting to this world the light of Christ.

3. THE CATHOLIC POSITION

In contrast to the intellectual, political and social revolutions, Catholic doctrine during this age of preparation changed but little. The upheaval of the Protestant Reformation did have some effect in this field, but the changes occurred not so much in positive papal doctrine as in the opinions of theologians and in those of the general body of the faithful.

The most remarkable of these developments was in the field of religious tolerance. As late as the fifteenth century, heretics were being burned. In the sixteenth and seventeenth centuries Catholic and Protestant alike were engaging in wholesale religious massacres and wars. The very horror and fruitlessness of such happenings eventually called forth some salutary reconsiderations of the principle of intolerance. The ideal of one religion under one head was not abandoned, but sound theological reasons for tolerance soon were rediscovered, and they came to be accepted by both sides. Joseph Lecler, in his excellent study of tolerance and the reformation, lists four such arguments which were developed then, and which meet every qualification for theological credibility.[1]

The first was derived from St. Thomas' reasons for leaving Jews and pagans in peace. Thomas argued that for the sake of a greater good, or to avoid a greater evil, these groups could remain unmolested.[2] Never having had the faith, they could—contrary to the heretics—be presumed to be in good faith. Reformation

1. *Op. cit.*, II, pp. 499-506.
2. IIa, IIae, q. 10, art. 9.

theologians, and practically all subsequent thinkers, argued that second-generation heretics fell into the same category.

The second argument is from Scripture. Carnal and bodily punishments for false prophets and blasphemers were allowable in the Old Testament, but the New Testament of Christ was founded in love and patient sufferance of injury. Hence the only weapons of Christ's Church should be spiritual ones, after the example of its divine Founder.

The third argument was an appeal to St. Paul's defence of, and respect for, the individual conscience. The pioneering efforts of Thomas as to the real nature of the conscience began to bear fruit during this period. The widespread spirit of the humanists gave support to the theologians' efforts.

Fourthly, the growing appreciation for the fundamental distinction between Church and State led thinkers to question that the State really had the power, much less the duty, to impose religous conformity on its citizens. This was one of the fundamental points among the French *Politiques,* a Catholic group active during the struggles of the sixteenth century. The movement counted in its ranks some of France's outstanding theologians.

These four arguments did not remain static after the Reformation period. They continued to be developed and clarified in the hands of Catholic thinkers, especially those in the countries affected by the Reformation. Spain and Italy remained largely unmoved by them. The popes themselves, while relaxing somewhat from their rigid pre-Reformation position, continued to condemn toleration in theory. A few grudgingly admitted its necessity in concrete cases.[3] But in spite of the popes' disapproval, it was the Catholic States of France and Poland which led the way in putting tolerance into practice.

In post-Reformation times the principle of tolerance became steadily more and more accepted by both theologians and states-

3. Cf. Lecler, I, p. 144 ff.

men. However, an established state religion remained the ideal of both Catholic and Protestant. England and the Scandinavian countries remained officially Protestant, and France and the Empire officially Catholic. But during the eighteenth, and especially the nineteenth centuries, toleration of minority religions took an increasingly firm hold in the laws and institutions of these nations. This was inspired by the deistic principles of the Enlightenment; but it soon was put on sound theological foundations by the theologians.[4]

In addition to the growth of tolerance, some small progress was made in the over-all doctrine of church-state relations. We recall that the end of the middle ages left Catholic church-state doctrine wavering between the hieratic theory and various slightly differing statements of an indirect power theory. During the Reformation Francis of Vittoria (1480-1546) rendered a great service by cutting out much of the remaining deposits of the hieratic doctrine. He spoke out strongly against the grave immoralities committed against the American Indians by Catholic princes in the name of religion. He categorically denied that either pope or Christian emperor had any political authority over these peoples, and hence had no right to wage war against them and take away their independence.[5] To take such a position required a great deal of courage and conviction. Only fifty years before, Pope Alexander had taught and acted in an opposite manner.[6] Francis placed great stress on the natural derivation of political power from the people governed. Two of his pupils at the University of Salamanca, Dominic Soto and Melchior Cano, continued and elaborated his teachings.

4. Cf. H. R. Schlette, "Tolerance," in *Handbuch Theologischer Grundbegriffe* (München, 1963), II, pp. 679-686.

5. Francis of Vittoria, *De Indis et de iure belli relectiones* (Washington, 1917), p. 231.

6. See *Inter Cetera* (*Acta Sanctae Sedis*, XXXIII), pp. 389-390.

But two Jesuits, both living and writing during the late sixteenth century and early seventeenth century, made the biggest contribution to the work of scrapping the hieratic theory. Francis Suarez (1548-1617) and Robert Bellarmine (1542-1621) were agreed in the general lines of their church-state doctrine. Both denied the pope any direct power in the temporal affairs of kings. This they did on the Thomistic grounds that the king's power comes from God through the people immediately. They left out what Thomas added regarding the special arrangement whereby in the Christian State the Pope acts as mediator between people and king.

Probably the most significant contribution of these theologians was their adjustment to the times of Thomas' classical abstract conception of the rightful places of Church and State in relation to one another. Aquinas had with great clarity and simplicity restated the very ancient doctrine that the king is supreme in temporal affairs and the Church in the spiritual, but that, since all things must be ordered according to their final end, the Church is superior to the State.[7] In so far as the Church has eternal life as her immediate end, whereas the State's goal is only a means to this final end, the Church has the power to direct the State in matters pertaining to man's supernatural goal. Thomas, living as he did in the hieratic era, concluded that popes enjoyed what amounted to almost universal power over kings.

The Reformation theologians, especially Bellarmine, emphasized the other side of the exact same conception. They stressed the fact that the king was supreme in temporal affairs. While admitting that the Church could and should direct the temporal power towards its final end, they made it clear that any specifically temporal measures required by the Church to accomplish her end were strictly accidental to her nature. Such measures

7. Cf. *Comment. super libros Sent.*, II, dist. XLIV, q. 2, art. 3.

could only be justified when they happened to be really necessary for the execution of her spiritual duties.[8]

In this way Bellarmine's writings, and to a lesser extent those of Suarez, tended to uphold the inviolability of the prince's authority and indirectly to censure the political pretensions of the popes. Nevertheless, these men all considered the pope's indirect power so real that, for a sufficiently grave spiritual reason, it could unseat kings and dissolve subjects of their oaths of loyalty. Thus, their contributions were comparatively small.

After Suarez and Bellarmine, Catholic church-state doctrine remained practically at a standstill. The next two hundred years, as we have noted above, witnessed one of history's greatest ferments in political theory and practice. Hobbes, Locke, Rousseau, Hume and Burke inaugurated or enhanced the movement towards modern political freedom through popular representation. But the papacy, who for a thousand years was such a powerful force in political theory and practice, wielded no influence in these affairs.

This was true not merely because the majority of the directors of this movement were Protestant or deistic in their religious outlook. The basic concepts of democracy and freedom were quite compatible with Christian doctrine. The popes, for reasons we are about to investigate, actively opposed and even condemned the whole trend. They supported the monarchy even when the individual monarchs were indefensible both in their private morals and in their public policies.[9] One might understand why the Holy See supported the Catholic king, James of England, against the parliamentarians. But why support Louis XIV in France? Why did they not at least support the good qualities of both sides and condemn the defects of both

8. Cf. "De Potestate Pontificis," *Opera Omnia,* II, V (Paris, 1870), pp. 155-156.

9. See, for example, H. Küng, *The Council and Reform* (New York, 1962), p. 122 ff.

sides equally, as the popes had done down through the ages?

That, of course, is the great question: "Why?" The phenomenon of papal recalcitrance in the face of political progress of the highest moral significance is beyond a doubt the outstanding church-state reality of the transition period. It has caused Catholic citizens since that time no end of anguished embarrassment, and turned sincere seekers for truth away from conversion to, or reunion with, the Catholic Church.[10] Why did the popes drag their heels at every turn during this gradual evolution? The answer is certainly complicated.

The standard answer of the Protestants and secularists has been that the Church is in its very essence absolutist or even totalitarian. The solution given by Catholics is that the French and English republican and democratic movements were basically anti-Catholic during that period. Surely both responses carry a good deal of truth. It is a fact that the Church is largely monarchical in its own social structure. Also, until the nineteenth century it had never given its approval to any type of civil government other than a monarchy. There were no others. Beyond a doubt these factors aid in explaining Rome's frozen attitude during transitional (or "preparational") times. The popes were men of their times, quite fallible as judges of political institutions.

The "Catholic answer" is also partially true. The drive towards democracy in England and France was always led by anti-Catholic forces, and in France it was greatly intensified by several basically unchristian concepts.[11]

Nevertheless, both of the foregoing explanations have serious faults. Any objective study of history and of Catholic doctrine will reveal that the Church is neither totalitarian nor absolutist by nature. Neither is it true that the movement towards democracy was essentially unchristian. The papacy *could* have sup-

10. This is Father Küng's whole point, *loc. cit.*
11. See Leclerq, *op. cit.*, p. 161 ff.

ported the French revolutionists' demands for "Liberty, Fraternity and Equality." It could have been made clear that these
laudable aims have a stronger foundation in Christian doctrine
than they have in naturalist and deistic philosophies.[12]

What, then, is the real reason behind the perplexing mystery
of the persistently conservative policies followed by the transitional popes? While granting both the above solutions their
proper weight in the matter, it now seems certain that neither of
them contain the really decisive factor.

The real problem was on the practical plane. With half of the
Church in republics and half in monarchies the Church could
only hurt one-half of her children by supporting the political
philosophy of the other. If she supported the monarchy in
France, all of her institutions and freedoms could be swept
away by the liberals. If she supported even the Christian ideals
of the liberalists she would be betraying the ancient alliances
with the Christian monarchs and subverting the very existence
of her own monarchical rule of the papal states.

The popes of this era were caught in the midst of a centuries-
long political transition wherein any positive alliance, such as
was customary and beneficial heretofore, would cause great
harm for Catholics under the opposing system. Southern Europe,
though by no means untouched by the new ideas, remained
firmly monarchical at the beginning of the crisis. France, the
only solidly Catholic country in northern Europe, remained
largely undecided between monarchy and republic even long
after the Revolution. Hence, for roughly a hundred and fifty
years, from the English Revolution in 1688 till after the final
triumph of republicanism in France in 1848, it seemed from the
papal standpoint that the monarchists would have a good chance
of winning out in the end.

The ultimate solution to the dilemma would be the realization

12. See Gustave Thibon, *Christianity and Freedom,* a symposium by
the *Centre catholique des intellectuels français* (London, 1955), pp. 1-17.

that the Church, by her very nature, stands neutral in the confrontations of various non-absolutist forms of government.[13] But the realization of this fact had not yet evolved.[14] The almost immemorial tradition of close union between Church and Christian monarchies obscured the biblical and patristic teaching that the kingdom of God is above the intricacies of the purely political.[15] As a result, the popes felt obliged to choose between the two systems. The odds were for a long time so overwhelmingly in favor of the monarchy that they were very slow in even realizing the existence of the dilemma.

It is only fair to say (once the fact of their blindness to the nature of the democratic revolution is realized) that the popes had sound pastoral reasons for siding with the monarchies. This is true not only because the majority of Catholics lived under kings and were more or less content with their lot. A still more important reason is that to support liberalism would have been to subvert papal political sovereignty in Italy; and to subvert this political independence would be to imperil the very existence of spiritual autonomy. The papacy had no realistic hope that its spiritual sovereignty would be respected by either monarch or parliament once it surrendered political command. This problem of papal political sovereignty constituted on every level an effective block against any objective evaluation of the democratic ferment.

Gradually the reaction against political absolutism became general even in the Germanic nations and in Italy. We have seen how Napoleon brought the new spirit with him wherever he went. It was only then, during the nineteenth century, that the full force of their dilemma began to dawn on the popes. The

13. Pius XII, Christmas Message for 1951: "Nevertheless the Church cannot renounce her political neutrality."

14. It is clearly indicated in the Scriptures, but it had not yet evolved a form compatible with modern society.

15. See Oscar Cullmann, *Dieu et César*, pp. 91-96.

reigns of Gregory XVI (1831-1846) and Pius IX (1846-1878)
epitomize in many ways the quandary in which the Holy See
found itself, and bring the matter to ultimate solution.

In the eighteen-thirties, the French priest de Lamennais led a
party of eminent French Catholics in their espousal of a Christian brand of political liberalism.[16] Through their organ, the
newspaper *L'Avenir*, they soon had all of Catholic Europe in an
uproar over the merits of such ideas as freedom of the press,
freedom of conscience, and separation of Church and State. De
Lamennais' writings were full of fire and genius, but they lacked
both prudence and theological precision. He left himself wide
open to his enemies, and they were not long in denouncing him
to Rome.

Pope Gregory could have curbed the undoubted exaggerations
in the movement without entirely contradicting his espousal of
liberalism. But Gregory, from his standpoint as a traditionalist
monarch, could see only dimly if at all the possibilities for good
within these ideas. The dilemma was only beginning to make
itself evident. De Lamennais was at least blessed with the genius
to see that the whole movement of western society had advanced
beyond the point of no return in its drive for human freedom.
The pope saw only a movement led by enemies of the Church
which had already caused havoc to the faith. The extremism of
L'Avenir did nothing to help him alter his views. The rash of
liberalist governments springing up in Belgium, Poland, and
even Spain, demanded an immediate decision on both the theoretic and practical level.

In 1832 Gregory made known his course of action. On the
practical level it was a wavering, precarious one. In the bull,
Sollicitudo Ecclesiarum, he gave *de facto* recognition to the new
liberalist governments, but at the same time he came out strongly
for the traditionalist monarchy and condemned the principle of

16. For a good account of this movement see Fliche-Martin, XX, p.
442 ff.

revolution. In 1832 his Encyclical *Mirari Vos* condemned in strongest terms the cherished ideals of de Lamennais.[17]

De Lamennais himself refused to submit and died in apostacy. His most famous followers such as Lacordaire curbed their zeal and were subsequently able to be of great service to the whole Church by serving their old cause with proper restraint and prudence. Gregory's best efforts were in vain, for at his death the new movement within the Church was stronger than ever.

Pius IX (1846-1878), with his long and eventful reign, sheds even more light on the dilemma which kept the papacy shackled to outmoded conceptions in church-state relations. At first Pius surprised the world by siding with the liberals. Nor was this a mere political move. Politically it would still have been wiser to remain a close friend with the monarchies who protected the pope's own realm.[18] Rather, Pius' liberalism was a sincere attempt to acknowledge, and adjust to, the new ideas. He granted freedom of the press, released all of the Vatican's political prisoners, and set up a constitutional government within his territories.

The results of these moves were disastrous to the papal monarchy. The pope's new friends soon showed that they would stop at nothing short of complete reunion of Italy under truly representative government. Nor would any questions of the morality of the means to this end detain them. This in itself proves how real were the dangers which Pius' predecessors feared so much. When, in 1870, Victor Emmanuel's troops entered Rome, the pope's spiritual independence went down with his political sovereignty. He became a "prisoner of the Vatican" and powerless against the intolerable pressures of his political masters.

But Pius recognized long before this event that a liberal papal policy would lead eventually to political annihilation. Only two

17. Cf. *Acta Sanctae Sedis*, 1831, IV, pp. 336-337.
18. See E. E. Y. Hales, *Pio Nono* (Garden City, 1954), p. 56.

years after the beginning of his long reign he alienated himself
from the Risorgimento movement by condemning its anti-
Christian elements and making clear his intention of retaining
ultimate power in his own realm. From then on the pope slowly
reverted to the policies of Gregory—not out of conviction so
much as out of fear of the spiritual harm which the new *Geist*
might bring.

It might have been possible for a diplomatic genius like Innocent III to have separated the good from the bad in the new
movement without losing everything in the process. But Pius IX
was no such genius. He lacked the suppleness necessary for successful diplomacy. As a result he ended by apparently condemning the whole movement to which he had originally given his
support: "(It is condemned that) the Roman Pontiff can and
should reconcile itself with liberalism and the new political
structure."[19] Such a position, which was held to the end of his
life, may have been understandable in its original context, but
given in the form of an encyclical to the whole world, it caused
no end of consternation and misunderstanding.

Such was the extent of the papal dilemma which lasted so
many years. Pius IX felt its full force and saw it solved when
the papal states were wrested from him.

Catholic doctrine on freedom in Church and State has remained
the same in essence throughout the centuries, but it has changed
immensely in its outward form. According to its very nature the
Church has always respected civil authority, demanded spiritual
autonomy, and interpreted public Christian morality for the
individual and for society. Of course the concrete constellation
of relations have changed radically as the State itself changed
and the Church grew and evolved. But no greater change in
constellations had ever been witnessed in Christian history than

19. *Syllabus Errorum*, lxxx, Denzinger, no. 1780, 300. See Hales, *Pio
Nono*, for a clarification of the actual origin and circumstances, p. 266 ff.

those witnessed by the age of preparation—and yet the Church itself remained still wedded to its medieval positions.

In the age of Constantine and in the middle ages the Church was in the vanguard of those seeking progress. But circumstances in the transition period left it in the role of the conservative. The loss of the papal states, however, marked the beginning of a new era. It marked, both for Europe and for the Church, the triumph of democratic ideals. It also was the end of purely political concerns for the Holy See, concerns which had so long clung like a dead weight to Peter's successor. Freed at last from its dilemma, the papacy began at once the task of adjusting Catholic church-state doctrine to the new political and social realities. The new era which followed is the main object of this essay. It is beyond a doubt the most significant period of development in the whole history of church-state doctrine. The entire chronicle of historical development up to this period has therefore been, in part, but a necessary preparation towards a better understanding of the significant doctrinal evolution which has taken place in our own century.

Chapter Five

Pope Leo XIII

When one writes history it is almost invariably in order to shed light on the contemporary scene. When the history of a doctrine is written, it always has as its ultimate end a fuller comprehension of the current form of that doctrine. Part Two of this essay is at once the modern chapter of a doctrinal history and a critical analysis of a doctrine in formation. The one reason why a careful investigation of the historical evolution of church-state doctrine is so necessary is precisely its critical importance for a better understanding of the modern forms of this doctrine. Pope Leo XIII may be said to have formally inaugurated the modern period. The last three sections of this study treat of three modern popes and a Council, and this influence on the direction of modern church-state doctrine. By studying, in the light of the material contained in Part One, the doctrines of Popes Leo XIII, Pius XII, John XXIII, and the Council's Declaration on Religious Freedom, we will be able to understand and judge the import of the teaching of our own day.

As in previous chapters, we intend to follow the lines of doctrinal development in religious freedom and Catholic church-state doctrine. But this object must now be seen in the kaleidoscopic social and political conditions of the twentieth century. Because the modern period is, for us, the terminal point of the development of this doctrine, it must be studied by a more critical method and in greater detail than was either possible or necessary for patristic or medieval times.

No one will deny that modern Catholic church-state doctrine

presents problems to any commentator or interpreter. The fact is amply proven by the realization that, during the two decades immediately preceding the Second Vatican Council, theologians writing on this subject were split into two warring camps.[1] The disagreement was so sharp that anyone seeking to throw light on the subject was immediately assumed to be merely taking sides, and so becoming nothing but a reinforcement for one side or the other. To avoid this pitfall, one of the first precautions is a judicious choosing of one's authorities. For the Catholic, at least, the safest source is papal doctrine. We have already seen that papal doctrine has always been the primary font of this doctrine throughout history. Popes both lead and represent the belief of the faithful. Faced with the panorama of almost infinite contemporary theological opinion in this matter, papal teaching acts as a barometer to measure the theological climate. Nothing could be more natural. That is the purpose of Peter's office.

1. The controversy is world-wide. Its two sides can be roughly distinguished by the stand taken on the question as to whether or not there exists an absolutely ideal system of church-state relations. Because of its importance, this controversy will be alluded to frequently in Part Two of this essay. The whole argument can be found in miniature form in two series of articles which appeared in two American theological journals some years ago. The conservative position (that a close and formal union between Church and State remains the unchangeable ideal form of relations) was defended by Msgr. Joseph Fenton; the opposite stance (that no one type or system of church-state relations could be called ideal for all times) was taken by Father John Courtney Murray, S.J. For the first view, see the articles in the *American Ecclesiastical Review*, especially the following: "Catholic Polemic and Doctrinal Accuracy" (September, 1954), 107 ff.; "The Relation of the Christian State to the Catholic Church according to the *Pontificale Romanum*" (September, 1950), 214 ff.; "Toleration and the Church-State Question" (May, 1954), 330 ff.; "The Teachings of *Ci riesci*" (February, 1954), 114 ff.; and "The Holy Father's Statement on Relations between Church and State" (November, 1955), 323 ff. For Father Murray's views, see especially the following articles which appeared in *Theological Studies:* "The Problem of Religious Freedom" (September, 1949), 409 ff.; "The Problem of State Religion" (February, 1950), 155 ff.; "The Church and Totalitarian Democracy" (December, 1952), 525 ff.; "Pope Leo XIII and the Order of Culture" (March, 1954), 1 ff. This is a representative (not a complete) list of their articles on the subject. They portray accurately the lines of the controversy in wider circles.

But even papal doctrine must be interpreted. And interpretations have always been conflicting. Historical method seems best suited to assure both accuracy and objectivity. The source of a great many of the conflicts seems to have been too little recognition of the typical twentieth century speed which has characterized the evolution of even papal doctrine. In the middle ages three-quarters of a century was a short period. Today it is enormous. This will become quite clear as we see the distance which separates Pope Leo XIII from John XXIII.

Another source of conflict is the fact that modern papal doctrine is often studied in the light of only the immediate past, that is, of the medieval and transitional periods. For a deep and accurate appraisal, doctrine must be studied in the light of its roots in Scripture, and in its total historical development. In this manner the progressions from Pope Leo XIII to Pope John XXIII are seen quite naturally as the latest dynamic surge in a two-thousand-year-old growth process.

When Pope Leo ascended the papal throne he found his office reduced in political influence to a position almost as impotent as it was in the days before the Edict of Milan. For centuries the Church had been seeing the pre-eminent place she enjoyed in the days of Christendom slowly being eroded away. This loss took place both invisibly, within the hearts of men, and visibly, as her institutionalized pre-eminence was whittled away by civil laws and revolutions. Pope after pope had protested this loss so constantly and vehemently that, especially at the time of Pius IX and his *Syllabus of Errors,* the Church began to take on, in the public forum, the appearance of a chronic and disillusioned prophet of doom.[2] No one had as yet seen that the undoubtedly sad politico-social situation had its positive side. It was to be years before this positive view was to be felt concretely in the realm of church-state relations.

The period of political transition from Christendom to the

2. See Section on Pope John XXIII, below, 269 ff.

modern State was, as we have seen, more or less complete. This change had involved a great deal of deterioration of Christian ideals. But it can by no means be called merely a deterioration. Indeed, it was seen by many—even then—as a positive thing. This was a time of crucial decision for the Church. It had to be decided whether or not it would retain in the popular image the figure of an aging system, grudgingly protesting change and civil progress. The encyclicals of Leo changed fundamentally the direction and place of the Church in modern society. In no area was their impact greater than in that of church-state relations.

Pope Leo XIII (1878-1903) came to the throne of Peter adequately prepared to do great things for freedom in Church and State. His contributions may seem singularly imperfect to post-Vatican II minds, and indeed they are. But when judged in the light of his immediate predecessors, Leo XIII was a daring progressive. A better schooling for the task would be hard to imagine. He had, from his earliest manhood, been outstanding for his keen intellect. His noble birth[3] assured him an excellent early education, and his own talents pushed him forward in his seminary days. He fell in love with Thomistic philosophy and theology at an early age and it was to remain a foundation of his tight logical thought for the rest of his life.

But he rarely allowed his love of speculative truth to separate him from the concrete reality of human life in society. His fine diplomatic record as Nuncio to Belgium bears witness to this.[4] In Belgium he learned liberalism at first hand, on both its philosophical and its political levels. Subsequently, as bishop of Perugia for twenty-two years, he put this knowledge to good use. There he was Ordinary in a province which had seceded from the papal states and was ruled by anti-Catholic liberals.

3. He was the son of Count Pecci, born March 2, 1810.
4. He began at the age of 33.

During these difficult years he perfected the art of meeting his
opponents on their own ground, and demanding for the Church
the liberty which they extolled so highly.

Thus, when Cardinal Joachim Pecci succeeded (February 20,
1878) Pius IX as Leo XIII, he already had outlined a remedy for
the doldrums into which the social doctrine of the Church had
fallen. On the very day following his election he sent messages
to the heads of State in Russia, Switzerland, and Germany, protesting the lack of liberty accorded to the Church. His first allocution was a protest against the loss of the Holy See's political
independence. But Leo did not by any means limit himself to
condemnations and protests. He supported his predecessors'
long list of rebukes and laments. But he did so only in conjunc-
tion with a bold and positive definition of the Christian moral
and dogmatic position regarding the modern world.

From his first encyclical (*Inscrutabili,* April 21, 1878) to his
last (*Annum Ingressi,* 1902) the very central aim of his pontificate remained the anchoring of the Church firmly in the modern world.[5] A tone entirely new for the Holy See pervaded both
his writings and his concrete policy. For the first time in history
the rights of the working classes were set forth clearly in a papal
encyclical—*Rerum Novarum.* Encyclicals followed devoted to
Christian marriage (*Arcanum Divinae,* February, 1880), and
the reunion of Christianity (*Praeclara Gratuationis Publicae,*
June, 1894). These slowly changed the notions of both Catholics and non-Catholics as to the place and function of the head
of the Church respecting vital social issues of the times. Men
received clear, unequivocal direction concerning their most
personal problems. Each encyclical was a neat stone cemented
into a growing edifice of teaching.

Leo's social pronouncements were held together by a clearly
enunciated scholastic conception of the natural and of the divine

5. See E. Gilson, *The Church Speaks to the Modern World:* The Social
Teachings of Leo XIII (Garden City, 1954), Preface, p. iii.

law.[6] They cover a wide range indeed. But at the very center of his attention was the new society itself, and the relations of the Church with that society on all levels. First his attention was directed to the precise nature of the current social evils, and to finding corresponding Christian solutions. Liberalism (*Inscrutabili*, 1878), socialism and communism (*Quod Apostolici Muneris*, 1878) and freemasonry (*Humanum Genus*, 1884) were each in its turn confronted with the Gospel.

Then followed a series of encyclicals which outlined a positive Christian adaptation to the new political structures. These helped immeasurably to bring the Church into firm contact with —and into participation in—the new world. At the center of this growing corpus we find Leo's leading declarations of the church-state doctrine. *Immortale Dei* (November 1, 1885), as *Inscrutabili* (1878) before it, clarified the Christian constitution of States. *Libertas Praestantissimus* (June, 1888) proposed a Christian alternative to the relativistic liberalist teaching on human freedom. *Sapientiae Christianae* (January 10, 1890) outlined the duties of Christian citizens.[7] Thus, only halfway through his long pontificate, Pope Leo had already forged a totally new political *Weltanschauung* for the Church.

With relatively few exceptions, the second half of his pontificate was devoted merely to perfecting and defending an already mature doctrine. In the aforementioned documents he had

6. Leo wrote during the strong revival of scholastic philosophy and theology in the Church, to which he contributed not a little strength. But he was himself influenced quite a bit in this regard, as in the substance of his doctrines, by his many advisers who were practically all fervent scholastics—notably Cardinal Cigliari. The influence of a popular movement in theology upon a pope's writing and thinking is a good example of the complicated ingredients which go into any pope's doctrine.

7. Numerous other documents (though especially the social encyclicals) contain much valuable church-state teachings. But they serve only to give depth to an amazingly complete outline already drawn in these three letters. For a list of the pope's major pronouncements on political matters, see J. García, *Doctrina Pontificia II, Documentos Políticos* (Madrid, 1957), pp. 7-8.

clearly outlined a church-state doctrine calculated to harmonize with a changed society. The principles involved were very old indeed. But Leo's predecessors were not always in the position required for a clear enunciation of principles. Alongside these outstanding writings one finds an equally impressive practical diplomatic adjustment with the nations of Europe. Thus, he synthesized on both the theoretic and practical level the whole question in a manner not attempted since Pope Gelasius.

He was able to penetrate beneath the anti-Catholic façade of the new political world. Without neglecting to protest its excesses, he had no small insight into the positive and irreversible progresses which the new world embodied. He gave recognition to these in the name of the Church, and offered a fundamentally new program towards a church-state rapprochement based partially upon these new but authentic values. This was evidently his intention from the beginning of his pontificate. We will first investigate what precisely his contribution consisted in. Then we will attempt to weigh carefully its true significance in the light of the growth-curve of the church-state doctrine as a whole.

A close examination of Leo's political writings shows little development, in the sense of marked changes in orientation and direction, between those written at the beginning and those written at the end of his reign. Rather there is evident a continually broadening panorama of almost identically orientated doctrine. Each of the four fundamental encyclicals mentioned above are meshed tightly with the others. All of them originated from a single source: a mastery of the traditional scholastic concept of the natural law and a consideration of the whole basic civil order in the light of this law. This law, he was convinced, would not really conflict with the divine positive law of the Church since both rested ultimately in the same eternal law of God. This principle is clearly indicated in his very first encyclical.

Since Leo's church-state doctrine does flow from this one source in a typical scholastic, almost syllogistic, form, we will examine it not in the chronological order of its appearance,[8] but in its logical divisions. It consists essentially in the development of two contrasting but nevertheless complementary facts: 1) the Church and the State are separate in their essence, 2) but they are coordinate partners in their destinies.

1. CHURCH-STATE AUTONOMY

According to both logic and importance, the first of Leo's contributions is his clear affirmation of the fundamental autonomy and independence of both Church and State.[1]

> The Almighty, therefore, has given the charge of the human race to two powers, the ecclesiastical and the civil, the one being set over divine, and the other over human, things. Each in its kind is supreme, each has fixed limits within which it is contained, limits which are defined by the nature and special object of the province of each so that there is, we may say, an orbit traced out within which the action of each is brought into play by its own native right.[2]

This conclusion as to the respective autonomy of the two authorities is the term of a simple line of reasoning. God placed within all men a natural desire to live in society: "Man's natural instinct moves him to live in civil society." This is impossible without the order which only authority can give. "Every body politic must have a ruling authority." Hence the State and its authority comes ultimately from God and is subject to him. ". . . this

8. This Leo himself advised against. See Gilson, *op. cit.*, p. 23-24.

1. The pontiff stressed more the complementary fact of the two societies' coordination; but in doing so he added nothing to the already existing doctrine.

2. *Immortale Dei*, Acta, V, 127, trs. E. Gilson, p. 167. Translations of citations from Leo XIII's encyclicals appearing here are taken from *The Church Speaks to the Modern World*, edited by Etienne Gilson (New York, 1954).

authority, no less than society itself, has its source in nature and has, consequently, God for its author." Hence the State possesses naturally—ultimately from God—all the instruments needed for its function as the protector of the common good.

The Church too has God as its author through Jesus Christ who established it with all the power and authority it needed to carry out its task of praising God and leading men to their ultimate supernatural end.

> This society is made up of men, just as civil society is, and yet is supernatural and spiritual, on account of the end for which it was founded, and of the means by which it aims at attaining that end. Hence, it is distinguished and differs from civil society, and, what is of highest moment, it is a society chartered as of right divine, perfect in its nature and in its title, to possess in itself and by itself, through the will and loving kindness of its Founder, all needful provision for its maintenance and action.[3]

Being established immediately by Christ and of a supernatural nature, the Church is "by far" superior in dignity.[4] From this mutual independence of both societies Leo drew several important conclusions. For the State it follows first that it is free to choose for itself the form of government which it considers best, without interference on the part of the Church. If it is not anti-Christian in form or spirit, the form of government is left completely in the hands of civil society. Secondly, the form of government being outside its jurisdiction, the Church has no objection to democratic forms of government,[5] and indeed, in certain conditions, a democracy is surely to be recommended:

3. *Loc. cit.* (Gilson, p. 168).
4. ". . . The Church is far and away the most distinguished . . ." *Ibid.*, p. 125. Leo's idea here is clarified by a parallel passage occurring in the encyclical *Libertas praestantissimum:* "They would take away from the Church her rights as a perfect society and would deny her the power to make laws to judge and to punish. They would allow her only the right to persuade those who voluntarily subject themselves to her" (Acta, VII, 223).
5. This is a break with the constant royalist tradition of the Holy See during hundreds of years.

Neither is it blameworthy in itself, in any manner, for the people to have a share greater or less, in the government: for at certain times, and under certain laws, such participation may not only be of benefit to the citizens, but may even be of obligation.[6]

Thirdly, since Christians are citizens, they must actively serve their country and should in all areas of natural learning, particularly the natural sciences, serve the interest of their country by helping to advance its natural well-being.

On the other hand, the Church also benefits from the liberty and rights of an independent society. Leo condemned liberalism for not according to the Church the benefits of freedom which it so loudly demanded for itself.

The drawing up of laws, the administration of State affairs, the godless education of youth, the spoliation and suppression of religious orders, the overthrow of the temporal power of the Roman Pontiff, all alike aim to this one end—to paralyze the action of Christian institutions, to cramp to the utmost the freedom of the Catholic Church, and to curtail her every single prerogative.[7]

Thus, according to the pontiff's conception, the true mutual recognition by both Church and State of each other's rights as autonomous societies works to the advantage of both.

Here we have not only Leo's clearest exposition of the foundation of Christian church-state relations,[8] but the clearest in the whole history of the Church. All accidental elements are stripped away and the universal abstract kernel of doctrine is exposed to view.[9] For this reason Leo's classical exposition of the funda-

6. *Immortale Dei*, Acta, V, 141 (Gilson, p. 177).

7. *Ibid.*, 136 (Gilson, p. 174).

8. This is a principle to which the pope returned time and again, notably in *Libertas* (cf. VII, 220 ff.).

9. Such abstraction and universality is, indeed, Leo's strength. But it also embodies a recurring weakness. Abstractions, precisely because they are abstract, take on a facility which is deceiving. For example, Leo claims that it is not difficult to determine what would be the form and character of the State, were it governed according to the principles of Christian philosophy (*Ibid.*, 120). But is it not really extremely difficult to establish any

mental autonomy of Church and State was most important.

One needs only to recall briefly Part One to realize that Leo is indicating a fundamentally new approach to the question. How vastly different from the writings and policies of Boniface VIII and Innocent III. How vastly different from all papal doctrine five centuries before and after Boniface and Innocent. Different, and yet the same. All these men admitted, and even insisted on, the fundamental separation of these two societies. They even guardedly admitted the theoretic independence of the civil authority in purely temporal matters. But a clear and abstract statement of the principle of the real independence of the State, though it could have worked wonders towards a reconciliation with the princes, never issued from their pens.

To find a similar statement of this church-state doctrine one must go back to the seventh century and Pope Gelasius.[10] After Gelasius' time, concrete, existential mixing of political and religious powers within the papal office so complicated the issue that during the thirteen hundred intervening years any clear enunciation of the mutual autonomy of the two societies would have undermined the whole medieval structure.[11]

---

society which even remotely approaches a full incarnation of these principles, or even to calculate its general outlines? However, the encyclical was of a polemical genre—aimed against the liberalists, and this explains some otherwise very remarkable generalizations. For example, in the same letter we read that it is very easy for all to find the true religion. None of the contemporary popes would have said this. But Leo was aiming at the European liberalists who were centered in Catholic nations. For *them* it was not difficult, he thought. Such abstractions are true only when read carefully, in their context. The same applies to Leo's great church-state principles. They contain gold, true; but the very nature of encyclicals demands that they be read in the context of their times. They are prudential statements not only of doctrine but of practical policy. And doctrine can be very much obscured by the policy demands of the times. An example of this truth for us is the encyclicals of Gregory VII. One would not call them inexact, but rather heavily coated with the policy demands of his age. The same applies even to the most abstract of Leo's political writings.

10. And see Murray, "The Church . . .," p. 559.

11. Cf. Dondeyne, *Faith and the World* (Pittsburgh, 1963), pp. 256-257.

This significant service to general Christian church-state doc-trine was motivated by another of Leo's characteristic traits. It was always his firm policy to go to great lengths in order to give his opponents due consideration.[12] The positive results were very obvious in his dealings with the nations of northern Europe.[13] The clear declaration of the absolute autonomy of the State in all political affairs was perhaps the crowning point of this policy. First, it dealt a serious blow to the liberals' contention that the Church wished to maintain an authoritarian control over the State, and over society on all levels. Secondly, it reassured and gave new hope to sincere but very confused Christians partaking in political movements and holding civil positions. They were assured that it was possible to be perfectly loyal to their politi-cal obligation without in the least compromising their loyalty to Christ. This seemingly self-evident fact was quite obscured in the liberalist battles at the turn of the century. The realization, fostered by so many of the great pope's writings, had the effect of initiating the dissipation of the defeatist, ghetto attitude of Christians.

Thirdly, the clear enunciation of distinction and autonomy for both societies marked the definitive burial of such outmoded ideas as the Church's power to depose kings and decide their succession. Though for centuries now these ideas had not been mentioned except by some theologians, their memory was kept alive by such broad papal hints as those found in Pius IX's *Syllabus of Errors*.[14] Though Leo retained as his right a wide power for the Church in political affairs having moral implica-tions, nevertheless he never once inferred that these rights extended into the very foundation of the State's duties. By deliberately emphasizing the State's independence, he laid the

12. At least in comparison with his immediate predecessors.
13. For example, Leo gradually persuaded Germany's Bismarck to soften his crippling repression of the Church (cf. "Leon XIII," *Dict. Theol. Cath.*, 345 ff.).
14. See, for example, No. XXIV (Denz., 1124).

foundation of a new era of mutual trust and respect between civil and ecclesiastical authorities.[15]

But there is another, more practical, reason for emphasizing the mutual independence of these two "perfect" societies. The Church had just lost her only sure assurance of keeping herself free and independent in the very center of her vitality. Since 1870 the pope's very palace had been subject to the whims of the Italian government. As it was considered subject to Italian law, the Holy See was far from being recognized as the head of a perfect, supra-political society, notwithstanding any Italian protestations of non-interference.[16] Seeing what had happened to the Church in France and Germany under the liberalist governments, Pope Leo recognized clearly the mortal danger that the political subjection of Rome constituted for the spiritual independence of the universal Church. This is a central theme in his encyclical *Inscrutabili*, in which he outlines the limits of the State's power. This fear colored Leo's whole church-state doctrine:

> The enemies of public order, being fully aware of this, have thought nothing better suited to destroy the foundations of society than to make an unflagging attack upon the Church of God, to bring her into discredit and odium by spreading infamous calumnies and accusing her of being opposed to genuine progress. They labor to weaken her influence and power by wounds daily inflicted, and to overthrow the authority of the Bishop of Rome, in whom the abiding and unchangeable principles of right and good find their earthly guardian and champion.[17]

For example, it explains the lavish praise he heaped on the Church as the great historical bearer of culture and progress. Though the Church surely has done its part in such matters,

15. See H. Küng, *The Council, Reform and Reunion* (New York, 1961), p. 128 ff.
16. Regarding Italian policies to the Holy See in Leo's time see McGovern, *The Life and Life-Work of Pope Leo XIII* (Chicago, 1903), p. 244 ff.
17. *Acta*, I, 45 (Gilson, p. 279).

Leo's claims often sound somewhat exaggerated to modern ears:

> Therefore, if the many blessings We have mentioned, due to the agency and saving help of the Church, are the true and worthy outcome of civilization, the Church of Christ, far from being alien to or neglectful of progress, has a just claim to all men's praise as its nurse, its mistress, and its mother.[18]

This same great fear made him "the prisoner of the Vatican," by his own choice. The loss of civil independence was certainly a serious threat, calling for uncompromising firmness. We have seen how past civil encroachment on the spiritual has always brought on direst consequences. History shows, too, that papal reaction to this threat tended always to take the form of exaggerated claims to power.[19] Leo scrupulously avoided this danger. But the threat also had another ill effect. His church-state doctrine, even though very abstract in nature, was very often to much too great an extent tailored specifically to the abuses of liberalism.[20]

Leo's doctrine on the distinction and autonomy of the two "perfect" societies cannot be called the highest one on his personal scale of values. But it deserves to be treated first in this history, because it was his most original contribution. The highest ranking theme by reason of Leo's own emphasis was the opposite side of the church-state ratio: the unanimity and cooperation which should exist between the two parties.

2. Church-State Cooperation

We have already seen how Pope Leo emphasized especially the need for cooperation (or "union") between Church and State.[1]

18. *Ibid.*, 44 (Gilson, p. 280).
19. Boniface's claims (cf. above, p. 311 ff.) were surely partially provoked by the dangerous totalitarian ambitions of Frederick.
20. This becomes especially clear when one sees how vastly different were the outlooks of Popes Pius XII and John XXIII, who had their independence assured by the Lateran Pacts.
1. Though the term "union" can mean almost anything from theocracy

This followed immediately from the fact that they are both
societies coming directly or indirectly from God and having,
each of them in its own way, mankind's eternal end as their
goal.[2] In their own way, then, both societies make their contribution, and in doing so they cannot reasonably be antagonistic.
The great bulk of Leo's church-state writings has as its aim
the defense of this one point: Church and State are *partners*.
Indeed all of the remaining facets of his doctrine on freedom
and church-state relations are but re-statements of this one
truth. It is not surprising, since he was combating powerful
enemies who taught exactly the opposite.

In this area Leo is not original. He is, in fact, fighting the same
enemy which his predecessors had been fighting for a hundred
years. Since the loss of papal civil independence, the task
seemed even more urgent. He makes use of all the traditional
arguments to prove the importance of church-state coordination.
He advances no new ones. Nevertheless, these old arguments
take on new power by reason of the form in which they are presented. They are not condemnations. They are religious instruc-
tions. They are not supported by, nor do they seek, military or
political might. Neither do they take place against a background
of underhanded diplomatic manipulations of the international
balance of power. Rather they are presented as simply the dictates of natural and of divine law.[3] Herein lies the strength and
psychological appeal they enjoyed in Europe at the turn of the
century.

---

to the most tenuous formal agreement, we will use it in the remaining part
of this essay in a specially defined sense. "Union" of Church and State
will refer to formal recognition of the Church by the State as the one
propagator of religious truth and the official religion of the land. This, as
we will see, Pope Leo taught to be the ideal, at least for his own day.

2. See O. Schilling, *Die Staats- und Soziallehre des Papstes Leo XIII*
(Koln, 1925), p. 50 ff.; and P. Tischleder, *Die Staatslehre Leo XIII* (Koln,
1925), pp. 285-293.

3. The treatment of this doctrine is found primarily in *Inscrutabili*
(*Ibid.*, 44-58).

Leo's four great political encyclicals all preached from difference points of view the necessity for formal church-state
coordination, or "union."[4] Therefore we will study each of them
in turn in order to see the central theme of one of history's
greatest exponents of Christian church-state doctrine. Three of
the four documents argued the necessity of church-state partnership from three separate points of view: a) from the nature of
the Church and of her authorities *(Inscrutabili);* b) from the
nature, authority and mission of the State *(Immortale Dei);* c)
from the nature, rights and duties of the citizen *(Sapientiae
Christianae).* These three letters comprise an acceptable outline of the pope's ideas on what should be the ideal relations
between the religious and the political authorities.[5] Having
seen already that Leo conceived the two as totally separate in
essence, let us now examine his conception as to how they,
nevertheless, can and should enter into intimate dialogue and
cooperation.

1. *Church-State Cooperation Necessitated by Authority of the
Church:* Pope Leo wrote his first encyclical on the evils afflicting
western society. *Inscrutabili* sees the anarchy of the times as the
direct result of casting off the Church's directive authority. God
has founded a Church and given it the direct guidance of his
Holy Spirit not only in order to guide the private individual but
also to illumine social entities, including the State. In other
words, society's evils are largely the result of the separation
between the Church and the State.

Any robust civilization, Leo goes on to explain, must rest on
three solid foundation stones: truth, justice and love. The
Church has ever been the friend and powerful support of the

4. *Diuturnum Illud,* June 29, 1881 (*Acta,* X, 10-51), may be considered
a fifth major political document, but it adds little of substance to the content exposed in the four encyclicals which we will study.

5. The fourth—*Libertas*—will be treated below in this chapter, "Human
Freedom and Church-State Theory."

State because she has ever imbued men with a knowledge and love of these virtues. The authority of the Holy See is the center of the Church's authority, and to refuse attention to its voice is to refuse one of the most powerful means of securing a social and political peace and prosperity. For this reason it is the pope's duty to fight to regain political independence in order to proclaim the Church's spiritual views on political matters. Leo saw this restoration as a *sine qua non* for a stable civil government. The encyclical ends with the pope expressing his hope that the nations now estranged may return to "respect" for (the political independence of) the Holy See.

> Great indeed and beyond the strength of man are these objects of our hopes and prayers, venerable brothers; but, since God has "made the nations of the earth for health," when He founded the Church for the welfare of the peoples, and promised that He will abide with her by His assistance to the end of the world, We firmly trust that, through your endeavors, the human race, taking warning from so many evils and visitations, will submit themselves at length to the Church, and turn for health and prosperity to the infallible guidance of this apostolic see.[6]

Pope Leo was not so naïve as to yearn for the "good old days." Nor is the encyclical merely a demand for a formal union with the State. It cannot be too often pointed out that the pope always wrote in a pastoral vein. This fact is perfectly clear from the direction of his policies in France and Germany, where he constantly urged support of the revolutionary regimes against the old pro-papal monarchies. The object of his lament was not the loss of political power but the loss of respect by public officials for the spiritual authority of the Church. Leo is above all proposing a program for renewed church-state cooperation. Conditioned by his times, the form of this program is church-state union. But first and foremost he pleads for the substance, not

6. *Inscrutabili Dei,* 55-56 (Gilson, pp. 286-287).

the form. His emphasis lies clearly on the cooperation which is contained within the union.

Leo's frequent references to the *ancient regime* must be interpreted in their context. As yet, Leo knew no modern democratic regime which embodied fully Christian ideals and Christian respect for religious authority.[7]

The doctrine, then, of *Inscrutabili* had two major parts: it taught the right to temporal independence and it refuted the liberalists' arguments against the pope's right to speak authoritatively on public matters. The first was a clear and open bid for the return of the papal states: the only assurance, Leo felt, of the spiritual freedom and independence absolutely necessary to his office.[8] The second was a general defense of a papal right and duty to instruct society on matters of public morality. It was also a statement of the duty of society (as represented by the States) to heed this teaching.

Leo did not, in this encyclical, directly demand formal relations and union with the State. He contented himself with deploring the liberalists' separation and lauding the effects of past unions. But the inference is clear enough. And his position on this point would be made clear in future announcements.

2. *The Nature of the State Demands Close Cooperation—or Union—with the Church:* The State, said Leo in *Immortale Dei*,

7. True, the United States possessed at that time a political system where religion was held in honor and where Catholics gave the greatest possible obedience to ecclesiastical law. But the United States had a system of separation of Church and State. And, surrounded as he was by the anti-religious separationist doctrines of the European liberals, Leo did not succeed completely in disassociating the two types of separation.

8. The eventual return of political independence to the popes by the Lateran Pacts actually fulfilled Leo's basic demand—but he had argued for the return of the whole "Patrimonium Petri" (*Inscrutabili*, 46 ff.). This is a good example of how embedded in their times were Leo's demands, even though his arguments were cast into the typically scholastic mold of metaphysical principles.

is a product of the natural law and as such receives its confirmation and autonomous authority from the divine author of that law. The next step in the pope's logic is of great import here. It leads to union of Church and State. The very fact of the State's ultimately divine origin, so runs the argument, demands that the State recognize and pay homage to its Creator. Both "nature and reason" show clearly that the State, no less than the individual, is obliged to accept and honor its Father.[9]

Here the pope states his central argument. The State is not an end in itself. It exists to serve man, who exists, in turn, to serve God. This Christian concept of the State stands in basic opposition to all totalitarian concepts in that the State itself recognizes the existence of a divine Being who is the ultimate ruler and end of all things. Next, the pope proceeds to describe how, in his mind, the State can best fulfill this obligation. It cannot justly be fulfilled in any manner at all which happens to suit the individual notion. God himself has revealed in what way he wishes man to carry out his religious duties:

> Since, then, no one is allowed to be remiss in the service due to God, and since the chief duty of all men is to cling to religion in both its teaching and practice—not such religion as they may have a preference for, but the religion which God enjoins, and which certain and most clear marks show to be the only one true religion—it is a public crime to act as though there were no God. So, too, it is a sin for the State not to have care for religion, as a something beyond its scope, or as of no practical benefit; or out of many forms of religion to adopt that one which chimes in with the fancy; for we are bound absolutely to worship God in that way which he has shown to be his will.[10]

Nor does Leo consider it difficult to determine which religion is really the one founded by God. But, continued Leo, the State's obligation does not cease with merely using religion as an instrument for giving its own homage to God. This very

9. *Immortale Dei,* Acta, V, 122-123 (Gilson, p. 164).
10. *Ibid.,* 123 (Gilson, p. 164).

homage to God entails respect for the rights of the true religion which is itself, like the State, a society with a definite sphere of sovereignty.

Recognizing the autonomy and right of the true religion, and watching over them, always results practically in a harmonious, friendly partnership *("colligatio")* between the two societies. Only a few sentences earlier he had described precisely what such a *"colligatio"* would consist in:

> So, too, is it a sin for the State not to have care for religion, as a something beyond its scope, or as of no practical benefit; or out of many forms of religion to adopt that one which chimes in with the fancy; for we are bound absolutely to worship God in that way which He has shown to be His will. All who rule, therefore, should hold in honor the holy name of God, and one of their chief duties must be to *favor* religion, to protect it, to shield it under the credit and sanction of the laws, and neither to organize nor enact any measure that may compromise its safety.[11]

In precisely chosen terms Leo informs the world that full union, formal mutual recognition, cooperation and protection between Church and State remained his ideal. Thus ends Leo's elementary teaching on the Christian State. He affirms clearly and unambiguously that States have a duty to accept what is commonly called "union" of Church and State.

The rest of the encyclical is taken up with a description of the opposing liberalist ideas of the State, and a refutation of them on the basis of the Christian ideal, and finally a resumé of the political duties of Catholics. *Immortali Dei* is surely Leo's most important political declaration. It contains a summary of his whole church-state *Weltanschauung.* And its outstanding feature is surely, at least for the present day, its apparently unquestioning affirmation of the formal union system as the Christian ideal.

Let us look at this more closely. The really crucial part in Leo's

---

11. *Loc. cit.* The italics are mine.

argument is his conclusion that the State's natural law obligation to recognize its God entails that it "embrace," "protect," and "shield with the command and authority of law" the true religion.[12] Did the pope mean that this followed inevitably and eternally from its natural law obligation, and that therefore any State of any Christian age, present, past, or future, would always have by its very nature a strict objective obligation to acknowledge its Creator through the Catholic Church, and to foster and protect her by its laws?[13]

Or was Leo intending to speak only to his own age—applying to this age a broad natural law demand for some type of acknowledgement of the divinity by the State? Or was it that, while believing his deduction from the general to the particular valid for all times, he simply did not foresee that changed circumstances and doctrinal developments (for example, the doctrine of the freedom of the human person) might create circumstances where his apparently universal deduction could not apply?[14]

12. His previous argument was limited to a plea for cooperation and coordination between the two authorities, as we have already seen. That raised no difficulty. But here the argument concerns primarily the State's duties, and argues that the State is obliged formally to foster the Catholic Church. This brings us to the central point of controversy.

13. Even though, as he himself said, circumstances may make exceptions necessary and good.

14. This last possibility is still quite within the bounds of orthodoxy. We must not forget that *Immortale Dei* was not a dogmatic definition. Encyclicals are, before all else, pastoral guide-lines, and Pope Leo's political encyclicals were eminently pastoral teachings concerning a current—and passing—problem called liberalism. Hence, though the doctrine was couched in Leo's highly scholastic, abstract terminology, still it does not deserve any great increase of longevity for that reason. Encyclicals cannot be *presumed* to be eternally àpropos, but must be considered according to what they themselves propose to do, and what place in the context of subsequent developments in the subject matter would indicate . . . Cf. C. Journet, *The Church of the Word Incarnate,* II, *The Apostolic Hierarchy,* pp. 350 and 449 ff. The absence of any clear claim to be speaking unchangeable doctrine, plus the nineteen-hundred-year tradition of doctrinal openness in the question under study, both speak in favor of not attributing to Leo's political encyclicals the unchanging quality of *credenda* doctrine.

The problem, put precisely, is this: does the State as such always have the duty formally to recognize the Catholic Church? By analysis of his thought we can arrive at a high degree of certainty about what Pope Leo thought on this point. But only by considering his thought, and that of subsequent popes, in the light of historical development, both prior and subsequent to his day, can we hope to assess accurately Catholic teaching on this point. The primary source remains *Immortale Dei,* since it is here that he treated the problem quite directly and completely.

Although its first part is composed in the form of a positive statement of doctrine, its final end is expressly to combat a particular current error. The abstract statements are tailored in form and emphasis to confront and to overcome these "new opinions." The "new law" of the liberalists is referred to in almost every paragraph. Another important point is the fact that Leo does not claim in his introduction that the propositions he is about to set forth are the unchanging doctrine of the Church. On the contrary, he describes his position as one which the Church "approves."

> The wicked proneness, however, to levy like charges and accusations has not been lulled to rest. Many, indeed, are they who have tried to work out a plan of civil society based on doctrines other than those approved by the Catholic Church.[15]

That is not the language in which unquestionable doctrine is propounded. It indicates that the teaching he is about to give does not possess real definition and finality.

> Nay, in these latter days a novel conception of law has begun here and there to gain increase and influence, the outcome, as it is maintained, of an age arrived at full stature, and the result of progressive liberty. But, though endeavors of various kinds have been ventured on, it is clear that no better mode has been devised for building up and ruling the State than that which is the necessary growth of the teachings of the Gospel.[16]

15. *Immortale Dei,* 119 (cf. Gilson, p. 162).
16. *Loc. cit.*

Leo describes his answer to the liberalists as one that "naturally flourishes" wherever the Gospel has been preached. He quite evidently has in mind the formal union of Church and State that began under Constantine and continued up to modern times. Thus he seems to be basing his argument on history. Our doctrine (he says in effect) is based upon that system which is the natural one because it has been in effect since that time, until the liberalists rejected it.

This is, to be sure, a powerful argument. But it hardly is one to use in seeking to make a doctrine officially unchangeable. It would not make the system beyond question—especially not after the circumstances that made it "natural" for a thousand years had ceased to exist.

We have already seen how Leo argued from the natural law to a conclusion that the State must recognize, and even unite itself with, the Church. But we must not fail to see this argument in its true context within the encyclical as a whole. The work was called forth by the total separation doctrine of the liberalists. First, Leo invokes the natural law as his authority for the Christian doctrine of a mutual cooperation and recognition between Church and State. But he goes a step further than cooperation and demands union.

With this background our difficult question can be resolved fairly completely. Leo himself firmly believed in union of Church and State. As a result, when arguing against the clearly unchristian doctrine of total separation, he pushed the natural law argument for cooperation to cover also his position on union. Tradition, of course, really influenced Leo's thinking. Cooperation and union had been synonymous up to this time. The boundary line ending what nature demands in church-state relations is always obscure and difficult to determine. His argumentation is therefore understandable. But both context and reason deny that union was necessarily an integral part of Leo's natural law argument. That is, his argument for cooperation would not have been weakened (indeed, it might have been strengthened) had it stopped short before union.

History simply had not shown Leo any choice between union and the liberalists' solution. Leo the pastor knew that enmity between Church and State was destructive of both the spiritual and political common good. But, like every pastor, the pope could only apply those remedies with which he was acquainted at the time.

To sum up: Leo, with some signs of hesitation, did maintain that his unionist position was based on the natural law, at least in so far as it embodied the degree of church-state cooperation which theologians of that age believed to be based on the natural law. He probably considered union the only solution.

But this conclusion is not without its difficulties. For the pontiff did have an example of a middle ground before him: the Constitution of the United States of America. Yet he rejected this as being no more than second best. In a letter to the American hierarchy he praised this country's laws and the people's faithfulness.[17] But he immediately added a warning: no one should conclude that the system of separation of Church and State enforced in that country would be universally good or lawful.

His statement that the Church in America would fare better under a system of union shows that he knew relatively little of conditions here. The history of the United States indicated clearly that the very unity and stability of the whole mode of government depends on this lack of favoritism to any one religious group.[18] The fact that the pope felt it necessary to warn against an opinion known to be popular among United States Catholics shows how strongly he held the opposite opinion.

And this does not weaken the contention that he saw no middle ground between full union and total separation. His

17. *Longinqua Oceani,* January 18, 1901, *Acta,* XV, 3-21.
18. See Murray, *We Hold These Truths,* pp. 45-78.

language to the American bishops discloses his ignorance of the fact that their system was, in truth, founded on religion, and that its statesmen felt a sacred duty to protect both religion and morality.[19] This ignorance is quite understandable, for to the Europeans at the turn of the century the United States was as relatively insignificant, at least in Catholic theology, as are the countries of South Africa today. That a system of separation could in fact have its very cause in a love and respect for God and religion had evidently not occurred to him.[20]

True, Leo said many good things about the American system. But one fairly advantageous democratic separation scheme in a new-born nation could hardly be expected to shake either the distaste and suspicion caused by one hundred and fifty years of anti-Church European democracy or his trust in fifteen hundred years of monarchical union. The pontiff was the prophet of a new age, but even he could not foresee the full effects of the democratic revolution.[21]

Leo, then, held that union was the ideal system. But careful notice must be given to the fact that in *Longinqua Oceani,* as

19. See Murray, *op. cit.,* pp. 28-30.

20. That he denied that the American system was ideal was surely wise. Not even American scholars themselves (e.g., Father Murray) consider it ideal. And the pope had the added worry of the effect such praise would have had on liberalist Europe's separationists.

21. Hans Küng expressed Pope Leo's situation accurately when he said: "A new age began for the Church and the Papacy. It cannot simply be separated from what went before; innumerable lines of continuity were preserved . . . The man of the new era was Leo XIII. The Church of the preceding period had been built like a fortress; . . . there had to be increased centralization to withstand the storm. Those outside could look only with dislike and suspicion on this grim, inhospitable fortress . . . Excelling his predecessors in flexibility of mind and by his sober readiness to meet others half-way . . . Leo XIII certainly did not demolish the fortress, but he threw open its gates and its windows . . . Individual measures, which may well be of disputable value in themselves, are less important than the fact that the whole atmosphere changed: fresh air blew through the Church, and men breathed more freely (*The Council* . . ., pp. 128-129).

indeed elsewhere, he did not choose to teach this as *credenda*.[22]

But we must next look at additional indications of Pope Leo's conviction that cooperation between Church and State was a necessary part of Christian doctrine. This additional evidence does not add or subtract anything from what *Immortale Dei* taught about the manner in which they should cooperate. That manner, as we have seen, was official recognition and protection of, or simply union with, the Catholic Church.

3. *The Necessity for Church-State Coordination is Indicated by the Duties of the Christian Citizen: Sapientiae Christianae* expounds the Christian concept of the citizen. It is a fresh presentation of Pope Leo's finely worked out concept of the Church in nineteenth century society. It is founded on the same Christian principles and presented in the same scholastic form which we have already seen. But because Leo's ideals are here approached from another direction, it gives us a more complete idea of the whole and a more thorough insight into the fine details of its construction.

Leo opened his discourse by observing that the new society and government with their complexity and manifold demands on the individual, could very easily appear as ends in themselves. Hence, he rightly observed, the citizen had to become more clearly aware of his true position in the world. The solid foundation on which the Christian outlook is based is the clear realization that by baptism he has been born again, and hence is a citizen of two fatherlands, one natural, and the other supernatural. He owes allegiance to both:

> But the man who has embraced the Christian faith, as in duty bound, is by that very fact a subject of the Church as one of the children born of her, and becomes a member of that greatest

22. One could say, on the other hand, that he *did* teach as *credenda* that separation was not the universal ideal.

and holiest body, which it is the special charge of the Roman
Pontiff to rule with supreme power, under its invisible head,
Jesus Christ.

Now, if the natural law enjoins us to love devotedly and to
defend the country in which we had birth, and in which we
were brought up, so that every good citizen hesitates not to
face death for his native land, very much more is it the urgent
duty of Christians to be ever quickened by like feelings toward
the Church. For the Church is the holy City of the living God.[23]

But the Christian's love for country and Church cannot come
into essential conflict, for both were given by the same original
source. We have every right to love ourselves, neighbor, and
country; but above all we must love our mother, the Church:

> Moreover, if we would judge aright, the supernatural love for
> the Church and the natural love of our own country proceed
> from the same eternal principle, since God Himself is their
> Author and originating Cause. Consequently, it follows that
> between the duties they respectively enjoin, neither can come
> into collision with the other. We can, certainly, and should love
> ourselves, bear ourselves kindly toward our fellow men, nourish
> affection for the State and the governing powers; but at the
> same time we can and must cherish toward the Church a feeling
> of filial piety, and love God with the deepest love of which we
> are capable.[24]

Here again we arrive at the ideal: two societies which com-
plement without contradicting one another.

As usual, in a very few paragraphs, the pope sketched out the
unchanging outlines of Christian social teachings. The complicated form of real, current embodiments of the two "countries"
follow soon enough. Working out the complexities on the real
level is the aim of the encyclical, but by prefacing it with the
usual abstract, ontological sketch we are given a glance at the
interior framework. It is these simple prefaces which make Leo's

23. *Sapientiae Christianae, Acta,* X, 13 (cf. Gilson, p. 251).
24. *Ibid.,* 14 (cf. Gilson, pp. 251-252).

political teachings clearer and more solid than any of his predecessors and successors. They left little room for procrastination by Catholics, and equally little space for suspicion of ulterior motives by governments. Today's reader may find them more than a little idealistic in their almost simplistic and categorical pronouncements. This was, however, the style and manner of thought of Leo's age. In spite of these weaknesses, there is much good to be found.

The pope brings his argument out of pure abstraction by quickly admitting, in practice, that apparently genuine conflicts do arise:

> For instances occur where the State seems to require from men as subjects one thing, and religion, from men as Christians, quite another; and this in reality without any other ground, than that the rulers of the State either hold the sacred power of the Church of no account, or endeavor to subject it to their own will.[25]

The alleged conflict of interests to which the pope referred is the charge being alleged by the liberalists. This is the difficulty which occasioned the encyclical. The modern citizen is faced often by this false conflict of powers because of the modern governments' tendency to deny that there exists any other public power whose rights it must respect. The rest of the encyclical consists of guidance for the citizen in fulfilling his twofold loyalty under such circumstances. We will list only the chief ones. They are essential elements in Leo's doctrine of concrete and practical church-state relations, and are to be found repeated time and again in his writings: 1) If the State demands anything against the Church or the Church's teaching, it is not treasonous to disobey; indeed it would be unpatriotic if one did obey since it is not for the common good. 2) A citizen is not a real Christian unless he permeates his social milieu, by word and example, with Christ's doctrine. But this must always be done under the

25. *Loc. cit.*

leadership of the bishops and the pope. 3) Obeying the Church, far from detracting from allegiance and service owed to the State, strengthens and perfects it, by engendering honesty, piety and hence the general common good. 4) The State has no authority in the realm of spiritual matters. 5) The Church cannot presume to favor any one form of government or political movement as such. 6) The pope and bishops have a divine right to regulate the actions of Christian citizens in so far as these actions have to do with faith and morals. 7) Charity must be the guiding principle of the Christian citizen's social and political activities.

Such was Leo's conception of the Christian citizen and his duties. Being a member of two basically complementary societies the Christian, by perfecting his loyalty to the higher one, is in reality preparing himself in the best possible manner to serve loyally also the lower one.

Modern statesmen were preaching a "new concept of political order." They declared that the ultimate criterion of law is in the will of the people. By thus refusing to take any account of the objective natural law, they were not only ignoring the just rights of the Church but were also actually wrecking the foundations of their own authority. By declaring themselves to be the only public authority and disassociating themselves entirely from the teaching authority of the Church, they were depriving themselves of the best ultimate support and guarantee of their stability and effectiveness.

The argument that Christians make the best citizens was the foundation of Leo's appeal for cooperation between Church and State. In fact, it is itself the doctrine of cooperation. To say with St. Paul, as Leo did, that "all power comes from God" (Rom 13:1) is one way of denying that the Church's powers and the State's powers are in any way antagonistic to one another. Rather, they are "born from the same eternal principle," hence are brothers and should cooperate, each on its own proper level.

This is Chistian church-state doctrine in its purest form, based on the Scriptures themselves.[26] Formal recognition and protection (that is, union) are clearly not ends in themselves; they are means of cooperation. Leo realized this much more clearly than did his predecessors. This is evident from the content of his political encyclicals. For their day, they were splendidly thought out and practical programs for cooperation. They spelled out what both citizens and States could do to achieve cooperation.

Too often, papal political teaching of the past had tended to be satisfied with demanding and commanding. Leo offered a concrete approach towards solving the church-state crisis. True, he too thought that union, by mutual formal recognition and protection, was necessary. Looked at in the light of the Second Vatican Council, this cannot be considered a contribution of lasting worth. His greatest contribution was his apologia for cooperation. The practical program he outlined for the realization of this end was especially tailored to his own times.

3. HUMAN FREEDOM AND SEPARATION OF CHURCH AND STATE

The necessary link between the doctrine of church-state relations and freedom of the human person has already been stressed more than once in this study. The whole drama of Christian church-state relations turns upon the question of how close these relations should be. In practice this question is intimately associated with the problem of how free and independent should be the State, the Church and the citizen. Any relationship, if it is to be genuine and fruitful, demands a certain mutual sacrifice of freedom on the part of the two related entities. Hence, in examining a given relationship, it would be foolish to ignore two associated problems: 1) How much freedom is essential to each party in order to operate effectively? 2) How

26. See Murray, "The Church . . .," 546 ff.

much freedom must both parties sacrifice in the interest of successful relations? The history of church-state relations shows
how important the association between relationship and freedom really is.[1] Every single conflict arose directly or indirectly
out of an insensitivity on the part of one party or the other
respecting its partner's freedom.

Pope Leo XIII was well aware of this connection. His encyclical *Libertas* dealt with this matter in typical Leonine fashion.
First he described and rejected the liberalist notion of separation. Then he took up, one by one, individual teachings of his
opponents and answered them. His manner of rejecting them is
almost shocking to post-Vatican II ears. The encyclical does,
however, end with a revolutionary (for that era) declaration on
tolerance.

It is the second half of the encyclical which is of particular
interest. After expounding the Christian *via media* between
license and despotism, the various general shades of liberalist
ideas of freedom are described and then the individual tenets
of the liberalist political movement are confronted. What is said
is of vital importance for our theme.

1. *Separation of Church and State:* The pontiff wastes no time
in arriving at what he considers the central bone of contention
between the concrete political expressions of the two opposing
conceptions of liberty. The dispute, so he thinks, is centered in
opposing concepts of the relationship which should exist between
religion (in all its various social manifestations) and the socio-
political plane of activity. This is indicated when he describes
the most moderate type of liberalism:

> There are others, somewhat more moderate though not more
> consistent, who affirm that the morality of individuals is to be
> guided by the divine law, but not the morality of the State, so

1. This freedom, was not, of course, the object of contention at all; what
is in question is the philosophical basis for moral freedom.

that in public affairs the commands of God may be passed over, and may be entirely disregarded in the framing of laws. Hence follows the fatal theory of the need of separation between Church and State.[2]

This last group of liberalists could even be Catholics. They recognized religion's authority in their own lives. The only thing which united them to the liberalist camp was their belief that the activities of the Church and the body-politic should be disassociated, at least to some extent.[3]

Leo makes it clear enough exactly what type of disassociation these liberals were recommending. It is absolute separation.[4] This is evident even in the above quotation. This "separation" holds it legitimate that the State[5] depart from (*discedere*) the commands of God: that is, "in no way" take note of them in making its laws.

Today everyone knows that there are many degrees of formal separation whose advocates are adamantly opposed to those who "consider in no way" the laws of God.[6] But the separation which Leo was attacking was definitely not of such a type. He makes this increasingly clear as he continues his argument:

> But the absurdity of such a position is manifest. Nature herself proclaims the necessity of the State providing means and opportunities whereby the community may be enabled to live properly, that is to say, according to the laws of God. For, since God

2. *Libertas, Acta,* VIII, 228 (Gilson, p. 69).

3. See J. Leclerq, *op. cit.,* p. 280. The author gives an excellent analysis of the encyclical as a whole, pp. 191-203 and 277-282.

4. See Murray, "Leo XIII, Government and the order of Culture," pp. 2-6.

5. The term used invariably is *"civitas,"* which is surely wider than just "State." But nevertheless the idea of State is surely included in his intention here. Often it seems to be the only meaning intended—but not always.

6. For example, Ireland, a country with a population almost completely Catholic, whose government scrupulously considers the Church's commands and principles—but who, nevertheless, is officially separated from her. See *Bunreacht na Heireann* (Constitution of Ireland), Dublin: Government Publications, 1956.

is the source of all goodness and justice, it is absolutely ridiculous that the State should pay no attention to these laws or render them abortive by contrary enactments.[7]

This passage contains two distinct arguments against separation. Both of them indicate clearly the type of separation envisioned. The first is the argument from the natural law. Nature demands that the State provide means whereby the citizen can live in accord with God's command; and the State which makes laws against God's commands acts against this command of nature. The pope is arguing against such States—and the description fits the various European States of the time.[8]

The second argument is based upon the existence of certain things, such as marriage and education, which pertain to the care of both Church and State. The separation attacked by Leo gives these matters exclusively to the State by refusing the Church any authority or control. Union, so says the pontiff, is necessary in order that harmonious arrangements be worked out in this area of mixed jurisdiction.

The argument, then, proceeds thus: liberalists say that true freedom demands separation of the Church from the State to the extent that the latter must refuse to consider *in any way* the commands of God or to allow the rights of the Church in mixed matters. This, Leo declares, is absurd because it destroys the natural harmony between the Church and State.

Neither in the discussion following—nor, in fact, anywhere in all of his writings—does Leo argue either for or against any of the types of separation other than the one just described. It is only logical to conclude, therefore, that Leo really knew of no other type, nor even conceived of the possibility of one essentially different. If he had understood the American type of separation, would he have given it a place in his consideration?

7. *Libertas,* 228-229 (Gilson, p. 69).
8. See Dondeyne, pp. 272-273, and also Murray, "The Church . . .," p. 533 ff.

Perhaps. But actually, as will become evident from an analysis of the remainder of *Libertas,* Pope Leo saw no need to go beyond the traditional Constantinian "formal recognition and protection" method in his search for an acceptable alternative to the liberalist separation. So widespread were the clearly unsound liberalist ideas, and so deeply rooted in tradition was Leo to the formal-recognition answer, that he apparently considered the whole question capable of definite settlement in terms of an "either-or" confrontation.

After defining and refuting in a general fashion the three liberalist positions, the pontiff begins discussing the various details common to all three forms. These details he divides into four "freedoms": freedom of worship, speech and press, teaching, and conscience. These four freedoms had been battle cries of the liberalist party, and in their liberalist sense they presumed that the State did not "embrace, protect, and shield by laws" any one particular religion. Leo rejected them all, expressly, in this, their political form.[9]

2. *Freedom of Worship:*

And, first, let us examine that liberty in individuals which is so opposed to the virtue of religion, namely, the liberty of worship, as it called . . . This kind of liberty, if considered in relation to the State, clearly implies that there is no reason why the State should offer any homage to God, or should desire any public recognition of Him; that no one form of worship is to be preferred to another, but that all stand on an equal footing, no account being taken of the religion of the people, even if they profess the Catholic faith. But, to justify this, it must needs be taken as true that the State has no duties toward God, or that such duties, if they exist, can be abandoned with impunity, both of which assertions are manifestly false.[10]

9. He likewise rejected them in themselves (but that is not our point here). See Murray, pp. 561-562.
10. *Libertas,* 229 (Gilson, pp. 70-71).

In justifying this rejection of public freedom of religion Leo appeals again to the nature of the State itself, as in *Immortale Dei*. But here he elaborates on this argument by explaining that the true religion pertains, before all else, to the common good, and so must be promoted by the State. Here is perhaps the clearest indication in the whole Leonine corpus that the pontiff considers formal union to be the ideal and necessary form of true Christian church-state relations. He drives home the point with force as he continues:

> Justice therefore forbids, and reason itself forbids, the State to be godless; or to adopt a line of action which would end in godlessness—namely, to treat the various religions (as they call them) alike, and to bestow upon them promiscuously equal rights and privileges. Since, then, the profession of one religion is necessary in the State, that religion must be professed which alone is true . . .[11]

True social freedom of worship, concludes the pope, must then be seen within the context of a State which "preserves and protects" the true religion. Again, however, what immediately precedes this declaration shows once again that the only alternative that he can imagine is a State in which religion is "disregarded":

> For public authority exists for the welfare of those whom it governs; and, although its proximate end is to lead men to the prosperity found in this life, yet, in so doing, it ought not to diminish, but rather to increase, man's capability of attaining to the supreme good in which his everlasting happiness consists: which never can be attained if religion be disregarded.[12]

3. *Freedom of Speech and Press:* Here, as above, the social and political forms of freedom are the primary concern. And, though not expressed, the limitations which the pope placed on this freedom would seem to apply especially to the propagation of religious error:

11. *Ibid.*, 231 (Gilson, p. 71).
12. *Loc. cit.*

We must now consider briefly *liberty of speech,* and liberty of the press. It is hardly necessary to say that there can be no such right as this, if it be not used in moderation, and if it pass beyond the bounds and end of all true liberty. For a right is a moral power which—as We have before said and must again and again repeat—it is absurd to suppose that nature has accorded indifferently to truth and falsehood, to justice and injustice. Men have a right freely and prudently to propagate throughout the State what things soever are true and honorable, so that as many as possible may possess them; but lying opinions, than which no mental plague is greater, and vices which corrupt the heart and moral life, should be diligently repressed by public authority, lest they insidiously work the ruin of the State.[13]

In accord with his ideal of formal and full acceptance of revealed truth by the State, the pope could draw but one conclusion: anything which contradicted such religious truths could not be freely discussed and written about.[14] But perhaps the most striking characteristic of Leo's doctrine here is that, for once, he seems to make no attempt to consider the problem from the point of view of his adversaries.[15] He does not allow any leniency on grounds of good intention or unavoidable ignorance.

13. *Ibid.,* 232 (Gilson, p. 72).

14. The qualifications placed on freedom of speech and press seem unduly harsh to contemporary thinking. But Leo was not speaking to the contemporary world and—an even more important factor—was himself not of the contemporary world. In this respect, and in regard to all the "freedoms" which he treats, he was more of a representative of the old type of pope than of the new type (which has its ideal representative in John XXIII). But this is true only relatively. For, in comparison with his immediate predecessors he was quite liberal on the issue. His encyclical, though not comparable to *Pacem in Terris,* gave freedom its first positive papal treatment, and thus prepared the ground for his successors. See also Jacques Leclerq, *op. cit.,* pp. 191-200: "With Leo XIII an evolution began to take place."

15. This aspect of the doctrine of freedom of speech deals only indirectly with church-state relations. But, though indirect, it is of utmost importance. It has to do with the right of men to be in invincible error in expressing their opinions and in living by them. The same importance must be given to the other types of freedom discussed below. There will be more detailed discussion of this matter in the conclusion to our study of Leo's doctrine.

4. *Freedom of Teaching:* From freedom of speech to freedom
of teaching there is but a single step. Pope Leo applies the same
principles:

> A like judgment must be passed upon what is called *liberty of*
> *teaching.* . . . From this it follows, as is evident, that the liberty
> of which We have been speaking is greatly opposed to reason,
> and tends absolutely to pervert men's minds, in as much as it
> claims for itself the right of teaching whatever it pleases—a
> liberty which the State cannot grant without failing in its
> duty.[16]

Truth is of two kinds, the pope continues, natural and supernatural. Natural truth is the very basis of society, and to allow
freedom to teach contrary to it would be ridiculous. Supernatural
truth is the exclusive teaching realm of the Church. Only she
has the right of authority to teach on matters of religious truth
and on morals. He objects to the State allowing any and every
opinion on religious truth to be taught, and demands that the
Church's own rights in this matter be free from the strangling
restrictions advocated by the separationists.

5. *Freedom of Conscience:* The freedom to follow one's conscience sums up the other foregoing ones. As Leo himself says,
the reasoning already presented is sufficient refutation of that
particular freedom which rests on the presumption that all truth
is relative. On the other hand, freedom of conscience is perfectly
legitimate and praiseworthy if it means that everyone in a State
is free to follow God's actual commands.

> Another liberty is widely advocated, namely, *liberty of con-*
> *science.* If by this is meant that everyone may, as he chooses,
> worship God or not, it is sufficiently refuted by the arguments
> already adduced. But it may also be taken to mean that every
> man in the State may follow the will of God and, from a con-
> sciousness of duty and free from every obstacle, obey His com-

16. *Libertas,* 234 (Gilson, p. 73).

mands. This, indeed, is true liberty, a liberty worthy of the sons of God, which nobly maintains the dignity of man and is stronger than all violence or wrong—a liberty which the Church has always desired and held most dear.[17]

Leo, then, could see no grounds for allowing a State to guarantee the invincibly erroneous citizen the unqualified right to follow his conscience in matters of religion.

6. *Religious Tolerance:* Nevertheless the pontiff remained a realist. He recognized the incontrovertible fact that there can be situations where too summarily repressed falsehood could cause much more harm than good. He recognized that revolution thrived on rigid repressionism. For this reason he qualified with tolerance what, up to this point, might have seemed an unrealistically purist doctrine. The pope saw no choice but to be severe in his judgment of liberalism. It was an evil of passive potentiality and he, as few others, had the prophetic vision to see where it could lead.[18] But he tempered his severity with the understanding of a father.

Yet, with the discernment of a true mother, the Church weighs the great burden of human weakness, and well knows the course down which the minds and actions of men are in this our age being borne. For this reason, while not conceding any right to anything save what is true and honest, she does not forbid public authority to *tolerate* what is at variance with truth and justice, for the sake of avoiding some greater evil, or of obtaining or preserving some greater good.[19]

This statement qualifies his apparent total rejection of the four freedoms described above. This was no mere empty gesture in order to coat a bitter doctrine with a bit of sugar. His practical policies on the diplomatic level showed how consistently he

17. *Loc. cit.*
18. Just before his statement on tolerance, Leo makes a statement which is almost prophetic. It describes well the present Communist State (238).
19. *Ibid.*, 239 (Gilson, pp. 76-77).

practiced toleration himself. The history of his dealings with Bismarck's *Kulturkampf* in Germany, with the parallel movement in Switzerland, and with the liberalist governments in France show this clearly. Not only did he tolerate the basically anti-Catholic republic in France; he patiently persuaded an unwilling Catholic population to support this republic.

The defense given by the pope for his toleration is revealing. His customary appeals to the authority of his predecessors are conspicuous by their absence. There were no such precedents. In recognizing the fittingness of toleration for the "new law," with its political innovations such as separation of Church and State, Leo was making a definite break with precedent. And it is of truly epoch making proportions. He bases his decision solidly on the Gospel itself:

> God Himself in His providence, though infinitely good and powerful, permits evil to exist in the world, partly that greater good may not be impeded, and partly that greater evil may not ensue. In the government of States it is not forbidden to imitate the Ruler of the world; and, as the authority of man is powerless to prevent every evil, it has (as St. Augustine says) to overlook and leave unpunished many things which are punished, and rightly, by Divine Providence.[20]

Lest anyone be led to believe that this tolerance might totally exclude his ideal of union, the pontiff concludes this section as follows:

> But to judge aright, we must acknowledge that, the more a State is driven to tolerate evil, the further is it from perfection; and the tolerance of evil which is dictated by political prudence should be strictly confined to the limits which its justifying cause, the public welfare, requires.[21]

The principle of tolerance was, of course, not unknown before Leo. But no pope had as yet applied it explicitly to separation

20. *Libertas,* 239 (Gilson, p. 78). See J. Lecler, "La papauté moderne et la liberté de conscience," *Etudes,* 1946, II, 289-309, especially pp. 305 and 306.
21. *Libertas,* 240 (Gilson, p. 77).

of Church and State, freedom of conscience, and the like. In doing so Leo was, for the second time,[22] making history in the realm of church-state relations. Supported, as it was, by a determined, realistic policy, it marked the beginning of the end of the old uncompromising enmity between the Catholic Church and the new political order.

This was no accident on Leo's part. He had repeatedly and vociferously renounced all desire for political power himself,[23] and had ceased to interfere in the politics of other nations. His principle of tolerance, even though it gave liberty a very qualified approval, was enough eventually to turn the tide away from the liberalists' unmitigated opposition to the Church.

While denying that the separation of Church and State could be the ideal of Christian politicians, his principle of tolerance gave assent to such aspirations on a conditional basis. As a result, it formed a sort of charter of rights and encouragement for an ever-increasing number of Catholic politicians and statesmen. It gave hope and encouragement for a whole Catholic world that had already too long been held on the sidelines of political activity by its ecclesiastical superiors' uncompromising opposition to the new forms.

Compared to the Second Vatican Council's Declaration on Religous Freedom, Pope Leo's pronouncements on tolerance seem negative and incomplete. They do, however, deserve a prominent place in history because they served as the necessary bridge between medieval intolerance and modern recognition of man's right and duty to follow his conscience's dictates in matters of religion. Without the foundations begun by Pope Leo, the modern doctrinal structure would have been impossible.

22. The first time was his clarification of the State's right to autonomy. See above, pp. 185-187.
23. He made it clear enough that his demand for the restoration of the papal states was based only on a desire for political independence which would safeguard his spiritual independence from the pressures of political leaders.

Chapter Six

Pope Pius XII

Between the reigns of Leo XIII and Pius XII there occurred only one event of major importance for our theme. But it was of truly epic significance. This was the signing of the Lateran Pacts in the reign of Pope Pius XI, in June of 1929. This event appeared at the time as the only possible peaceful settlement of the feud between Italy and the Holy See, unsettled since the seizure of Rome by the troops of King Victor Emmanuel in 1870. Thus, by the agreements in 1929, the Vatican was recognized as a sovereign State with the full immunity and independence due to such a status.[1] Indemnity was paid for various seizures of Church property and general accord was reached on the relations which were to exist between the State of Italy and the Italian Church. These factors in themselves were of great importance for the Church, but the significance of the Lateran Pacts reached far beyond a mere settlement between Italy and the Holy See. The signing of these pacts was the outstanding achievement of Pope Pius XI. It was the beginning of a new era for the Church in general, and particularly for the development of Catholic church-state relations.

Of lesser importance for Catholic church-state doctrine were the pontificates of Popes Pius X and Benedict XV. The former, following closely the inspired program of Leo XIII, continued the fight against the liberalists. He condemned in the strongest

1. For a description of these agreements see A. Blat, *Jus Concordatarium Postbellicum Conlatum cum Codice Iuris Canonica* (Romae, 1938), pp. 17-30, and A. Giannini, *Il cammino della Conciliazione* (Roma, 1947).

terms the French government's separation laws. The laws scrapped France's concordat with the Holy See, despoiled the Church of all property, and arranged that the State take complete control of education.[2] Continental liberalism was, however, changing its form. Pius X condemned as "Modernism"[3] the philosophical and theological outcroppings of that doctrine, which extolled unlimited freedom in all fields. Leo had encouraged the growth of an orthodox movement embodying the best of liberalist objectives, and he thereby had robbed the extremists of large numbers of followers in every European nation. The extremists' movement, on the other hand, deprived of the balancing factor of the more conservative element, became ever more extreme and eventually swung towards—or metamorphosed into —the beginnings of the socialist and communist movements of today.[4]

Pope Benedict XV had little to say on the question of church-state relations. He was content to follow the paths of Leo XIII. However, in a consistorial allocution,[5] he introduced a concept which was to grow ever larger in the future. He took note of the rise of numerous new republics with regimes vastly different from those they had replaced, and affirmed the mutual need for both Church and State to establish contact with one another. But he rejected the old custom whereby Church and State exchanged many mutual privileges. Rather, he said, new agreements should be worked out which would embody the mutual cooperation so necessary for the well-being of both societies.[6]

2. See H. Wagnon, *Concordats et droit international* (Gembloux, 1935), and C. Seignobos, "L'Evolution de la IIIe Republique," in E. Levisse, *Histoire de France contemporaine*, VIII (Paris, 1921), pp. 193-249.

3. See "Modernisme: Préparation," *Dict. Theol. Cath.*, X, 2013-2019.

4. John Courtney Murray, "The Church and Totalitarian Democracy," p. 550 ff.

5. *In hac quidem*, AAS, XIII (1921), 521-524.

6. See Garcia's Introduction to *Non abbiamo bisogno*, pp. 578-579; Leclerq, *op. cit.*, and Murray, "Contemporary Orientations of Catholic Thought on Church and State," *Theological Studies*, X (1949), 224.

Pope Pius XI made two other notable contributions to the Catholic church-state doctrine besides the Lateran Pacts. First, he inaugurated the movement called Catholic Action. He emphasized the important effects this Catholic layman's crusade could have for revitalizing the internal relationships between the religious and political life of all nations. Secondly, in his two letters, *Mit Brennender Sorge* (1939) and *Non Abbiamo Bisogno* (1938), he became the first pope to confront the modern totalitarian State, and to declare its essential incompatibility with the Christian doctrine of human dignity and freedom of conscience,[7] and with the Church's rights as an independent society.

The similarities between Pope Leo XIII and Pope Pius XII are remarkable. They extend from noble birth, high intelligence, excellent schooling, and successful diplomatic careers, down to pontificates of similar length, and include a similar doctrine. One of the greatest similarities of their doctrine is the fact that both are extremely well adjusted to their contemporary social realities. They both showed themselves unswervingly determined to exercise their office as spiritual leaders in order to illumine the massive social and political problems of the modern era.

Eugenio Pacelli was born of noble parents in 1876, and received his clerical education at the Seminario Romano and at the Gregorian University. He was ordained in 1899, and within two years was appointed to serve at the Vatican in the Secretariat for Extraordinary Affairs. He became Nuncio to Bavaria and was consecrated Archbishop in 1917, at the age of forty-one. After serving brilliantly in various diplomatic posts, mostly in the Germanic countries, Pope Pius XI made him his Secretary of State in 1930. Upon the death of Pope Pius XI he was elected on the first ballot to the papacy on March 3, 1939.

7. Concerning *Mit Brennender Sorge* García says: "With words at once energetic and moderate the pope totally condemns the Nazi ideology and its concrete applications" (*Doctrina Política,* p. 642).

From the time of his election to his death in October, 1958, he flooded the world with a volume of writings and addresses which rivaled those of Leo XIII both in sheer quantity and in importance. High on the scale of value were his social teachings, among which his church-state doctrine was surely outstanding.

The doctrine of Pope Pius XII regarding relations between Church and State by no means form a closely knit corpus, like those of Pope Leo XIII. Rather, they take the form of scattered allocutions, addresses, and informal talks given to audiences of extremely diverse composition. Pius' writings are not characterized by Leo's stiff scholasticism. His doctrine has a more natural, almost sociological quality. It blends almost indistinguishably with that vast body of Christian social teaching which occupies so large a portion of the twenty volumes of the great pope's speeches, encyclicals, and other personal documents.[8]

Nevertheless, the similiarity of idea content between the church-state doctrine of Pope Leo and Pope Pius is evident. Like his three immediate predecessors, Pius XII referred to Leo as his master in church-state matters. His own doctrine is, to speak generally, but a continuation without unnecessary repetition of the teachings of Leo XIII. But it is set in, and adjusted to, the time and circumstances of its author.

It is precisely the time and circumstances which gave Pope Pius' genius an advantage which favored significant maturation in church-state doctrine.[9] Leo, as we have seen, was burdened with the necessity of mixing his Christian doctrine with polemics against the Holy See's political enemies. Pius had been freed of this unbalancing factor by the Lateran Pacts. Our treatment of Pope Pius' doctrine will open with a discussion of the effects

8. *Discorsi e Radiomessaggi di sua Santità Pio XII*, 20 vols. (Tipografia Vaticana, 1939-1958). For a good summary of his social doctrine see A. Utz and J. Groner, *Relations humaine et societé contemporaine: Synthése chrétienne, directives de S.S. Pie XII* (Fribourg, 1956-1962), 3 vols.

9. See Leclerq, *op. cit.*, p. 203 ff.

of this change. It is clearly discernible in Pius' doctrine, and is
of great importance for our theme.[10] Our second section will deal
with the revolutionary, "universalist" church-state relationship
established by Pius with the nations of the world. The third and
final chapter will consider the more traditional facets of Pope
Pius' doctrine.

1. Beyond Politics

When Pope Pius ascended the papal throne, the Lateran Pacts
were less than ten years old. It was as yet impossible to assess
either the true significance of this accord, or its durability.
Already under Pius XI Mussolini and the pontiff had accused
one another of violating it.[1] Il Duce's totalitarian politics raised
grave fears the world over that the new Vatican State would
remain a frail bark to be tossed around at will on the sea of
anticlerical politics. Nevertheless, the Holy See's political independence was already at least a legal reality, and the new pontiff did not fail to see the tremendous importance of this fact.
From the very beginning he presumed both its justness and
reality, and wasted little time in defensive polemics. Rather he
turned his attention almost immediately to the vast labor of
speaking words of peace and reconciliation to a world drawn
up for battle.

Throughout the Second World War he occupied a post over-
looking the battle. And he demonstrated an absolute independence and neutrality unique in the long history of the papacy.[2]

10. The Lateran Pacts might be considered a *sine qua non* for the
developments described below in this chapter, "Beyond Politics."

1. The clearest accusation on the part of the pope is his *Non abbiamo
bisogno*.

2. He was so careful to maintain this neutrality that he left himself
open at times to charges of neglecting his spiritual duty in the name of
political neutrality. This is exemplified by the charges made in the recent
drama by Hochhuth, *Der Stellvertreter*. See a comment in *The Catholic
Mind* (December, 1963), 4-9.

After the end of hostilities, throughout the remainder of his twenty-year pontificate he never once descended from this supra-national post of observation and counsel.

The Italian Republic which replaced Mussolini's Fascist regime incorporated the Lateran Pacts into its very Constitution[3] and soon showed itself very respectful of the Vatican's independence and dignity as a sovereign State. Thus the Holy See's position of independence, having survived its first trial, became ever more widely accepted as normal and permanent. Pius had a deep awareness of this fact and he was proud of it. His conception of his position as head of the Vatican State is very important for a proper evaluation of his whole church-state position. It is best grasped in his own words:

> When you enter upon the terrain of the Vatican City you do not merely enter into another sovereign territory. The whole atmosphere which you breathe here is more spiritual and hence different from that of other political capitols . . . The Holy See is the supreme authority of the Catholic Church, and hence of a religious society. Its goals are situated in the supernatural and in the next life . . . Political events influence the Church and the Holy See as well, but only indirectly or in the measure in which they alter the situation of the Church in some country.[4]

Pope Pius' whole social doctrine grew in influence and prestige as the Vatican became thoroughly known in this, its new role.[5] Let us examine this new *Gestalt* of the Holy See in the light of history.

During the first eight hundred years of its existence the throne of Peter remained relatively free of any distinctly political orientation. Even after the Edict of Milan the popular image of

3. See M. Searle, *Religious Liberty: An Inquiry* (New York, 1945), p. 134.

4. Allocution to the officials of the Roman Rota, October 29, 1947, AAS, XXXIX (1947), 494-495.

5. During its first fifteen years its true nature was obscured to a large extent by its proximity and "alliance" with the Italian Fascist regime.

the papal office remained that of a purely religious, even charismatic, leader. We have seen how pope and bishops alike received honors and privileges from the Roman emperors precisely because of their prestige as being men of God, untouched by the sordidness and corruption inevitably attached to politics. Because of this aura of the supernatural, they were able to remain for a goodly number of centuries largely out of range of imperial influence on their office, even though they were technically subjects of the emperor.

After the acquisition of the papal states, however, the picture began to be altered almost immediately. As soon as Charlemagne became firmly master of his own territory, he began to undermine seriously the pope's own political power. His successors for one thousand years eyed with the same longing the political pearl which the papal states constituted. Equally enticing were the political advantages deriving from a manipulation of papal spiritual functions. The popes fought back with whatever instruments were at their disposal. Spiritual, military, and diplomatic weapons were wielded with ever greater finesse. Thus arose the medieval image of a pope. He was a spiritual leader, yes. But also a prince, a noble, and a man of immense wealth, splendor and power. As such, his doctrine on church-state relations, being rooted as always in the temporal milieu, necessarily carried overtones reflecting his non-spiritual powers. As a result the papacy gradually lost that aura of a selfless mirroring of Christ's doctrine which characterized the social teachings of the early occupants of Peter's office. Surely, this sad development was caused chiefly by ambitious, rapacious kings and emperors. Pope Gregory VII wanted, above all, spiritual freedom but was forced to fight for this right with the most unlikely weapons. But whatever the origin, the fact of strong worldly overtones in the papal church-state doctrine certainly cut heavily into the popes' effectiveness as spiritual leaders. The image of the pope as a temporal sovereign strongly compromised most sincere efforts to instill

Christ's spirit into the affairs of nations.[6] The image retained its harmful effect right down to the year 1870.

It was only in the reign of Pius XII that another popular image of the pope began to manifest itself. Now the pope's position was a balanced one. He had his independence, but it did not carry with it the sovereignty over vast areas and the temporal concerns which necessarily accompany such sovereignty. He was free from political pressures on his religious office, but likewise free from personal political interests to safeguard. Never in the history of the papacy did a pontiff speak so fearlessly and yet so selflessly to the princes of the world.

From the point of view of the sovereigns, however, there was also a great change. Nations could see for themselves the military helplessness of the Vatican. They could also see the relative fruitlessness, if not the impossibility, of trying to use the Vatican for their own political ends. For all practical purposes it was a purely religious entity. True, they might gain political advantages from being on good terms with the Catholic Church. But Pius made it quite clear that friendliness with the Catholic Church had to be bought with a demonstration of friendliness to the dictates of the natural law.[7] Since the Vatican had little either to gain or lose, to give or to receive, in the temporal sphere, nations and governments began to listen with a changed attitude to the social doctrine of the pope. His international image had indeed changed. Those who heeded him did so for moral reasons. Those who ignored him likewise based their decision on motives other than his temporal position.

Pope Pius' church-state doctrine was, then, spared the circumstantial impediments suffered by the teachings of his prede-

6. See the description of Innocent III given above, pp. 102-103. See also K. Rahner, *Theological Investigations*, II (Baltimore, 1963), pp. 99-100.

7. See his Christmas message to the world, December 25, 1951, AAS, XLIV, 6 ff. See also J. Calvez and J. Perrin, *The Church and Social Justice* (London, 1959), pp. 39-53, where numerous quotations from Pius on the natural law are cited and analysed.

cessors. Pope Leo's doctrine had been compromised by his battle for independence, which too many interpreted as a longing for the fleshpots of the papal states. The medieval popes (even those who were innocent) suffered from a similar suspicion: that of defending wealth and power by an appeal to the necessity of spiritual independence. Pius' doctrine, perhaps, as yet tended to reflect to some degree the overtones of his chief master in these matters, Leo XIII. But they were nevertheless more advanced in every respect.

Because Pope Pius' church-state teachings were relatively free from political overtones, they may be considered as normal.[8] That is not to say that they were *average*. Indeed they are quite exceptional when compared to the teachings of his predecessors during the second Christian millenium. But we must consider St. Peter's own inspired respect for civil authority (1 Pet 2:13-15), and the broad, selfless, Christ-like attitude toward the State found in the New Testament and in the early Church. When these things are remembered, it seems wholly proper to call Pius' apolitical teachings *normal*. This truth will become clearer as we study his doctrine in detail.

2. THE NEW UNIVERSALIST TEACHING

We have seen how the social doctrine of Leo XIII laid the foundations for a program of Christian influence in modern society. Pope Pius' pontificate is outstanding for having carried forward

8. Compared with the papal teachings of the previous thousand years they were free from politics. The very nature of church-state relations makes a completely a-political doctrine next to impossible. Religion is a social thing in its inner nature, and has profound effects on the political life of a nation in spite of sincere efforts to remain above the purely political. The history of the United States' political system shows this clearly. For example, the Catholic faith of President Kennedy was one of the most important political factors in his campaign for election. Even in atheist Russia the very fact of religious suppressionism makes religion a political factor of great importance. Thus Pope Pius knew his politico-religious

this program in an unprecedented, and in an unforeseeable, manner. Citing Pope Leo's example as a precedent and an authority, he pleaded for justice to workers, the sanctity of marriage, and the dignity and freedom of the human person.[1] He sought to bring Christ to the modern world, using modern channels and methods. He opened the Vatican radio station, and labored diligently to build and improve the Catholic press.

His doctrine on freedom in Church and State forms an integral part of this program. He was interested in bringing the light of Christ and his peace-giving love into the troubled deliberations of modern nations. His fundamental outlook on the problem is a very simple one. He seems to have considered the Church as Christ's continued presence on earth, and as such the necessary instrument by which nations may share in Christ's light. This clearly Christlike spirit shining through the writings of Pius XII is no doubt one of the chief reasons why his cause is already up for canonization. Church-state relations were largely Christ-state relations. This, of course, is what Catholic church-state doctrine has always professed.

The doctrinal and moral principles which Pius offered the world were rarely startling for their newness. They are largely traditional. Still, there is a difference. The revolutionary quality of Pius' teachings lies in the fearless universalism with which he applied simple Christian norms to literally everything in the modern world. We have already seen how his teachings were not restricted by the usual political considerations accompanying past papal doctrine. There was also a breadth of vision and interest reaching far beyond the boundaries of the Catholic Church. This lent Pius' viewpoint something of the old selfless

doctrine would have purely political repercussions, and he could not ignore their importance. Nevertheless, this type of political overtones is of a different order entirely than those created by the former position of the papacy as sovereign of the papal states.

1. The most famous of the many treatments of this last subject is the pontiff's Christmas message for 1942, AAS, XXXV, 9-24.

aura possessed by his patristic forebears. Thus, his political doctrine by-passed old limitations and acquired an expansiveness
which effected an important change of orientation for all the
traditional questions.

The great danger to be avoided in ferreting out exactly what
Pius thought about the Church's relations with States is to limit
one's self to those passages where he spoke of formal relations
between the Church and traditionally Catholic States. We shall
examine the traditional aspect later, but it by no means exhausts
the pontiff's teachings on our subject. First we must investigate
the doctrine which Pius addressed to the States of the world.

Since he was no longer limited, as were his predecessors, to
addressing one State at a time, Pius addressed the world on
politico-moral questions. By doing so he re-established contact,
or relationships, with States in a new manner. Even before
World War II the pontiff sensed a fundamental shifting in the
political attitudes of the world.[2] After the war he threw himself
unreservedly behind the movement for an international body
which materialized in the form of the United Nations. Likewise
he supported vigorously the movements for a politically united
Europe, and for the independence of former European colonies.

These great shifts were forming a "new world." Pius stayed
completely in step with this progress, not only by supporting it,
but by adapting traditional church-state doctrine so as to make
it an adequate instrument in mirroring Christ's light to the new
socio-political reality. It is this new adaptation which is the
subject of consideration in the present chapter.

The pope spoke to the world as a divinely appointed head of
the Church. He labored constantly to open up new channels
whereby Christ's doctrine might acquire new influence in moral
and ideological aspects of political affairs. His addresses to
statesmen and to the world, and his commentaries on political
events, were themselves a relationship with States. They were

2. *Summi Pontificatus,* AAS, XXXI (1939), the section concerning international order, 440 ff.

religious advice offered to States by the Church in the person of its head.

In reality they differed only in form from the various bulls and edicts addressed in former ages to princes. Both situations involved the Church's moral and doctrinal magisterium offered to the civil authority as guidance toward achieving its own ends. Indeed the form which Pius' advice took was more important than the traditional exchanges of ambassadors between the Holy See and Catholic countries. This is true because the service rendered and the light given was often world-wide. Let us examine the various parts of this new style of church-state doctrine.

To Pius, the whole human race formed but a single family, and the Church was its divinely appointed herald of religious truth.[3] Into the framework created by this insight he inserted such doctrines as the supra-nationality of the Church, its political neutrality, and its guardianship of human dignity and brotherhood.

1. *The Church and pope are supra-national and politically neutral:* It is supra-national, he said, both because it must be the mother of all nations and because its destiny is to exist in all nations.[4] These truths pertain to the essence of church-state doctrine. They come under this heading even though they were offered to both Catholic and non-Catholic lands alike.

In his Christmas message for 1951 Pope Pius declared, among other things,[5] his Church's political neutrality:

3. Christmas message to members of the Curia, December 24, 1948, AAS, XLI (1949), 10.

4. Christmas message to members of the Curia, December, 1945, AAS, XXXVIII (1946), 18. Another very important address on this subject was Pius' address to thirty-two newly created cardinals (from five different nations scattered over the whole globe), February 20, 1946 (AAS, XXXVIII, 141-151).

5. This address contains his clearest exposition of the nature of his universalist church-state doctrine. See quotations and comments below, p. 236 ff.

Now those who wrongly consider the Church as a kind of earthly power, of a sort of world empire, are easily induced to demand also from her, as from others, the renunciation of her neutrality and a definite election in favor of one or the other side. However, there can be no question of the Church renouncing her political neutrality, for the simple reason that she cannot serve purely political interests.[6]

He goes on to make quite precise the Church's true stance regarding political affairs:

Whoever then would wish to detach the Church from her supposed neutrality, . . . would not make the Church's cooperation in the work of peace easier. For any decision on the Church's part, even in political questions, can never be purely political, but must always be *"sub specie aeternitatis,"* in the light of the divine law, of its order, its values, its standards.[7]

The great pontiff returned repeatedly to this subject throughout his lengthy career.

Other popes had, of course, declared the Church's non-political nature. But two circumstances made Pius' statements unique. First, no other pope had actually been so free of political ties and temporal power. Secondly, no other pope had spoken, literally to the entire world, of his own and his Church's purely spiritual ambitions. Pius' Christmas messages especially were beamed to all parts of the world from the Vatican radio station. Here was a concrete and living relationship established by the pope with the civil authorities of the world.

2. *There is a need for peace and mutual brotherly comprehension among individuals and societies:* Another key point to the pope's universalist church-state doctrine was his plea for world peace both within and among nations. Christ had preached the brotherhood of all men and had amply fulfilled the prophet's

6. Christmas message to the world, December 25, 1951, AAS, XLIV (1952), 6.
7. *Ibid.,* 7.

title of "Prince of Peace." His Church never ceased to spread both individual and social peace wherever genuine Christian faith penetrated. But again it was Pope Pius who created a new medium for this age-old service to nations. On countless occasions before, during and following the Second World War, he sent out urgent calls to heads of governments for peace. This existential relation of Catholicism's head with governments was truly a universal one. Peace required a close union of all men and this was what the pope, as the spiritual father of all, desired most of all.[8]

One of the most powerful instruments for realizing both peace and brotherhood was, Pius often repeated, an international organization for States. By its means immoral aggression could be policed so that all nations could advance in mutual knowledge and respect. For this reason he became one of the world's staunchest supporters of the United Nations:

> Already, in our Christmas Message of 1939, we expressed a desire for the creation of international organizations which, while avoiding the lacunae and defects of the past, would be really capable of preserving peace according to the principles of justice and equity, against all possible threat in the future. Since today, in the light of such terrible experience, the desire to secure a new world-wide peace institution of this kind is ever more occupying the attention and the care of statesmen and people, we gladly hope that its actual achievement may really correspond in the largest possible measure to the nobility of its tranquility and security in the world for the benefit of all.[9]

Little concrete and measurable results can be assigned to Pius' indefatigable calls to peace and brotherhood among nations. It was no doubt considerable. These calls had the side-effect of strengthening greatly the pope's new relationships with States

8. Christmas message to the world, December 24, 1950, AAS, XLIII (1951), 57.
9. Radio message, September 1, 1944, AAS, XXXVI (1944), 257. (English translation in the *Catholic Mind*, October, 1944, 585.)

of the world. Slowly they drew the attention of the world to this
voice crying in the wilderness the eternal message of Christ.[10]
Political leaders of all faiths and all continents began to be frequent visitors at the papal apartments of the Vatican. Secular
newspapers unfailingly featured his major addresses. The international prestige of the pope soared to heights not known since
the early days of Christendom.

This influence of the Church and its doctrine on political
events was informal. But it was undeniably a real and very
important church-state relationship. What Pius said on the Catholic Church's political neutrality, on peace and brotherhood,
affected markedly the exchanges between Catholicism and political bodies, and the results were unquestionably positive.

3. *Every individual has a right to a just freedom of conscience
and of religion:* Perhaps the most important teaching in Pius'
universalist doctrine was his affirmation of all men's right to
freedom.[11] We have seen how, for centuries, one of the greatest
barriers between the Church and the rising democratic governments was the conflict over the nature of human freedom. Both
sides had progressed greatly towards a *détente* by the time of
Pius XII. Nations such as France and post-war Germany and
Italy no longer were ruled by rationalistic and anti-Catholic
liberalism. On the other hand, these new governments were not
ready to allow religious censorship of press, speech, and cult
such as Leo XIII had advocated. Catholic theology, as we have
seen, had undergone development of its own in this regard. Pius'
statements both to the world at large and to the Church marked
the beginning of the end of old hostilities in these matters.

10. See B. Häring, *Das Gesetz Christi* (Freiburg i/Br., 1961), 3 vols.,
III, p. 157 ff.
11. See Lecler, "Pie XII et la tolérance," *Etudes,* 1954, II, 241-9 '.
The author shows clearly the characteristic of Pius' appeals for freedom
which we have termed "universalist."

Though it would be Pope John XXIII and the Second Vatican Council who finally brought this doctrine to maturity, it was Pius XII who provided its decisive change of course.

Leo XIII had admitted almost grudgingly the basic compatibility between sane democratic concepts on human freedom and Christian doctrine. Pius praised these ideals[12] unhesitatingly as being positively good and completely in accord with the Christian spirit:

> The origin and the primary scope of social life is the conservation, development and perfection of the human person, helping him to realize accurately the demands and values of religion and culture set by the creator for every man and for all mankind, both as a whole and in its natural ramifications.[13]

Lest there be any doubt to his meaning, he added:

> He who would have the star of peace shine out and stand over society should cooperate, for his part, in giving back to the human person the dignity given to it by God from the very beginnings; . . . He should uphold respect for the practical realization of the following fundamental personal rights: the right to maintain and develop one's corporal, intellectual and moral life, and especially the right to religious formation and education; the right to worship God in private and public and to carry on religious works of charity . . .[14]

Two years later, again on the occasion of his Christmas message to the world, he insisted once more on the same dignity, liberty, and equality for all citizens:

> In a people worthy of the name the citizen feels within him the consciousness of his personality, of his duties and rights, of his

12. See Leclerq, *op. cit.*, p. 203 ff. Commenting on one of Pius' letters written while yet a cardinal, Leclerq notes, "He does not leave the impression that he is afraid of freedom . . . nevertheless such an attitude, new as it was, did not go so far as to break with tradition" (p. 204).

13. Christmas message to the world for 1942, AAS, XXXV, 12 (cf. *Catholic Mind*, January, 1943, 48).

14. *Ibid.*, 19 (cf. *Catholic Mind*, January, 1943, 55).

own freedom joined to respect for the freedom and dignity of others.[15]

In 1950 he became even more explicit about man's rights to freedom:

Everyone has, and should keep, his liberty of movement toward the common good. Furthermore, there are certain rights and liberties of individuals—of every individual—of the family, which the State should always protect, which it may not violate or sacrifice in the name of an alleged common good. To cite a few examples: we believe in the right and liberty to venerate the true God, the primary right of parents over their children, and over their children's education.[16]

Pius did more than demand that the State respect the individual's right to a just freedom of conscience and religion. (This was, of course, to the Church's advantage.) He also admitted that the Church must also respect the conscience of the individual. We will see how the great pontiff denied that the Church despised men's freedom to follow their consciences in other religions. Without this second assurance of security and universality, Pius would never have gained the confidence of either States or individuals. Because of it, he was able to bring the Church into closer rapport with modern States than it had ever enjoyed before. Doubts and suspicions remained on both sides. But at last it could be said that in an increasing number of nations the Church and the State were friends. And, of course, friendship is of the essence of good relations between two rational beings, whether they be individuals or societies.

A lack of due freedom of action has been the cause of the destruction of church-state accord from the very beginning. Totalitarian disregard for the rights of both individuals and societies has been the perennial obstacle to church-state friendship.

15. Christmas message to the world, December 24, 1944, AAS, XXXVII (1945), 14 (cf. *Catholic Mind,* February, 1945, 68).

16. Allocution to graduates in the administrative sciences, August 5, 1950: Discorsi et Radiomessagi . . ., XII, 160.

Pope Pius' fervent espousal of human dignity and freedom was a significant and necessary step towards the resumption of fruitful cooperation between Catholicism and civil authority, especially in modern democratic States.[17]

Such, in brief outline, was the new universalist church-state doctrine which Pius offered for the first time to the world. What is its essence? What makes it different from previous church-state doctrines?

First, it is most important to see that it did not differ essentially from traditional church-state doctrine. It was a new type of relationship, of rapport, between the two societies. But the substance was the same. Christ's Church was reflecting the light of divine truth on the troubled affairs of nations and between nations.

The difference lay in the almost unlimited scope of influence which this new universalist doctrine enjoyed. It was addressed to, and heard by, all nations. But its universality was not due simply to the instantaneous and global diffusion made possible by modern communications. At the heart of the characteristic difference of the new approach was its adaptation to the whole world. Pope Leo (and most of his many predecessors) had spoken of peace, love, and even of freedom. But their doctrine was geared especially to Catholics and addressed specifically, in the form of encyclicals usually, to Catholic States alone. Their tone and their form restricted the effectiveness of their arguments to a narrow band of nations. They demanded not only formal relations, but formal union of States with the Church.

Pius' universalist relationship, on the other hand, addressed Catholic and non-Catholic States alike. He placed no conditions, explicit or implicit, on his doctrine. He based it on the universal natural law. It was Christian doctrine supported by the full authority of the Church's highest doctrinal tribunal, yet adapted

17. See Calvet and Perrin, *op. cit.*, pp. 101-132; and García, *op cit.*, pp. 868-871.

to all men. But, after the example of Christ, it was addressed to all men of good will as the "good news" capable of changing the face of the earth. Indeed Pope Pius was the herald of the *aggiornamento* spirit.

The ultimate significance of this new method is nothing other than a revolutionary adaptation of the perennial church-state doctrine of Christ to modern times. Pope Pius offered Christ's message of truth, peace, and love to nations in a new way. He did not cease to advocate formal relationships, but he saw how obsolescent this instrument had become in the new order of things. So he simply forged a new informal relation adequate for the needs of the moment. We will see how durable his new tool would be.

Pope Pius' intention to create such a new instrument can be seen in each of the citations just given. There is one text, however, where he brings his ideas into sharper focus than usual. In his Christmas message of 1951 he analyzed in a beautiful and deeply theological manner the foundations for the Church's relations with the State. His address was on world peace, and he felt called to justify the Church's claim to be heard by nations on this and similar political problems having moral implications.

His first argument is, in essence, identical with Leo's. The Church is a visible and independent society and so necessarily encounters the State. Formal ties are never mentioned except indirectly, perhaps, as part of the "external relations" between the two bodies. But the pontiff brings forth a new title for church-state relations. It deserves a high place in the history of the doctrine for its beauty as well as for the depth and the breadth it adds to church-state relationships in general:

> And since the Church and the States live together, besides these external and what might be called natural relations, there are others, too, interior and vital relations, which have their principle and origin in the person of Jesus Christ as Head of the Church. For the Son of God by becoming man, and truly man, has by that very fact entered into a new relationship, a truly

> vital relationship, with human society, with human nature. And this is true whether we consider human nature as a single unit implying equal personal dignity in all men, or human nature as found in multiple particular societies, especially those societies which, within the fundamental unity of human nature, are necessary to effect or at least perfect external order and sound organization.[18]

Christ's own relations with the State and other public societies are the model and forerunner of the Church's relations.

> With them, as societies which exist for maintaining peace, Jesus Christ, the Prince of Peace—and with Him the Church in whom He continues to live—has entered into a new and intimate relationship which elevates and strengthens society. This is the basis for the singular contribution which the Church by her very nature makes to the cause of peace, that is, when her life and her action among men occupy the place that is their due.[19]

And just what is this place due the Church? It is a relation of illumination:

> And how will all this come about except through the continuous, enlightening and strengthening action of the grace of Christ on the minds and hearts of citizens and statesmen, so that in all human relationships they recognize and pursue the purposes of the Creator, so that they strive to enlist the collaboration of individuals and nations for effecting these purposes, so that within, as well as among, nations they practice social justice and charity?

The allocution ends by laying down four practical ways in which the Church (using the pattern just described) will, in fact, contribute to world peace: 1) by suffusing society with Christian morality; 2) by condemning the arms race; 3) by promoting true liberty; and 4) by offering the world the peace-preserving services of the Holy See.

Here we have in outline the whole theology of Christian

18. Christmas message to the world, December 24, 1951, AAS, XLIV (1952), 10 (cf. *Catholic Mind*, April, 1952, 252).
19. *Ibid.*, 10 (*Catholic Mind, loc. cit.*).

church-state relations both new and traditional, both formal and informal. By becoming man, Christ entered into contact with society with the aim of enlightening and redeeming it. The Church, as Christ's continued presence on earth, has an identical mission. The outstanding quality discernible here is surely the universality of such a doctrine's scope. The Church must shed its light upon all nations. All States benefit equally from the impartial love and peace of Christ. No condition of formal relations are laid down: but the possibility is not excluded. The foundation of such a relationship is supernatural—the incarnation of Christ—but the practical program of peace and freedom are commonsense dictates of the natural law.

Of course, the new relationship could never replace individual relationships between the Church and each State. There will always be problems particular to individuals or to groups of nations, Pius feels, where the more traditional and more formal relations will be necessary. Pius was merely answering the needs of the times in supplying new forms for new church-state situations. He was following logically his own conception of the Church as never "becoming petrified in any one moment of history":

> The Church . . . [does not] become petrified, so to speak, in any one moment of history . . . On the contrary, bent over mankind as she is with constant attention, listening to each one of its heartbeats, she recognizes all of the treasures which can be had by man only under the supernatural light of Christ's doctrine and from the supernatural heart of his divine love. Thus the Church in her progress follows without halt and without mistake the providential highway of the times and circumstances. Such is the profound meaning of her vital law of continual adaptation.[20]

These words aptly sum up the attitude which caused Pope Pius to give the Church a new, "universalist" orientation in church-state relations.

20. *Ibid.*, 11.

The fundamentally revolutionary direction which this universalist doctrine gave to Catholic church-state relations must be
carefully noted and weighed. By addressing Catholic church-
state doctrine to the whole world, Pius did nothing less than
change and reorientate the whole Christian attitude in this
matter.[21] Before, the doctrine was addressed to Catholics in a
manner which made it almost totally inapplicable to all but a
very few of our modern political systems. Both political and
psychological factors prevented the popes from exercising their
universal fatherhood in this delicate realm. The twentieth century man quickly acquired a broad world-embracing outlook on
political matters. Pius immediately availed himself of the possibilities this new spirit offered for widening the scope of papal
teaching to hitherto undreamed-of dimensions.

It is important to recognize that these universalist teachings
of Pius constituted an authentic, though new and as yet widely
misunderstood, relationship between the Church and the States.
Church-state relations are in essence the vital contacts and
influences mutually exercised and received by the two authorities involved. In the past when Europe constituted a Christendom, this contact was formalized and codified. It became traditional to emphasize the formalities involved in this exchange,
often to the almost total exclusion of the vital substance of true
church-state relations. Exchange of ambassadors and signing of
formal agreements often came to be accepted, even by theologians, as the essence of the matter. The political and religious
revolutions of the past two hundred years, however, brought an
end to these formalities in the States containing over half the
Church's membership.

A further technical revolution made possible new contacts
between Christ's Church and civil authority. It was Pope Pius

21. Of course, this trend had been steadily advancing in this direction
with each pope since the time of Leo XIII. But Pope Pius XII was provi-
dentially prepared by circumstances, and by his deep social awareness, to
make the trend still more marked and, apparently, irreversible.

who spearheaded the drive to realize and strengthen these contacts. The moral influence brought to bear on civil governments by this new contact is surely hard to evaluate. But by common consent of Church and State it is immense.[22] If this novel type of church-state relationship had been a charism of Pius XII, one might perhaps dismiss it as simply a part of papal social doctrine having little to do with real religio-civil relations. But it by no means ended with Pope Pius. On the contrary, it has grown, as we shall see, even greater in scope and effectiveness, so that it seems today to be rapidly absorbing (though it will probably never completely absorb) the more traditional form.

3. Perspectives on the Past

At first sight, Pius' treatment of traditional church-state questions seems rather far removed, if not wholly separated from, his universalist teachings. Actually, however, the pope did all in his power to keep the two levels in harmony. This was by no means always an easy task. He was busy building up a realistic program for world-wide, mutual comprehension and cooperation between Church and modern States. On the other hand, he had inherited a traditional outlook on the relations between the Church and so-called "Catholic" States. Evolving both policy and principle to do justice to both types of State was, in reality, an impossibility, but Pope Pius achieved considerable success at it.

In order to appreciate better the significance of this problem of the two facets of Pius' doctrine, a clarification of its full *Sitz im Leben* seems necessary.

If any one trait characterizes the whole corpus of Pope Pius' writings, it is his conviction that the light of Christian doctrine

22. A good example of this effect was the reception by Pope John XXIII of the Balzan Peace Prize in 1963. Pope John attested that it was not himself alone who had merited this civil recognition of beneficent relationship and influence on society, but his predecessors from Leo XIII to Pius XII. See below, p. 279.

is capable of illumining even the most complex and technical of modern problems. The massive twenty volumes of messages contain discussions of such widely differing topics as atomic physics and depth psychology, football and natural childbirth. His treatments show how deep was his interest in, and contact with, the modern world. He was determined to be literally all things to all men.

What especially sharpened this resolution were the charges, coming simultaneously from many quarters, that the Church has lost relevance to the modern world: the Church was a medieval relic. During Pius' pontificate communists and anti-Catholic Christians, as well as a large segment of the entire intellectual world, tended to take this attitude. Pope Leo had already recognized that modern society had refused the Church its place in public life. Pope Pius was determined to win back that place by demonstrating the Church's relevance and society's need for it. This, no doubt, motivated his internationalization of Christian church-state doctrine.

Many Protestants were convinced that the Church advocated as an ideal the State's cooperation in the repression of other religions wherever feasible. The communists, of course, collaborated in this accusation. Thus the Church was denounced on two sides as an enemy of the rights of man.

We have already seen Pope Pius' reaction to these accusations. By coming out strongly on the side of human rights and freedom he both condemned the current totalitarian States' suppression of Catholic rights and denied that the Church wished to exercise a totalitarian repression itself. Unfortunately, however, Pius' bold stand on human religious rights could not change ancient religious laws and customs embedded in the traditions of States in southern Europe and South America. Neither could it change the opinions of many influential theologians who, like Pope Leo, did not believe that these laws violated human dignity.

The result was that, even while Pius wrote and spoke, an

international theological feud of major proportions was raging between liberal and conservative theologians. The liberals applied Pius' universalist doctrine universally. The conservatives believed that the restrictive laws on the other religions, enforced by various church-allied States, constituted part of the ideal church-state union. The one side argued that a system refusing equal civil rights to its citizens respecting public preaching and worship could not be considered an absolute Christian ideal. The other side argued that only the State positively favoring the Catholic Church could be considered to have the ideal system.[1]

This bitter argument could not have been unknown to Pope Pius, though he never publicly commented on it. Evidently he felt that the time was not yet right to decide the issue definitively.[2] Nevertheless he could not limit his church-state doctrine

1. Besides the articles by Msgr. Fenton cited above, this position is presented in many other Catholic writers: F. Martinez, *Naturaleza juridica y derechos de la Iglesia* (Pamplona, 1954); E. Guerrero, "Mas sobre la libertad religiosa en España," *Razòn y Fe*, 149 (1954), 331 ff., and "Con la libertad del acto de fe no es incompatible el estado catòlico," *ibid.*, 151 (1955), 475 ff.; A. Messineo, in various articles in *Civiltà Cattolica*, among which are vol. II, 497 ff.; IV, 314 ff., and 562 ff.; 1951, II, 126 ff., and 585 ff.; 1952, I, 129 ff. See also the speech of Cardinal Ottaviani as it appears in *L'Osservatore Romano* (March 3, 1953), 1.

2. It was not a question merely of ending a theological feud. Rather, it was a real practical dilemma, not totally different from that dilemma faced by Pius IX. The doctrine of the right and duty of man to follow even an erroneous conscience had long since been commonly accepted, even if not universally. But in overwhelmingly Catholic countries like Spain and Italy Pius thought it unrealistic to demand immediate respect for this right in the field of public propagation of non-Catholic religions. As in the middle ages, a common religion remained a powerful, and perhaps necessary, political bond and stabilizing force for the whole community. The issue was complicated. Both sides in the controversy had weighty arguments. Pius could not suddenly disown a system which even so recent a predecessor as Leo XIII had considered the best. On the other hand, neither could he deny the justice and basically Christian nature of the universal movement to freedom of speech, press and religion. "Cooperation" between Church and State—the rock on which the conservatives build their case— was acceptable as an ideal for both sides. It was simply New Testament doctrine. Pope Pius used this idea of cooperation in order to buy time until history could help clarify more precisely the degree of cooperation to be considered the ideal.

to the universalist plane, and so he treated in guarded tones the traditional doctrine on various occasions. This is the doctrine that we are about to study.

He never once came out clearly for either one side or the other on disputed points. In fact, on various occasions his statements seemed a bit ambiguous. Nevertheless, he managed to present the first broad outlines of a solution to the problem. By maintaining steadfastly a position in favor of religious liberty on the one hand, and close church-state cooperation on the other, he was able to agree apparently with both sides of the argument while actually steering a middle course between them.

Pius did not a little towards constructing a system involving the key elements of both these viewpoints. This middle course, though at times disconcertingly vague, did much to prepare the way for Pope John and the Vatican Council. His traditional doctrine falls easily under four essential concepts: 1) the Church's sovereignty and rights; 2) due cooperation between Church and State; 3) dissenters' rights to religious freedom; 4) the question of the ideal form of church-state relations. This last point, however, is so complicated as to require a special chapter for its consideration.

In treating Pius' traditional doctrine, we are dealing with a controversial subject. It is therefore of maximum importance to note carefully what the pontiff said and what he did not say. On various occasions he expressed himself on the subject with a fair amount of precision. His most complete treatment was given in an address to a congress of historians on September 7, 1955. In this address the pope outlined his whole position, touching on each of the major problems involved. It deserves special attention.

In the pre-Christian era public authority, the State, was as competent in the religious domain as in profane matters. The Catholic Church was aware that her Divine Founder had transferred to her the sphere of religion, the religious and moral direction of men to the fullest extent, and independent relations between Church and State, and this history has strongly attracted the attention of scholars.[3]

After the prehistory, he continues with an outline of Pope Leo XIII's summary of church-state principles:

While Church and State are independent powers, they should not because of this ignore one another and still less fight one another. It is far more in conformity to nature and the Divine Will if they cooperate in mutual understanding, since their activities apply to the same subject, namely, to the Catholic citizen. Certainly cases of conflict remain possible, and when the laws of the State do harm to divine law, the Church has a moral duty to oppose them.

Then the pontiff attacks the knotty problem of the medieval hieratic theory and practice. He explicitly rejects Boniface VIII's conception that the State was subject to the Church.

. . . This medieval conception was conditioned by the times. Those who know its sources will probably admit that it would undoubtedly have been more astonishing had it not appeared.

Continuing, he comes next to another central church-state problem—freedom for other religious groups:

Let no one object that the Church herself scorns the personal convictions of those who do not think as she does. The Church has considered and still considers that the willing abandonment of the true faith is a sin. When, beginning about 1200, such a defection entailed penal proceedings on the part of the spiritual as well as the temporal power, it was only to avoid the destruction of the religious and ecclesiastical unity of the West. To non-Catholics the Church applied the principle contained in the Code of Canon Law: "Let none be forced against his will to embrace the Catholic Faith" (Canon 1351). She believes that

3. Address given to the Tenth International Congress for the Historical Sciences, September 7, 1955: AAS, XLVII (1955), 676 ff. (cf. *Catholic Mind,* December, 1955, 746). See Leclerq's comments on this important address, *op. cit.,* pp. 205-207.

their convictions constitute a reason, although not always the principal one, for tolerance.

Next comes a summary of principles in the light of modern circumstances:

> The historian should not forget that, while the Church and State have known hours and years of conflict, there were also, from the time of Constantine the Great until the contemporary era, and even recently, tranquil periods, often quite long ones, during which they collaborated with full understanding in the education of the same people. The Church does not hide the fact that in principle she considers such collaboration normal, and that she regards the unity of the people in the true religion and the unanimity of action between herself and the State as an ideal.
>
> But she also knows that for some time events have been evolving in a rather different direction, that is to say, toward the multiplicity of religious beliefs and conceptions of life within the same national community, where Catholics are a more or less strong minority.

Finally, the pope mentions and comments on the use of concordats as a means of church-state agreement:

> In the history of relations between the Church and State, the concordats, as you know, play an important part . . . In concordats let us say, the Church seeks the juridical security and independence necessary to her mission.

A careful analysis of the whole address indicates that Pius stressed here all four points. But they all recur frequently in his other treatments of the matter. Let us now look at the four concepts in the light of some parallel references. These will furnish a more precise insight into the full pattern of Pius' thought.

1. *The Church has sovereignty and rights:* Regarding the sovereignty and rights of the Church, Pius said in the first encyclical of his pontificate:

Indeed, our Our great predecessor, Leo XIII, wisely taught in
the Encyclical *Immortale Dei,* it was the Creator's will that civil
sovereignty should regulate social life after the dictates of an
order changeless in its universal principles; should facilitate the
attainment in the temporal order, by individuals, of physical,
intellectual, and moral perfection; and should aid them to reach
their supernatural end.[4]

Here, then, he does not seek to improve on Pope Leo's classical
statements found in *Immortale Dei.* When this subject comes
up for discussion he treats it slightly, and simply refers to Pope
Leo's documents.

2. *Church and State must cooperate:* Regarding the second
point, he is consistently much less emphatic in his defense of
the traditional system than was Pope Leo. But he does repeatedly reiterate Leo's rejection of absolute and cold separation:
"She [the Church] cannot in principle or according to the thesis,
approve a complete separation between the two powers."[5]
Another important text for Pius' church-state doctrine indicates
more clearly the same difference between himself and Leo on
this point. It reflects the manner Pius typically chose to reconcile the universalist and the traditionalist facets of his doctrine,
and deserves careful attention. When addressing the Holy
Roman Rota on October 29, 1947, he analyzed the likenesses
and differences between the juridical authority of the Church
and that of civil law. First he says:

This last difference between the two societies, based upon their
respective ends, undoubtedly excludes that violent subjection
of the Church to the State, that forcible inclusion of the Church
within the State as a part of it, which is contrary to the nature

4. *Summi Pontificatus,* AAS, XXXI (1939), 445-446 (cf. *Catholic
Mind,* November, 1939, 905).
5. Allocution to the Fifth National Convention of Italian Catholic
Jurists, December 6, 1963, AAS, XLV (1953), 802. See Leclerq, 210 ff.
for his remarks on this important address. And see also Murray, *We Hold
These Truths,* p. 61, 75.

of each, and which, in the early stages at least, all totalitarianism tends to achieve. But it does not exclude every kind of union between the two societies, still less does it require between them a cold and detached attitude of agnosticism and indifference. This is an erroneous conception of the doctrine that Church and State are two perfect societies really distinct. Such a view would fail to account for the many forms of union, historical and actual, more or less advantageous, which have existed between the two powers; above all it would leave out of account the fact that Church and State both have their origin in God and that both are concerned with the same subjects, human beings, and with their dignity, whether natural or supernatural.[6]

So far, one would see almost an accord with Pope Leo. But when he goes on to explain the nature of the union between the two societies, one sees a marked difference of outlook. He uses Leo's analogy of the union of soul and body.

> May we not see here in some respects an analogy with the relation between body and soul. Their joint activity is such that a man's psychological character is constantly influenced by his temperament and physiological conditions, while on the other hand moral impressions, emotion, and passions react so powerfully upon physical sensibility that even the features of a man's countenance are modelled by the soul, which, as it were, imprints its own likeness on them.[7]

But the common point of comparison of this analogy is different from that of Leo. Leo intended to emphasize that the type of union between the two parts of the analogy was similar.[8] Pius, however, changed the analogue. The point of similarity that he sees between the two unions is not the type of union but the

6. Allocution to the officials of the Sacred Roman Rota, October 29, 1947, AAS, XXXIX (1953), 494-495 (cf. *Clergy Review,* March, 1948, 197).

7. *Loc. cit.*

8. Leo, by this analogy, emphasized the *closeness* which should characterize the union between the Church and the State. He went on to give such examples of this closeness as the prohibition by the State of public cults other than the Catholic one.

effects of the union. The major effects of the union are, says
Pius, that the two parts—soul and body, Church and State—in
both cases have a profound effect on one another. They influence
each other profoundly.

In thus stressing the influence between the two parts, Pius
was, in fact, emphasizing the *difference* between the two societies, and between their respective juridical structures. When
he takes up Leo's analogy he merely wants to assure his audience
that in emphasizing the difference he is not denying the necessity for coordination.

In this different application of the body-soul analogy one sees
mirrored Pius' delicate compromise position between Leo's iron-
willed adherence to the medieval ideal of full union on the one
hand, and the modern cooperation-only view, on the other. He
softened Leo's rigidity while retaining the major part of his
doctrine. He takes a compromise position in the theological
feud. This finely balanced position becomes more evident later
on in the same address when he states:

> In saying this we are not overlooking the practical difficulties
> which, in spite of everything, modern life presents to the judi-
> cial power of the Church; difficulties which under certain aspects
> are greater than those that confront civil tribunals. It is enough
> to mention in this connection certain spiritual values in regard
> to which *the judicial power of the State acknowledges less obli-
> gation, or even maintains an attitude of deliberate indifference.*
> Typical of such difficulties are crimes against the faith or cases
> of apostasy, cases involving "freedom of conscience" or "reli-
> gious toleration," and also matrimonial cases. *Here the Church,
> and consequently the ecclesiastical judge in like manner, is
> unable to adopt the neutral attitude of states of mixed religious
> profession;* still less unbelief and religious indifference. The
> Church can let herself be guided only by the essential end which
> God has given her.[9]

Pius carefully avoids judging the morality of the State's remain-

9. *Ibid.*, 496. Italics are mine.

ing aloof in matters such as liberty of conscience. He merely emphasizes that the very purpose of ecclesiastical judges forbids that they imitate the State in this aloofness. In the following paragraph he emphasizes strongly the "profound difference of end" which must regulate the respective stances of the two societies on such religious matters.

> We are thus constantly meeting the profound difference between the judicial power of the Church and that of the State which their different ends entail. There is no reason, of course, why the one should not avail itself of the results achieved by the other, whether in the theoretical field or in that of practical experience; but it would be wrong to try to transfer mechanically all the elements and laws of the one to the other, still more to put both on the same level.[10]

He clearly holds that the "profound difference of end" fundamentally limits to the temporal, common good of its citizens the State's obligations regarding religious matters. But, although the difference be great, the two juridical systems must remain cooperative. How different from Leo.[11]

This shows how Pius' universalist view of church-state relations (which leads him to preach respect for human rights in religious matters) had great influence on his conception of how the narrower, traditionalist doctrine of church-state union would be put into practice. But it did not cause him to abandon the traditional manner of thought. He was in favor of close collaboration between Church and State. But he refused to conclude that this *"plein comprehension"* between the two societies required either of them "to transfer mechanically all the elements and laws of the one to the other," or to wish "to put both on the same level."

Thus, one gains more insight into the delicate balance Pope

10. *Loc. cit.*
11. See above, p. 232 ff. Pius nowhere even implies that the State *must* "worship God in the manner revealed by God." His expressions of the norm always stop short of this.

Pius would have exist between separation and union. It is not an easily acquired insight because Pius, it seems, did not wish to clarify all the problems it contained.

3. *The Church recognizes dissenters' rights to religious freedom:*
This third fundamental church-state principle shows clearly the pope's intention to coordinate his traditionalist doctrine carefully with that more general doctrine propounded to the world. We have seen how Pope Leo's interpretations of tradition's lessons respecting freedom of religion were relatively stringent. But Pius interprets the same history more liberally. In the address to the historians he denies that Leo's doctrine of cooperation between Church and State implies a contempt on the part of the Church for men whose religious convictions differ from its own, and specifically speaks out for tolerance. On numerous occasions before this Pius had proclaimed the rights of man. Here, in a specifically traditional treatment of church-state relations, he renews this proclamation.

In doing so he became the first pontiff to more or less directly disown the medieval tradition of State repression of heresy.[12] He cites the legislation of canon law against forced conversion as an indication of the Church's respect for conscience's inviolability. But there can be no doubt as to his real meaning. Already two years before, in his famous allocution on tolerance, he had made a similar declaration, again in connection with church-state matters:

> Hence the affirmation: religious and moral error must always be impeded, when it is possible, because toleration of them is in itself immoral, is not valid *absolutely and unconditionally*. Moreover, God has not given even to human authority such an

12. See Cardinal Bea, "Religiöse Freiheit und Wandlungen der Gesellschaft," 321-333 (especially 330 ff.). See also J. Lecler, "Pie XII et la tolérance," 247 ff., and "La papauté modern et la liberté de conscience," by the same author, in *Etudes*, 1946, II, 289-309; finally, see Murray, "Contemporary orientations . . .," 181 ff.

absolute and universal command in matters of faith and morality. Such a command is unknown to the common convictions of mankind, to Christian conscience, to the sources of revelation and to the practice of the Church . . . The duty of repressing moral and religious error cannot therefore be an ultimate norm of action. It must be subordinate to *higher and more general norms,* which *in some circumstances* permit, and even perhaps seem to indicate as the better policy, toleration of error in order to *promote a greater good.*[13]

We note that Pius' argument for toleration lacks something in clarity and absoluteness of tone. But such hedging is understandable in the light of what his predecessors had to say on the matter, and in view of the theological feud raging around the subject.

There is, however, one allocution in which he treats the matter more clearly. In 1946, in his address to the Holy Roman Rota, he stated in quite a definitive manner the Church's espousal of the principle of freedom of conscience for non-Catholics. He admitted frankly that the repressive actions of the Inquisition were not called for by purely theological implications:

It is doubtless true that the tribunal charged with the defense of the faith may in the course of the centuries have assumed forms and used methods uncalled for in the nature of things, yet explainable in the light of special historical circumstances. But it would be fallacious to argue from this against the legitimacy of the Court itself.[14]

He admitted also that, according to the more developed doctrine of his day, the Inquisition exceeded its just limits:

Though the "modern conscience" may be of the opinion that the punishment of offenses injurious to Faith in days gone by sometimes went beyond the limits of justice, society generally

13. To the Catholic Jurists of Italy, 799 (cf. *Catholic Mind,* April, 1954, 248). See Cardinal Bea's excellent commentary on the difficult points of this famous allocution, *op. cit.,* 329-330.

14. Allocution to the members of the Holy Roman Rota, October 6, 1946, AAS, XXXVIII (1946), 392 (cf. *Catholic Mind,* March, 1947, 130).

today, in contrast, shows itself too insensitive and indifferent to these same offenses.

The ever-increasing contacts and indiscriminate mingling of various religious denominations within the same national groups have induced the civil courts to apply the principle of "tolerance" and "freedom of conscience." In such circumstances, let us add, Catholics are in duty bound to practice political, civic and social tolerance with respect to the faithful of other denominations.[15]

He declared that, even for the statesmen, it is a moral duty to guarantee freedom of conscience in modern States where many religions live side by side. He even quotes Lactantius[16] (who spoke before the Edict of Milan and took a position directly opposed to Augustine's stand, and that of the whole Middle Ages), who denies that any force should be employed in the defense of the Christian faith. Finally, in order to make the record completely clear, he quotes from a note sent by his Secretary of State during January of the same year to the Yugoslav legation at the Vatican. The note, a response to a routinely forwarded diplomatic inquiry, reads in part:

According to the principles of Catholic teaching, conversion should be the result not of coercion from without but of sincere interior assent to the truths taught by the Catholic Church. That is why the Catholic Church grants admission to those adults desiring to be received or to return to her only on condition that they are fully conscious of the meaning and effect of the action they propose to take.[17]

Pius denied that the Church teaches that States are obliged to distinguish between religious truth and falsity. Nevertheless the Church, as a society expressly founded to teach religious truth, has a duty to judge in these matters:

15. *Loc. cit.*
16. Pope John XXIII was to cite the same author. See below, pp. 281-282.
17. *Ibid.*, 394 (cf. *Catholic Mind,* March, 1947, 132).

The Catholic Church, as we have said before, is a perfect society, based on truth infallibly revealed by God. Whatever is opposed to this truth is necessarily error; and error may not be accorded objectively the same rights as truth. Thus freedom of thought and freedom of conscience are essentially limited by the veracity of the God of Revelation.[18]

The intent behind these insistences on religious toleration and freedom is clear. Given, as they all were, in a context dealing with traditional church-state doctrine, they were intended to emphasize and develop a principle which Leo XIII had already declared: respect for human dignity must always play an important role in all church-state matters. Both the theology and the experience of freedom had advanced much since Leo's day. Pope Pius was determined to bring to the attention of even those nations where close church-state union was in effect that this new and deeper awareness of human rights could no longer be ignored. He had already proclaimed this principle to be fundamental in international relations between States and society on all levels. In these three addresses he made advances of truly historical importance towards incorporating the same principle in the church-state relations of largely Catholic nations.

But although of greatest importance, the documents we have just looked at were not of a definitive nature. None of them contained a universal, apodictic affirmation of freedom of conscience

18. *Ibid.*, 394-395. How different from the middle ages. Yet, as Pius himself so clearly points out, it has not been a change so much as an evolution. The extraneous political circumstances have changed, so that the civil and social order do not require a forceably maintained religious unity. Today heresy has few civil repercussions in most parts of the world. A reason even greater than this, however, is the fuller maturation of the totality of St. Paul's and Thomas' notion of the human conscience and its right to freedom and respect. Without a clear notion of this growth, the appearance of Pius' "new" doctrine on freedom of conscience is difficult to reconcile with tradition. But when seen in its true historical evolution the pontiff's firm insistence that the Church has always upheld individual rights is quite understandable. They were upheld to the degree that general cultural levels and doctrinal development permitted. In this sense, the pope's new doctrine is also a traditional one. Cf. Leclerq, *op. cit.*, p. 353 ff.

such as will later appear in *Pacem In Terris*. They were, like
Leo's teachings before them, carefully in step with their times.
They were calculated to refute accusations of Catholic totalitarianism and intolerance, but were so worded as not to disrupt
systems founded more on medieval than on democratic principles. By thus emphasizing tolerance and freedom, the pontiff
made it clear that no discussion of Christian church-state doctrine could be carried on without including these truths within
the formula. Any weighing of separation vs. union would in the
future have to make use of the scales of human dignity.

4. THE IDEAL CHURCH-STATE RELATION?

The fourth point in Pius' traditional doctrine touches directly on
the focal point of the then current theological feud. What is the
ideal in church-state relations? In the address to the historians
cited in the last chapter the pontiff answered that the ideal is
two-fold: the unity of all people in the true religion, and the
"unanimity of action" between that religion and the State. At
first glance it would seem that Pius is reiterating Leo's old
ideal of complete and formal union with and protection of the
Church. But when compared to the latter's "embrace, protect
. . . and shield by the authority of law," Pius' formula is clearly
more general. It surely does not explicitly reject Pope Leo's conception. But does it imply that formal union in the traditional
sense is the *only* way of achieving the ideal? Might "unanimity
of action" between the Church and a State be conceivable without formal union? Let us see what Pius said about the question.

First of all, there are several other phrases parallel to "unanimity of action" which give us a more precise understanding of
the pontiff's meaning. One such reference occurs alongside the
"unanimity" clause in the same address. The pope says, "Church
and State . . . should not . . . ignore one another and still less
fight one another. It is far more in conformity to nature and the

Divine Will if they cooperate in mutual understanding . . ."[1]
Again the phrasing is somewhat ambiguous. But this passage is
easier to interpret in favor of the possibility of a non-unitive
unanimity than the other phrase. There are others, however,
which seem to indicate the contrary. Pius voiced on several
occasions a high esteem for systems of the past which were formally and totally unitive, even to the exclusion of other religions.
For instance:

> Nor can one let pass unnoticed, or without recognizing its bene-
> ficient influence, that close union which, until the French
> Revolution, marked the mutual relations in the Catholic world
> of the two divinely established authorities: the Church and the
> State. The intimacy of their relations on the common ground of
> public life generally created an atmosphere of Christian spirit.[2]

Yet Pius nowhere takes up Leo's plea that the State favor the
Church over other religions. We have seen how he positively
denied that the State should suppress other religions. Further,
he affirmed that "union" between the two powers can take many
forms.[3]

Two questions arise. First, does the pontiff speak here only of
the "forms of union" consisting in complete union in the same
sense as Leo XIII? It is quite evident from the context that
neither here nor elsewhere is his intention so narrow. He is
rejecting "cold separation" and adding "multiple" types of union
which, both in his day and in the past, were successful. Surely
he does not mean only those medieval forms by which the State
wed itself to the Church to the total exclusion of civil recognition of other religions and sects. He speaks also of "present
forms." But scarcely a single modern nation fulfills even Leo

1. Allocution to the Historians (see above, p. 243 ff.).
2. Allocution to the First International Congress of Lay Apostles, October 14, 1951, AAS, XLIII (1951), 785 (cf. *Catholic Mind*, February, 1952,
116).
3. See p. 246, and note 8.

XIII's ideal of union to the extent of joint church-state censorship and repressive control of other religious concepts. Therefore at least some modern forms of union are good and fruitful,
in Pius' estimation, without the old coercive elements.

The second question is whether Pius limited his ideal of
"unanimity of action" to *formal* church-state relations. Certainly
there is no question that Pope Pius heartily approved of formal
relations between Church and State.[4] But there is a vast difference between formal relations and formal union. The various
concordats and diplomatic exchanges between the Vatican and
the most diverse nations of the world all come under the notion
of formal relations. But for the vast majority of these exchanges
there is no question of formal union, which entails not only
formal contacts but also full acceptance by the State of the
Church's claim to exclusive possession of full religious truth.

Now, Pope Pius described his ideal as "full unanimity of
action." But we have seen that Pius did not consider this ideal
to be limited to the medieval concept of formal and complete
union. We have seen, too, that he did approve of formal relations. The important question remains to be answered: Did he
consider formal relations as such a necessary part of his ideal?
The sum of pertinent writings will also give us a clearer idea of
Pius' over-all convictions as to what is, and what is not, ideal in
Catholic church-state relations.

To begin with, knowing, as he surely did, the theological battle raging over the matter of what is the objective ideal, it seems
that the pontiff would have been quite specific in his terminology
if he intended to limit the ideal to formal relations. But, as a

4. For proof of this one need only examine a few of the pontiff's many
addresses to his diplomatic corps and to individual representatives of
States. These addresses frequently express gratitude for good relations and
recognize explicitly the benefits, both national and international, which
flow from such a system of formal relations. A good example is the pope's
Allocution to his Diplomatic Corps on February 25, 1946. It concerned
the aids to world peace which flow from relations between the Holy See
and the various countries represented.

matter of fact, Pius praised in glowing terms the religious pro-
visions of one State which, though its citizens were overwhelmingly Catholic, united itself neither by concordat nor by constitution to the Church. Regarding the State of Ireland and its
Constitution, which guarantees civil equality to all religions and
the formal establishment of none, Pius said:

> Your Constitution [Bunreacht na h-Eireann] is intended to be
> an instrument of Prudence, Justice and Charity at the service of
> a community which has never, through its long Christian his-
> tory, had any doubt about the eternal, as well as the temporal,
> implications of the common good, which it professes to seek
> through the conjoined prayer, toil and oftentimes heroic sacri-
> fice of its children.
>
> Grounded on the bedrock of the natural law, those funda-
> mental prerogatives which your Constitution undertakes to
> assure to every citizen of Ireland, within the limits of order and
> morality, could find no ampler, no safer guarantee against the
> godless forces of subversion, the spirit of faction and of violence,
> than mutual trust between the authorities of Church and State,
> independent each in its own sphere but, as it were, allied for
> the common welfare in accordance with the principles of
> Catholic faith and doctrine.[5]

Here Pius' idea of mutual trust between Church and State—
"independent . . . but as it were allied for the common welfare"
—seems to fulfill every requirement he set elsewhere for full
"unanimity of action."[6] There is little substantial evidence that
his notion of unity was limited to formal ties either by constitu-

5. Address to Prime Minister E. De Valera, October 4, 1957, AAS,
XLIX (1957), 952.
6. There even seems to be a good likelihood that Pius deliberately left
his terminology vague enough to accommodate itself to new forms of
union. That it *is* a type of union (though a moral one only, it is still much
more a real one than many formal unions) is unquestionable. Enda
McDonagh brings this out nicely in his doctoral dissertation (as yet unpub-
lished), presented to the Canon Law faculty of the University of Munich:
Church and State in the Constitution of Ireland (Münchener Bibliotek,
Juris Canonici).

tion or concordat.[7] It is true, however, that Ireland does have diplomatic relations with the Holy See. But these diplomatic relations are more in the nature of relations between two independent States than relations between the Church and the State.

If the pontiff's various words of praise for union revealed no restriction to formal union or even formal relations, neither do his condemnations of separation include all forms of separation. One searches for such a restriction in vain when one examines his various explicit rejections of separation. We have seen how, in his address to the Italian jurists, he explicitly rejected separation, but significantly qualified his rejection with an adjective: "*complete* separation."[8] Speaking to the International Congress of Lay Apostles, he noted that the United States' Constitution and the French Revolution were the beginning of an ever-widening trend towards separation:

> At the end of the 18th century, a new factor came into play. On the one hand the Constitution of the United States of America —a country which had an extraordinarily rapid development and where the Church soon began to grow considerably in life and vigor—and on the other hand the French Revolution, with its consequences in Europe as well as overseas . . . led to the detachment of the Church from the State.[9]

He affirms that this concrete trend, which began at this point, had unsound effects for the Church. But he is careful not to condemn the whole movement as Pope Leo tended to do. Neither does he imply that a system such as Ireland's, though necessarily rising out of this movement, carried with it the evils which usually accompanied the separationist movement. The pontiff surely makes a valid point here. The atmosphere and the public psychology created by a State which formally recognized the Church was a great aid towards guarding and strengthening the faith. This was the thinking of the age of Christendom.

7. Ireland has no Concordat.
8. See above, p. 246. He similarly qualified all similar rejections.
9. *Op. cit.*, 785 (cf. *Catholic Mind*, February, 1952, 116).

Must State approval of religion necessarily be absent from even a most Christian country which, nevertheless, is not officially and legally "Christian"? In the address cited, the pontiff's point of emphasis was the vocation of the lay apostle. He pointed out that the aid which formal church-state union had furnished religion in ages past, must now be supplied by the lay apostle. He in no way implies that this new Christian dynamism could not be as effective as the medieval one in the task of integrating Christ and society.

> Without taking effect everywhere at the same time and in the same degree, this separation everywhere had for its logical conclusion the leaving of the Church to assure by her own means freedom of action, accomplishment of her mission and defense of her rights and liberty.[10]

From no matter what angle one examines his writings, one cannot declare Pius XII to have sided definitely with either one or the other factions in the great theological feud. He neither affirms nor denies that formal State recognition or State discrimination in favor of Catholicism is the ideal. He praised the good points of both the formal and the informal systems of church-state relation. But his ideal of full mutual comprehension between the two authorities fell short of any one system of relations.

When the fact of the pontiff's official reserve is considered in the light of the whole historical evolution of church-state doctrine, its immense importance becomes evident. From the fourth until the nineteenth century official, formal recognition had never been questioned, because of the nature of the monarchical form of government. No alternative except denial and rejection of the truth of the Church had ever presented itself, nor was even seriously imagined.[11] Even after the modern age was well

10. *Loc. cit.*
11. This seems to be what K. Rahner had in mind when he wrote: "Since the line of demarcation between coercion and freedom has in the nature of things a variability determined historically and by circumstances, and since this change in situation can bring with it not only the right but

established, Leo XIII and his immediate successors firmly
rejected the alternative offered by the liberalist democrats. But
Pius withheld judgment. And he did so in spite of the considerable division caused by the argument among theologians pro-
longed by such a lack of decision.

It is important to know that Pius *did* withhold this judgment;
but it is also necessary to ask why he did so. His motive could
scarcely have been a lack of knowledge on the subject, nor a
want of ability to make firm decisions. His vast corpus of social
and political teachings and his firm, clear decisions in any number of areas, belie any such explanations. In searching for the
answer, careful consideration must be given to the social and
political development which had occurred in the Christian
world since Pope Leo's day.

Leo had given his blessing to the new social structure in so far
as it was not dependent on relativistic liberalism. As a result,
vigorous Catholic movements sprang up all over Europe and
elsewhere, with both intellectual and practical strains working
hand in hand.[12] In countries like Belgium, Germany, and France,
such Christian movements soon became powerful forces in
governments, or at least in the political battlefield. The experience had a maturing effect on both the opposition, who had to
cede some degree of respectability to this new form of Christian

in certain circumstances also the absolute moral duty of shifting the
boundary between freedom and coercion—and this even in favour of a
greater freedom—the Church is not simply absolutely bound to old ideals
of protection for the Catholic religion by the State; she is not bound by
ideals which restricted non-Christians in their freedom . . . Neither the
Holy Empire nor the sectarian, territorial State with special privileges for
the Church as the State-religion need nowadays be the Christian ideal in
our country. Although there can be no right to a false cult *as such,* there
can certainly be a right to scope for freedom within which a false cult is
possible, and within which it would not be permitted to suppress this false
cult by external force merely because it is false when (and because) this
would be possible only by a restriction of what is a legitimate scope for
freedom in a determined historical situation" (*Theological Investigations,*
II, *Man in the Church* [Baltimore, 1963], pp. 262-263).

12. See Jacques Leclerq, *op. cit.,* pp. 217-218.

action, and on the movements themselves, which quickly purged themselves of unworkable theories and schemes.[13]

A new age for Christians rose out of this movement. It was an age of militant Christianity accepting the facts and circumstances of modern democratic society, becoming part of these elements, and bringing Christ to them. Catholic action and Catholic individuals took their place in all social endeavors beside men of all faiths. They demanded and received attention and acceptance not only on the basis of dogma, but on their tangible records of accomplishment and on their capabilities. Nowhere were they an overwhelming force, but everywhere they made themselves heard, even under the suppression of Hitler and Mussolini.

By the time Pope Pius had had time to find himself and hammer out a firm policy, World War II was over and the political climate was indeed new. Not only were Christian theorists and technicians firmly a part of social and political structures in both the old and the new worlds; the old and the new worlds had become one, with the founding of the United Nations. Christianity found itself a free force moving and working in a world made both new and one by the miracle of modern communications and modern toleration of new ideas. Pope Pius had the genius to see this revolution before it was fully a reality. He showed himself indeed a representative of Christ by throwing all the influence of his person and office behind not only the United Nations but also the whole direction of the new order in general, which was Christian in fact though not in name.

He aimed at unity, liberty, and peace. This was itself a new relationship between the Church and the States of the modern world. Before his death he added, in this manner, a whole new story to the traditional Catholic church-state edifice. His addition was a doctrine teaching cooperation and even formal rela-

13. For a fine long-ranged description of this whole trend see Dondeyne, *Faith and the World,* p. 195 ff.

tions with States, but stopping short of any union which would violate the consciences of other religious groups. In a prudent and gradual manner he set about conciliating the narrower, more traditional, forms and doctrines of church-state relations, so that no contradictions would separate the old from the new.

Though it may be questioned whether he actually abandoned Leo's ideal of formal union, it is hardly questionable that he re-tailored Leo's concept considerably. He certainly explicitly rejected (where Leo even obliquely praised) State repression of heresy and other violations of the human person. Catholic thinkers and workers had by this time matured enough to begin to show the world that, in general, what the Pope spoke was not just words but genuine Catholic doctrine and practice.

In the light of this development, Pope Pius' tacit break with a thousand-year-old tradition idealizing formal church-state union is seen in its proper perspective. The ideal of all men united in the true faith remained as firm as ever. This was simply following Christ's own words. Also unchanged was the ideal of coordination, both formal and informal, between the Church and the State. But the inexorable experience of history had altered the elements involved in any further elaboration of this doctrine. It no longer seemed easy to detail how coordination might be achieved in the ideal manner. The full complexity of the various sociological and civilizational influences working in society and history itself had begun to be realized. As a result one notes clearly in the papal documents a new hesitancy to declare in detail the technical forms of ideals not only in church-state relations but in all similar social phenomena.

Such are, in outline, the most plausible reasons why Pope Pius refused to come out solidly in support of Leo's ideal of formal and complete union of Church and State. He followed his brilliant predecessor's general doctrine in its outlines and adhered closely to its principles. But a deeper cognizance of the nature of modern democracy and modern social circumstances in general, plus his superior appreciation of the doctrine of human dignity and freedom, prevented him from declaring formal union to be the ultimate in objective ideals.[14] By so deciding, he provided Catholic church-state doctrine with a truly historical development.

These observations complete the treatment of Pius' doctrine on traditional church-state doctrine. It may be said by way of summary that he held intact the whole corpus handed him by tradition, while at the same time contributing in a unique manner to adapting this corpus of doctrine realistically to modern times and political circumstances.

Pius XII was, even more than Pope Leo XIII, the pope who sought to prove that the Church was not a stranger in the modern world. His deep interest in, and understanding of, his times enabled him to see old problems from new points of view. Thus, he was able to enlarge the Church's political doctrine to embrace the widened horizons of his day.

History favored him with a reign unclouded by polemics and the kind of purely political concerns which had weighted down his predecessors for more than a millennium. Time had all but healed the wounds left by the seizure of the papal states. The Lateran Pacts, standing with new firmness after World War II, gave him political independence, and at the same time gave the world assurance that his doctrines had purely spiritual ends. Thus enjoying a general world prestige rarely equalled in papal history, he addressed his social doctrine not only to the faithful but to all nations.

14. As we have mentioned before Pius' change had much to do with his acceptance of democracy as a form of government. As Leclerq points out, *op. cit.*, p. 211: "But to understand completely the attitude of Pius XII one must always bear in mind another element. Pius XII, as we have seen, accepts democracy. He no longer envisages any other type of government, but rather he searches for the conditions necessary for a sound democracy. Democracy is based on the equality of men. . . . But this supposes individual freedom, especially freedom of opinion."

What he taught concerning the relations between religion and civil authority had a universal character which appealed to both the States and the organizations of States; to both Catholics and men of all religions, or of no religion at all. Such a doctrine must be acknowledged to be an innovation in Catholic church-state teachings. It constituted a major turn in the long and intricate line of development of this area of Christian doctrine.

But the "new look" given church-state matters by Pope Pius was carefully worded so as not to conflict with the essential elements of the more traditional doctrine. The pontiff took Pope Leo as master, but he gave depth and breadth to his inheritance. His was a great contribution to church-state teachings. Though his doctrine was, in substance, traditional, it was in three ways also almost revolutionary: 1) He expanded the scope of Leo's doctrine, making it applicable literally to the world. He reversed Leo's doctrine on freedom of press, speech, and worship.[15] Without differing from Leo in principle on the matter of freedom, he nevertheless succeeded in reversing the practical application of these principles in favor of far greater freedom of press, speech and conscience. 3) He neglected, even under the pressure of a world-wide theological argument over the issue, to affirm that formal church-state union was the ideal system of church-state relations.

We have already sufficiently examined the development of Pius' universal doctrine and also his failure to affirm formal union as the ideal. By way of conclusion we will summarize briefly the growth-curve of the key to both of these doctrines: the socio-religious notion of freedom.[16]

15. Leo's basic message was, in spite of his best efforts, somewhat negative. Pius emphasized the necessity and goodness of these freedoms.

16. By becoming the first pope in history to defend the right of all men to freedom of press, speech and religion, Pius made a universalist church-state doctrine possible. This possibility—and its actualization—in turn made impossible the unconditional acceptance of the system which, during a whole era, his predecessors had considered an ideal. Cf. Rahner, *op. cit.*, pp. 262-263.

Not since the time of Constantine had a Catholic leader come out in favor of all men's right to freedom in following the religious dictates of their consciences. Since that time Catholics had tended more and more to isolate themselves from the rest of the world. Their treatment of Jews and non-believers had encouraged the rest of the world to turn away from all involvement with the Christian world. What Islamic and Jewish leaders had to say was presumed by Christians to be of no interest to them, and among non-Christian leaders the same was true. Persecutions by one led to persecutions by the other, so that an almost impenetrable cultural and intellectual barrier remained around Christendom.[17] This barrier had been broken down in the economic, cultural, and intellectual fields, but it remained largely intact in religious matters until Pius' pontificate.

By admitting the basically Christian nature of religious tolerance, and insisting on charity and openness to men of all faiths, Pope Pius made possible for the first time a universally applicable doctrine of new relationships between religion and civil governments.[18] In so doing he widened to an almost incredible degree the horizons of the Church's own traditional church-state teachings.

But what was the foundation on which Pope Pius based these innovations? What made it possible for him to encourage a substantial freedom of press, speech, and conscience, while his predecessors as late as Leo had constantly rejected them? The answer lies in the history of the development of the Christian

17. Dondeyne (*op. cit.*, p. 18) describes the removal of barriers thus: "Medieval man lived in a world that was spiritually homogeneous. He was in his religious thinking and acting a child of his milieu. If he wished to adhere to another view than that held by his neighbors, he had to become a revolutionary and was treated accordingly. Technology, however, has wiped out the frontiers that formerly separated men, countries and peoples. Man has become a citizen of the world."

18. Referring to this "new look" created by Pius XII (*op. cit.*, p. 210) Leclerq says: "He never alludes to the formation of a Christendom, nor to the problems of a Christian State. He does not even mention them. One gets the impression that an entirely new leaf has been turned."

doctrine concerning the human conscience. Had the Christian appreciation of conscience remained at its Augustinian level, or even on the level achieved by St. Thomas, the progresses achieved in Christian church-state relations, here recorded, would have been impossible.

Existential relationships between the Church and any State are basically a question of freedom: freedom for both Church and State to fulfill their missions.[19] Without mutual respect for the rights and even for the weakness of another, constructive relationships are impossible. That is why any treatment of church-state relations without a careful consideration of the doctrine of conscience and of its authority would necessarily be incomplete.

We have examined the new orientations concerning conscience given to the Church by St. Thomas. He was the first to declare that even an insuperably ignorant or erring conscience must be followed. We have seen, too, how Catholic theologians during the Reformation began to apply this for the first time to dissident Christians. They considered men's consciences to be sacred and inviolable even though in error.

The American and French revolutions provided the first testing ground where Catholics could experience in a living, existential manner the practical consequences of true freedom of conscience.[20] In a relatively short time all of Europe rang with the cry for the freedom and equality of every individual. Catholics were a part of this general social drive. It acted as a spur for

19. The whole outline of church-state history shows this truth clearly. Either kingly suppression of ecclesiastical rights or ecclesiastical denial of royal rights lay at the root of all church-state quarrels. Regarding the latter type of suppression K. Rahner illustrates our thesis by saying: "However, since the Church is always also a Church made up of sinful men, even as far as the holders of her authority are concerned, she can also in her individual actions offend against her own principles and against the freedom of the individual both within and without. This has happened often enough in the course of history" (*op. cit.*, pp. 99-100).

20. See Leclerq, *op. cit.*, p. 175 ff.

a re-thinking of the traditional deposit of theological opinions on the civil freedom of press, of speech, and of religion.[21]

Again and again popes were required to discipline erroneous, exaggerated attempts to find the Christian golden mean in these matters. Gregory XV, Pius IX, Leo XIII, and Pius X each were required to repress overambitious Catholics on questions concerning freedom. But they could not, even had they wished, stem the steadily growing tide of the theology of freedom. Men like Lacordaire and Dupenloup of France, and Cardinal Gibbons of the United States, were the forerunners of legions of lay and clerical thinkers of the twentieth century who threw their whole effort behind defending and developing the theology of the Christian conscience and its rights.[22] Vermeerch's work on tolerance[23] was the first of whole libraries issuing from the best thinkers in the Church. And always the problem of man's right to follow a sincere conscience was accompanied by a questioning of the laws existing in Catholic countries which seemed to hamper this right severely for non-Catholics.

During Pope Pius XII's pontificate the majority of the most famous names in theology reasoned as follows: Since Christ showed the greatest possible respect and forbearance to men of all creeds, and St. Paul taught the inviolability of the erring conscience, then Catholics must consistently reflect this tolerance in all its many applications. Hence, any undue pressure on dissident Christians, whether applied by civil or ecclesiastical law or custom, is unworthy of Christ's followers.[24] Thinking and

21. Not only the whole movement of Catholic Action, but likewise the presence of many outstanding Catholic statesmen and other officials within public life, thoroughly at home in the drive for liberty, attest to this phenomenon of Christian agitation for soundly reasoned doctrines of human liberty.

22. See John Tracy Ellis, "The Issue of Religious Freedom," *American Benedictine Review*, XIV (December, 1963), 509-511.

23. *La Tolérance* (Louvain, 1912).

24. See, for example, J. Maritain, *Man and the State* (Chicago, 1951), p. 76 ff., and J. Daniélou, "La liberté chrétienne et l'Eglise," in *L'Eglise et la liberté* (Paris, 1955), pp. 34-35.

arguing in this fashion, these men had the prestige and force of our whole modern civilization behind them. The outstanding thinkers of all religions and countries thought more or less as they.

This was the background on which Pope Pius built up his church-state doctrine. Hence, when he gave to the world new Catholic teachings on freedom and democracy he was not so much breaking with tradition as he was adhering to, and advancing, a living and dynamic tradition.[25] He was making official, and magisterial, theological opinion which originated with Aquinas' teachings on the human conscience and personality.

By the same token, when Pius inaugurated a universalist church-state doctrine and trimmed traditional concepts to mesh with it, he was *in* tradition, not severing himself from it. But when the total significance of Pope Pius XII's church-state doctrine is sought for, it must be said that he was in this respect more of a pioneer than a perfecter and consolidator. The innovations and readjustments he brought into traditional Catholic church-state doctrine were by no means complete, and not in all cases clear. He left much labor to be done by his successors and, as we shall see in the following chapter, this labor was not left undone.

25. As pointed out before, Christians from Paul to Augustine to Thomas to Pius IX sincerely protested that they were guarding the Christian concept of liberty, and—to the extent which times and circumstances allowed —they usually were. But the dialectic of force vs. freedom has, through the two thousand years of Christian history, refined the concept given by Paul so that Pius could not, without being false even to Augustine's ideals, fail to advance his practical teaching to match doctrinal development. This fits perfectly Newman's idea of doctrinal development: "This process, whether it be longer or shorter in point of time, by which the aspects of an idea are brought into consistency and form, I call its development, being the germination and maturation of some truth or apparent truth on a large mental field. On the other hand this process will not be a development, unless the assemblage of aspects which constitute its ultimate shape really belongs to the idea from which they start" (*An Essay on the Development of Christian Doctrine*, p. 61).

Chapter Seven

Pope John XXIII
and Vatican II

The final figure in the triad of modern popes who reformed Catholic church-state doctrine contrasts in many ways with his two predecessors. Angelo Roncalli was not born in a nobleman's palace. He was born, rather, in a tenant farmer's cramped quarters, at what must be considered near the bottom of the social scale. During his days in school and in the seminary he fared well in his studies.

The great amount of publicity given to Pope John makes a lengthy background unnecessary here. We will go immediately to his political background. Like Popes Leo and Pius he became skilled in diplomacy eventually, but his skill did not take the form usually expected. His success as an ecclesiastical diplomat lies in his emphasis of ecclesiastical qualifications over his diplomatic ones. In his eastern posts such as Bulgaria, as well as in Paris, he was considered above all else a father and pastor. Thus, the future Pope John made use of the simple traits of his rural background as effectively as Popes Leo and Pius used the aristocratic traits bred into them.[1]

The direction of Catholic church-state relations is usually set by popes. This is true not only of the doctrinal aspects of these relations but likewise of the more concrete policies and directions on the diplomatic level. Since the relations of the pope with nations are in themselves Catholic church-state relations, Pope John's distinctly un-regal, profoundly pastoral attitude itself did

1. See R. Rouquette, "Le mystère Roncalli," *Etudes,* 1963, III, 6-7.

much to impress upon the world the changes of orientation already given by Popes Leo and Pius.

These latter, as we have seen, had taught some rather untraditional things respecting our subject. But they taught them in a very traditional manner. Pope Pius had extended the scope of church-state relations to a world-wide, universal level. And he had emphasized human rights as a very pertinent part of politico-religious intercourse. He had also insisted on the basically spiritual, unpolitical nature of his office. But he kept untarnished the splendid traditions of protocol, insignia, and the general atmosphere of the days of papal monarchical splendor. This was understandable: not only was he indeed an independent and sovereign ruler, but he knew it to be urgent that nations not be allowed to forget this fact during the turbulent times in which he reigned. His continued monarchical stance no doubt helped the world at large to realize that the independence embodied in the Lateran Pacts was not a mere formality.

Pope John, however, before he uttered a word on the question, made it evident to all that his position as a sovereign paled into insignificance before the all-consuming exigencies of his office of spiritual father and shepherd. His paternal love often made him forget his role of monarch.

Pope Leo had recognized the advent of a new kind of State, but he had demanded that the political stance of the papacy be not changed. Pope Pius had recognized the fundamentally altered political position of the papacy, but he saw fit to keep intact the traditional trappings of the monarchy. Pope John, by his whole comportment and by his teachings, continued along the road opened by these previous pontiffs and presented the world with a papal image adequately adapted to the changes wrought by time. The instinctive recognition by the whole world of the singular fittingness of this image accounts, in part at least, for his phenomenal impact upon the world.[2] This simple change

2. Pope Paul VI has continued this de-politicalization of the papal

of conduct was evident from the beginning of his pontificate,[3] and was prophetic of the total church-state contribution that Pope John would offer the Church.

Pope John's church-state doctrine differs from that of Leo and Pius in that it is almost entirely an indirect one. Not once did he even employ the phrase "church-state relations." But to conclude that he said nothing or accomplished little in this field would be very erroneous. The truth is just the contrary. It was Pope John who, more than any pope for centuries, brought the various elements of the complicated problem into adjustment with the circumstances of his time.[4] In typical Joannine style, however, he accomplished this, not by complicated formulae solemnly proclaimed, but by simple, often wholly unspectacular, action.

Pope John was himself a historian, and one can see the effects of history's lessons in his church-state actions. Throughout the long chronicle of history we have seen how several problems unavoidably reappeared. The chronic, old quarrel over the jurisdictional frontiers between Church and civil authority has remained at the root of most of these difficulties. Repeatedly, States of one type or another would fall victim to the totalitarian ambition to be supreme director and final arbiter in every area of their citizens' lives. By thus overstepping an admittedly dim frontier of jurisdiction, such rulers infringed on the rights of both Church and individuals to freedom of action in pursuing their proper tasks. Thus, a single double-barrelled cause of church-state strife is seen: 1) violating the jurisdictional frontiers, and 2) disregarding the rights and freedoms of others.

---

office. See, for example, his address to the Roman nobility, *Osservatore Romano,* January 15, 1964, 1.

3. What Father Tucci says of his words concerning peace is true of all his politically orientated doctrine: "John XXIII follows fully, though according to his own inimitable style, in the steps of his great predecessors." "La Chiesa e la Pace," *La Civiltà Cattolica,* 114 (1963), II, 210.

4. See A. Cardinal Bea, "Religiöse Freiheit und Wandlungen der Gesellschaft," *Stimmen der Zeit,* CLXXIII, V, 321-333, esp. 330 ff.

This was a stumbling block over which the Church itself had fallen on more than one occasion.[5] And part of the cold, suspicious attitude of secular society toward the Church in modern times is traceable directly to precisely this failing. Historian Pope John knew this lesson well, and said so publicly.[6] He knew well how to detect the undercurrents of history running in the flow of day-to-day events, and he seemed determined to do what he could towards adjusting the channel of the church-state stream. Though he chose not to make an issue out of it, the fabric of his actions and writings show clearly his intent to put the politics and religion of his times into a more suitable relationship.

Let us examine, then, his own words and actions, letting them reveal the mind of one of history's really influential popes in the matter of re-molding the practical forms and ideals of Christian church-state relations. These words and deeds fall naturally into three divisions: 1) John formally closed the era of papal political power. 2) He emphasized the new universalist type of church-state relationships, bringing its emphasis on religious freedom to maturity. 3) He redefined the scope of formal relations, limiting their purpose to the advancement of spiritual and temporal wellbeing in individual countries.

1. THE NEW PAPAL DIPLOMACY

Of all Pope John's references to religio-civil phenomena, none reoccurred more frequently, or was as strongly emphasized, as

5. "However, since the Church is always also a Church made up of sinful men, even as far as the holders of her authority are concerned, she can also in her individual actions offend against her own principles and against the freedom of the individual both within and without. This has happened often enough in the course of history" (K. Rahner, *Theological Investigations*, II, *Man in the Church* [Baltimore, 1963], pp. 99-100. See also Y. Congar, *Lay People in the Church* [Westminster, Md., 1957], pp. 89-90.).

6. See Pope John's Allocution at the opening of the Second Vatican Council, October 11, 1962.

his assurance that the political power of popes was gone forever. On numerous occasions the holy pontiff called attention to this fact.[1] We recall the agonized cries of Pope Pius IX on the occasion of the political spoliation of the papacy. The contrast afforded by Pope John is immense. He acknowledged the fact of his political impotence with a profound sigh of relief. In most humble and fatherly terms he repeatedly expressed joy that the passing of temporal power had left more power and effectiveness to the real, the spiritual, cares of his office. At the very beginning of his pontificate, as he was solemnly taking possession of the papal throne in the Lateran Basilica, he said:

> Along the way, this entry of the new Pontiff has lost the pomp it knew in ages past; but it has gained ever so much in spirituality and deeper meaning!
> It is no longer a prince arrayed in the trappings of external power that people see, but a priest, a father, a shepherd.[2]

Another equally moving testimony of his relief at the passing of temporal power is furnished by the account of his intention of changing the symbolism of the papal tiara. When the citizens of the province of Bergamo wished to present him with a tiara he refused at first, begging them rather to give the money to the poor. When they insisted on offering something both to the poor and to their beloved fellow countryman, he accepted. But at its presentation he declared that each age should give its own symbolism to the three-fold crown. Whereas Boniface VIII had made it symbolize the pope's temporal power, he said, for modern popes it should symbolize the theological virtues: faith, hope and charity.[3]

1. For example, see the following citations in *Discorsi, Messaggi, Colloqui del Santo Padre, Giovanni XXIII* (Vatican, 1958-1962), 4 vols.: I, 38, 653 ff.; III, 204 ff.; and IV, 581-582.
2. Address given at the Basilica of St. John Lateran, *Discorsi*, I, 38. (This address was not printed in the *Acta Apostolici Sedes*. For the English translation, see *The Pope Speaks*, V [Summer, 1959], 283.)
3. See *Discorsi*, I, 653-658.

Still another important manifestation of the pontiff's views on this matter is found in his address to his diplomatic corps in December of 1962. He mentioned that the Church was interested in the general peace and welfare of all men, but that it nevertheless had no purely terrestrial goals of its own:

> Often We have recalled that the Church does not pursue earthly goals alone; nor does she aspire to any temporal domination. The golden rule left by her divine Founder is the Lord's Prayer, the sublime prayer which establishes the true hierarchy of values: first, God's name, His kingdom, His will; then, each day's bread and other necessities.[4]

Still another example of this occurred when the pope described Innocent III's homily on the Gospel. Innocent had used the text relating Jesus' promise that Peter would be a "fisher of men," and he had illustrated therewith the temporal power of Peter's successors. John, however, anxious to point out the transitory nature of such interpretations, declared the papal office to be: "Much more noble today and worthy of authority than it was in the days of its earthly powers."[5]

Pope John was known throughout the world for his beautiful humility. Disclaiming all intent to temporal advancement of any kind was a favorite way of manifesting his lowliness.

Not content with merely disclaiming political ambitions, John sought prudently to begin to erase from the papal image all the vestiges of past political glory. He refused to allow the cardinals to perform the ancient sign of vassalage contained in the rite of kissing the toe of the newly elected pontiff. By frequently leaving the Vatican for pilgrimages and works of mercy, he ended the long token of protest against the Italian State in remaining a "prisoner of the Vatican." These changes in the symbolism of the papal tiara and in the ceremony of taking possession of the

---

4. AAS, LV (1962), 46-47 (*The Pope Speaks*, Vol. VIII, No. 4, 393).
5. Sermon given at St. Peter's Basilica, June 28, 1962 (*Discorsi*, IV, 413).

Lateran throne are all examples of the zeal with which the pontiff went about dismantling the accumulations of a thousand years of papal temporal power.

Coming, as it did, at the end of almost a century of steady papal political decline, these changes did not attract great attention. But when one looks at them from a broad historical viewpoint, their significance is very great indeed. They were nothing less than the direct reversal of the trend already begun in earnest by the pope called Hildebrand. We recall how, in the face of the strangle-hold over the spiritual realm which the emperors and kings of that age possessed, that pontiff had set about methodically building up an arsenal of arguments and proofs for papal power. Roman law was resurrected and applied to the papacy. Biblical texts were called upon to support the extension of the pontiff's power well beyond the limits of spiritual jurisdiction. Over the centuries such argumentation and practice was so woven into the warp of tradition and of theology that any separation of the pope's spiritual concerns from his many-sided political involvements seemed a hopeless task indeed.

The sediments of Hildebrand's great drive resisted the harsh purges of history, and remained a living part of all the Church's relationships with States. Even the Lateran Pacts did not erase the image of the pope as a great political power—at least not from the popular mind. But Pope John was able to convince even his enemies of the selfless aims of his political doctrine.[6]

History had removed the reason for Hildebrand's type of defensive tactics. John was determined to rid his office of an armor which now served only as a hindrance to his efforts at a renewed relationship with the civil power.

In the process of disclaiming political power, however, the pontiff did not in any sense leave the impression that he was

6. Even Premier Khrushchev urged his nomination for the Balzan Peace Prize. See R. Kaiser, *Inside the Council* (New York, 1963), p. 44.

abandoning also his duty to teach on the moral aspects of politics and on the political duties of Christians.[7] In his fervent rejoicings over the end of political power, he was careful not to sacrifice any of the traditional authority to judge and direct in the moral aspects of these matters.

2. UNIVERSALISM ACHIEVED

We have already seen how Pope Pius XII, during his long pontificate, forged a doctrine concerning church-state relations which was applicable and, in fact, applied to *all* nations and groups of nations. This universalist view fulfilled a need in the modern Church, for it has to deal now with a world made small and bound together by a revolutionized technology and political configuration. Such an ecumenical church-state arrangement seemed made especially for Pope John's great heart. He demonstrated time and again how his paternal spirit could not be kept confined to those individuals, or those nations, already within the Church.

Not only did he adopt and continue this informal type of relationship; he showed clear signs of an intention to integrate within its framework the more traditional formalist system. In a world rapidly becoming united in a hundred different ways, John seemed to have quietly worked out for himself a uniform, integrated doctrine wherein the Church's policy would be the same, at least in basic content and emphasis, toward both Christian and non-Christian governments.[1]

Pius was careful that there was no contradiction between the political doctrine he addressed to the world at large and that which he addressed to the Christian leaders. But the two facets remained largely separate, and disparate, in many ways. Pope

7. Letter to the Latin American Hierarchy, December 1, 1961: *Discorsi*, II, 984, ff.

1. A prime example of this is found in the encyclical *Pacem in Terris*, which argues from the natural law in a manner capable of being understood by all types of modern leaders.

John, such seems the burden of all his pertinent pronouncements, simply did not see any need to continue the dualism. When addressing the world at large, he reemphasized Pope Pius' cherished ideals: peace between the Church and State, neutrality, supra-nationality, freedom, and peace among nations. When speaking to the faithful, whether members of his curia or Catholic heads of State, his doctrine did not change markedly in either tone or language. The most outstanding example of this integralist tendency is found in his great encyclical *Pacem in Terris*. Here he addressed both Catholic leaders and non-Catholics: the hierarchy and all "men of good will." He argued from a law "written in the hearts of men." He used Scripture and his own authority to underline this natural law.

> But the Creator of the world has imprinted in man's heart an order which his conscience reveals to him and enjoins him to obey: "They show the work of the Law written in their hearts. Their conscience bears witness to them" (Rom 2:15).
>
> And how could it be otherwise? For whatever God has made shows forth His infinite wisdom, and it is manifested more clearly in the things which have greater perfection.[2]

The holy pope preached peace, brotherhood and freedom to the world and to the Church in one and the same exhortation. This was a thing quite impossible under the old unionist ideal, which would exclude a part of mankind from the civil equality advocated in John's encyclical. Not once did the pontiff praise, in the manner of Pius XII, the past forms of union. In fact, he never employed the term "union" at all.

His idea of relations, as we will see, never exceeded that of simple, mutual understanding and benevolence between Church and State. Completely informal discussions with political leaders were used to settle problems as often as formal diplomatic channels. No concordats were signed under his reign. Diplomatic relations were established with new nations, but the ideas

2. *Pacem in Terris*, AAS, LV (1963), 258 (cf. *Our Sunday Visitor* edition, p. 6).

offered by the pontiff to these new—African and Asian—nations
were remarkably close to those offered to the representatives of
traditionally Christian populations.

This integration of two parallel branches of Catholic church-
state doctrine was accomplished by actions, not by words or
declarations. The pope made no direct renouncements of past
papal policy, and no direct pronouncements in favor of any one
school of thought in the matter. But, by emphasizing in season
and out a unilinear doctrine concerning the proper rapport
between the Church and States, he tended to leave past compli-
cations behind simply by ignoring them.

Let us now look at Pope John's universalist church-state doctrine in its concrete forms. It was pointed out that by universalist
doctrine we mean that type offered to all nations and expressed
in a manner adapted to the special needs of such a large and
varied audience. It is a doctrine offered by the Church either
directly or indirectly to heads of the various nations and their
people, which lays down the general norms regulating the contacts and cooperation of States among themselves and with the
Church. One of the chief differences between this new style
church-state doctrine and the older, narrower one is that its
major goal is to achieve, not formal and legal accord, but informal mutual understanding and peace. Such doctrine would not
oppose formal types of accord so long as these would in no way
impinge on the rights of any individuals and thus thwart and
cancel the very substance on which the wider, deeper accord is
based.

The major points which went to make up Pope Pius XII's
universalist doctrine have been listed. Pope John carried each
of these doctrines forward. He brought the doctrine of the freedom and brotherhood of all men to a maturity which would have
been considered unthinkable only a few years before his reign.

First, let us hear him on the neutrality of the Church before
all nations and before all types of government:

The Church, as you know, does not intend to pronounce upon the *forms* of association which this or that government should take for itself. But she never ceases to work towards mutual comprehension, good accord, and life in common, both peaceable and serene for the whole grand family of man.

. . . The Church then respects and *esteems* very greatly the characteristics and the noble traditions of each ethnic group, but she desires above all to see that all of them communicate with one another in a spirit of true fraternity.[3]

Shortly after this pronouncement the pope rendered beautiful testimony to two universalist themes at one time. He affirmed the neutrality of the Church, and also its concern for peace and brotherhood among all men. The occasion was his reception of the International Balzan Peace Prize.

The fact that a pope was chosen for this great honor is in itself eloquent testimony to the reality and effectiveness of the papacy's new relationship with the modern political world. He acknowledged that it was not himself alone who deserved this honor. The modern popes from Leo XIII to Pius XII, he said, deserved a large share of the honor and credit. Thus, on one occasion we see both the Church and modern States giving assent to the presence of a relationship between them which is quite different from forms familiar up till now, but which was clearly accomplishing goals totally impossible for traditional forms of intercourse.

By far the most eloquent evidence for John's enthusiastic pursuit of the new universalist manner of mirroring Christ to civil authority is found in his encyclical on peace. Here the great pope appeals for peace and brotherhood among men, and for freedom of press, speech, and conscience. His appeal had a positive and mature quality which far surpassed any similar treatment of the subject in the whole history of the papacy. The doctrinal elevation, combined with the practical wisdom which shines out in this document, has astounded the world. It was this document

3. Address to Ambassadors, AAS, LV (1963), 171-172.

which merited for its author the international prize for peace just referred to.[4]

Pacem in Terris itself is another example of an existential relationship between the Church and modern States. It is the Church's application of the wisdom of Christ to modern political problems on a truly world-wide scale.[5] The encyclical aims at a Christian exposition of the natural law principles governing relations between citizens and the State, between one State and another, and between individuals through their States and the international community of peoples.

It lists four great virtues which should serve as the pillars of the social order: truth, justice, charity, and freedom.[6] It is most interesting to note that both Leo and Pius XII spoke of the first three of these virtues in the same context. But the last one, freedom, is Pope John's own contribution. The seed planted by Leo in *Libertas,* and watered by Pius in his many allocutions on human dignity, we now see bearing mature fruit in the writings of Pope John.

The doctrine of human freedom outlined in *Pacem in Terris* is surely one of the most outstanding contributions of the encyclical. Because of this great contribution, the document becomes a real milestone in the history of church-state doctrine. By proclaiming human liberty one of the foundation stones of public

4. L. Cardinal Suenens, "The Meaning of *Pacem in Terris,*" *The Catholic Mind,* September, 1963, 5: "The papal document of which I shall speak is unprecedented in history . . . It was born of a great trust in God and, at the same time, of a trust in man, in that which is best in him." (Translation of an address given to the United States Committee for the United Nations in his capacity as the Holy Father's personal representative.)

5. "It is addressed not only to the five hundred million members of the Church whose beloved shepherd is the successor of St. Peter, but it is framed as an 'open letter to the whole world,' as a dialogue with all men of good will. It has been greeted with unanimous acclaim by the press of the whole world, and has aroused responsive echoes among all the nations of the earth. It speaks in a language that is simple, direct and man-to-man" (Cardinal Suenens, *op. cit.,* 5).

6. *Pacem in Terris,* AAS, LV (1963), 266. These four fundamental virtues are reiterated time again and form the *leit motif* of the encyclical.

order on all of its levels, Pope John inaugurated a new era in the relations of the Church with nations.

We have sketched the gradual, centuries-long flowering of the Christian teaching on human dignity and freedom, and have pointed out its effects on church-state relations at every step along the way. One sees the close relation of the two sister-doctrines very clearly in *Pacem in Terris*. Clearly, the rapport between the Church and the State ranks high among those intra-state relations dealt with in Part Two of the encyclical. But the pope declares freedom of conscience and of worship to be one of the main guide-lines for such relations. He begins by asserting only broad principles:

> First of all, it is necessary to speak of the order which should exist between men. Any human society, if it is to be well ordered and productive, must lay down as a foundation this principle, namely, that every human being is a person, that is, his nature is endowed with intelligence and free will. By virtue of this, he has rights and duties of his own, flowing directly and simultaneously from his very nature, which are therefore universal, inviolable and inalienable.[7]

There follows a listing and clarification of the inviolable rights mentioned. Immediately after the right to food and shelter the pope lists man's rights of conscience. First among these he declared to be the right to a sane freedom of inquiry, speech and press:

> By the natural law, every human being has the right to . . . freedom in searching for truth and in expressing and communicating his opinions, and in the pursuit of art, . . . and he has the right to be informed truthfully about public events.[8]

Then comes his first of several treatments of freedom of religion:

7. *Pacem in Terris,* AAS, 259 (cf. *OSV,* p. 7).
8. *Pacem in Terris,* AAS, 260 (cf. *OSV,* p. 8). How different from the old liberalist freedom, which recognized no objective standard other than the will of the people.

Every human being has the right to honor God according to the
dictates of an upright conscience, and therefore the right to
worship God privately and publicly. For, as Lactantius so clearly
taught: "We were created for the purpose of showing to the
God who bore us the submission we owe Him, of recognizing
Him alone, and of serving Him. We are obliged and bound by
this duty to God; from this religion itself receives its name."[9]

John bases this bold and completely unambiguous affirmation
on man's natural law right to freedom. But it is significant to
note that the patristic authority he chooses had written before
the Constantinian period, and had taken a stand almost directly
contrary to Augustine, Thomas, and practically every theologian
of the entire unionist era.

The pope recognizes, then, the authenticity of that tradition
which upheld the inviolability of man's religious convictions,
even though that tradition had been a tenuous one during half
of the life-span of the Church. Later, when treating specifically
of Catholics' relations with non-Catholics, the pontiff makes
even more emphatic his doctrine in this regard:

However, one must never confuse error and the person who
errs, not even when there is question of error or inadequate
knowledge of truth in the moral or religious field.

The person who errs is always and above all a human being
and retains in every case his dignity as a human person. And
he must always be regarded and treated in accordance with
that lofty dignity.[10]

This declaration is of such importance for our theme that we
must take stock of its historical significance. Though its precise
context here is the regulation of all public and social contacts
between Catholics and non-Catholics, it certainly holds good for
that particular contact wherein the Church (especially Catholic
heads of State) meet other religions (especially non-Catholic
citizens).

9. *Ibid.*, 260-261 (cf. *OSV*, p. 8).
10. *Ibid.*, 299 (cf. *OSV*, p. 50).

The pope makes it clear that the principles involved are "inherent in human nature itself." They are "dictates of the natural law." Taken as it stands, as a statement of abstract principle, this declaration marks the final step in the maturation of a doctrine inherent in the teachings of St. Paul and slowly, almost tortuously, evolving down through the centuries, gaining ever-increasing momentum since Leo XIII. The same principle, looked at in the light of its importance as a key concept in Christian church-state teaching, has an epoch-making quality. To appreciate its impact one need only imagine how different the history of church-state relations in the middle ages might have been had John's insight been already available at that time. What changes might it have wrought in the doctrine of Augustine, Gregory the Great, Charlemagne, and the scholastic theologians.[11]

Like many other great historical developments in Christian doctrine, John's "*magna charta* of human dignity and freedom" (Cardinal Wyszynski) cannot fail to have far-reaching effects, not only in church-state matters, but in any number of other Christian teachings and practices. In at least two important areas it affects the subject of our essay in a vital manner. Perhaps the most important effect is its bearing on the long disputed question concerning the proper treatment of religious minorities within States of overwhelmingly Catholic populations. If the "erring person" must "always be regarded and treated in accordance with [his] lofty dignity," there can no longer be any question of either direct or indirect civil discrimination against either himself or his religion.[12] Pope John himself made this application in the encyclical:

11. Of course, such anachronistic conjectures can rightly serve no other purpose than to highlight the relatively embryonic state of the Christian awareness of human dignity in those days. To condemn as erroneous the repressive measures of those men might be compared to condemning as heretical the polygamy of Solomon.

12. This same idea is implied in Cardinal Suenens' remarks (p. 6) on

One of the fundamental duties of civil authorities, therefore, is to coordinate social relations in such fashion that the exercise of one man's rights does not threaten others in the exercise of their own rights nor hinder them in the fulfillment of their duties. Finally, the rights of all should be effectively safeguarded, and, if they have been violated, completely restored.[13]

The second major effect on our subject of the pontiff's principle of human freedom is that it assures a great respect for the independence, integrity and competence of individual representatives of State authority. Again, it is the pope himself who made the inference. Regarding these individuals whose competence it should be to judge the general ethical acceptability of various political and economic movements, Pope John declared:

> But to decide whether this moment has arrived and also to lay down the ways and degrees in which work in common might be possible for the achievement of economic, social, cultural and political ends which are honorable and useful, are problems which can only be solved with the virtue of prudence, which is the guiding light of the virtues that regulate the moral life, both individual and social.[14]

But, continues the pope, such judgment must always proceed according to Catholic principles, and be subject ultimately to ecclesiastical authority:

> . . . in accordance with the principles of the natural law, with the social doctrine of the Church, and with the directives of ecclesiastical authority.[15]

Relations between the Church and civil rulers in the past have been repeatedly strained by the readiness with which ecclesias-

---

the encyclical: "Those rights, he declares, are valid and necessary in all latitudes and longitudes, without regard to place, or to racial, political, ideological or religious differences. Respect for those rights is at the foundation of every social structure."

13. *Pacem in Terris*, 274 (cf. *OSV*, p. 22).
14. *Ibid.*, 300 (cf. *OSV*, pp. 51-52).
15. *Ibid.*, 300-301 (cf. *OSV*, p. 52).

tical authority has rushed in to judge complicated political questions. This contributed in no small measure to a spirit of distrust, if not downright enmity, on the part of civil rulers toward the Church.[16] By recognizing the dignity and competence of those "who live and work in the specific sectors of human society in which those problems arise," Pope John applied his own *magna charta* to another traditional sore spot in church-state relations. In the same vein he denied his own competence to speak authoritatively concerning such things as the manner in which civil authorities should fulfill their function, admitting the great role which the historical background of each individual nation plays in such matters:

> It is impossible to determine, once and for all, what is the most suitable form of government, or how civil authorities can most effectively fulfill their respective functions, i.e., the legislative, judicial and executive functions of the State. In determining the structure and operation of government which a State is to have, great weight has to be given to the historical background and circumstances of given political communities, circumstances which will vary at different times and in different places.[17]

Throughout the whole length of the document, John bases his program for peace especially on human dignity and freedom. Peaceful relationships on all levels of modern society, he declared time and again, rest upon the four great foundation stones mentioned above, but freedom is given special stress.

A final note on Pope John's universalist doctrine in *Pacem in Terris* is provided by his support of the United Nations:

16. K. Rahner's comments on this matter are very illuminating: "Then . . . we Christians need not nowadays nor in the foreseeable future demand any patronage for the Church by way of political coercive measures from the State . . . There would be no harm if we . . . were to re-examine our situation and practices to see whether we do not here and there still hold fast to things from that bygone age which are or were historically justified, thus giving grounds for continued anti-clerical feelings to the detriment of Christianity's real power for winning souls" (*Theological Investigations*, II, pp. 262-263).

17. *Pacem in Terris*, 276 (cf. *OSV*, p. 24).

As is known, the United Nations Organization (UN) was established on June 26, 1945. The United Nations Organization has as its essential purpose the maintenance and consolidation of peace between peoples, fostering between them friendly relations based on the principles of equality, mutual respect and varied forms of cooperation in every sector of human society.[18]

Here again he highlights especially the promotion of human dignity afforded by that organization's famous Declaration of Human Rights:

An act of the highest importance performed by the United Nations Organization was the Universal Declaration of Human Rights, approved in the General Assembly on December 10, 1948.[19]

Pacem in Terris carries church-state implications which are very wide and deep. We have here attempted an analysis only of its significance for the universalist area of that doctrine. Already its influence is being felt within the traditional relationships between the Church and the so-called "Catholic" nations.[20] Its chief effect, however, is extremely difficult to either analyze or evaluate. This is the subtle, though marked, change of fundamental tone, or *Weltanschauung*, in political matters which since the appearance of *Pacem in Terris* has permeated the whole direction of papal political affairs. The change is as radical as that made by Pope Leo. But, far from being contrary to Leo's new orientations, it marks the final coming of age of a new spirit of optimism and "at-homeness" in the face of the new world. Leo himself gave such a spirit its first impetus.

The same, never fully expressed, universalism can be found scattered throughout all of Pope John's writings and actions. It is visible in his addresses to heads of State and in his addresses to the Council Fathers. One sees it in the unprecedented audi-

18. *Ibid.*, 295 (cf. *OSV*, p. 45).
19. *Loc. cit.*
20. The recent betterment of the situation of the Protestants and Jews in Spain is a good example.

ence given to Premier Kruschchev's son-in-law, A. Adzhubei. He was always open, as a spiritual father, to anyone, and showed great eagerness to contribute both to the natural and the supernatural welfare of men. Like Christ himself, John "went about doing good," and was so busy with trying to cure the ills of the world that he had little time to indulge in any pessimistic disillusionment.

In the realm of politics this attitude made him an eager co-worker in any worthwhile project. To accomplish the task he made full use of whatever instruments the modern world placed within his reach: the United Nations, modern travel, the Council. And he gloried in the ingeniousness of modern technology, which helped supply excellent means for his apostolate. In such a manner Pope John XXIII brought into its own the universalist church-state doctrine and practice which his predecessor had conceived.

3. THE END OF AN ERA

We have already mentioned that Pope John did not so much as employ the phrase "church-state relations." Only on rare occasions did he allude to the subject in its traditional meaning. He never made it the topic of an address or formal communication. But no pope, surrounded as he is by ambassadors to the Holy See, and occupied by the cares of his own representatives to nations, can avoid taking a position on this issue. Hence, it is not too difficult to determine, at least in broad outline, Pope John's convictions. Indeed, the very fact of the complete absence of formal discussion on such an important and debated question indicates, in itself, a very definite position on the matter: knowing the delicacy of the matter it seems that he decided, in perfectly sound diplomatic style, to make his contribution in an indirect manner.

1. *The Traditional Doctrine Itself:* One of the best sources for the pope's traditionalist doctrine is his addresses to the ambassadors and heads of State received at the Vatican. His relationship with the representatives of traditionally Catholic nations were naturally somewhat different from those with his diplomatic corps as a whole, and with representatives from predominantly non-Catholic countries. Let us look briefly at the first category.

In addresses given to such political visitors as the president of Argentina, of Peru, and of Italy itself, the pontiff followed an unchanging pattern in his references to past and present formal relationships. He praised the benefits which flowed from the mutual cooperation enjoyed at the time of his meeting with the dignitary, and expressed the desire that friendly relations continue. For example, he said to President Frondizi (June 18, 1960): "We would like to take this opportunity to recall the climate of harmony existing between this Apostolic See and the nation of Argentina: harmony which we trust will become each day more firm and more perfect."[1] He spoke in similar terms to President Manuel Prado of Peru on February 22 of the same year:

> We would like, along these lines, to acknowledge the respect and the collaboration which the Church and her institutions find in the public authorities of your nation, and especially in your excellency himself. The activities and initiatives which have benefited by this can develop more easily as a result, and can bring to the population the favorable influence of the doctrine and action of the Church by means of her spiritual and moral assistance.[2]

It is to be noted that the pope praises not only relations here, but also the "collaboration" between the Church and the Peruvian State. This is an important addition. As it stands, this might

1. AAS, LII (1960), 529.
2. *Ibid.*, 95-96.

mean anything from mere formal diplomatic relations to the fullest union excluding other religious beliefs. As a matter of fact, however, the Constitution of Peru guarantees freedom of conscience to all its citizens (though the Church is favored considerably in many of its institutions).[3] But Pope John is careful to make explicit the type of collaboration which he was praising:

> We are confident, in particular, that the Church will find with the authorities of your State all the aid necessary to assure the young generation a solid Christian formation, thanks especially to religious education in the schools and the protection of public morality against the perils which menace it from all sides.[4]

In countries such as the United States, aid by the State to religious education is generally considered contrary to freedom of conscience, since by it the State is supporting a specific creed. Even though it were offered to all religious schools, whatever the creed, argue many, it would still be prejudicial to sincere atheists. Such argumentation has never won any sympathy from any section of the Church. Even in *Pacem in Terris* Pope John made it quite clear that sane and just freedom of conscience in no way rules out religious education, but rather is quite reconcilable with it.[5]

What the pope said to President Prado, both regarding support for religious education and civil protection of Christian morality, is of considerable importance here because it makes precise the exact outlines of the pontiff's convictions in the realm of practical church-state relations. While upholding freedom of conscience, rejecting specifically various current forms of violation of this freedom, he nevertheless maintains the traditional, Pauline, balance between freedom and authority. Protecting public morals is an essential part of every State's duty, and pub-

3. See L. Pfeffer, *Church, State and Freedom* (Boston, 1953), p. 231.
4. Allocution to the President of Peru, AAS, LII (1960), 96.
5. *Pacem in Terris*, 277.

lic morals cannot be allowed to fall into ruin simply because they are Christian. Only when they are so exclusively Christian that sincere non-believers reasonably take issue with them could the enforcement of Christian morals come into conflict with freedom of conscience.

Likewise, Christian education furnishes a very sound basis and motivation for both good public morality and sound respect for that public morality. Thus, in upholding a nation's tradition of support for Christian education and morality, Pope John was definitely not contradicting his declaration of freedom of conscience. He was merely completing and explicitating it. Only if he were to forbid State support for the schools of other religions (or other concepts of public morality within the realm of the natural law) would he involve himself in contradiction. This he never did. What the pontiff gives us here is a typical expression of the Church's traditional church-state teaching as it applies to education and public morality. It is abundantly evident in the teachings of both Leo and Pius. But again, with John, it takes on new meaning, depth and beauty because of its configuration with his great advances in the doctrine of freedom of conscience.

Another facet of traditional church-state relations was illumined by Pope John in his address to Amintore Fanfani, then the president of the Italian council of ministers. He broached the delicate subject of the unification of Italy and the Lateran Pacts in a manner calculated to lay to rest any lingering doubts as to the Church's complete satisfaction with the outcome of both issues. He calls the solution providential. Here, once again, we see evidence of a new and joyful atmosphere being created by the wisdom of "good Pope John":

All of the remainder of that historic period was, in the designs of divine Providence, a preparation for the victorious and peace-bringing era of the Lateran Pacts. These pacts which the wisdom of another Pius, whose motto was "The peace of Christ under the rule of Christ," would have hailed as an indication of a new horizon, ended in the final celebration of a true and perfect unity of race, of language and of religion which had been the ardent desire of all the better Italians.[6]

In all such addresses John's tone is irenic, and fraternal. No trace of wounded dignity or overtones of diplomatic superiority remain. Noteworthy also is the lack of references to past political glories such as abounded in Pope Leo, and are present also in Pius XII. John referred to the past only in order to note the spiritual mission of the pope and to recall with gratitude the passing of political worries from his office.

Let us turn now to the pontiff's addresses to those individuals not representing Catholic nations. One of the most important gauges of Pope John's doctrine concerning the end and purpose of the Vatican's diplomatic system (which had for centuries been almost the sole instrument for Catholic church-state affairs) is found in two Christmas allocutions given to the whole diplomatic corps. Here he surpassed both Leo and Pius in the simple precision with which he described the *raison d'être* of the Vatican's formal diplomatic endeavor. It existed, he said, for the benefit of the spiritual power of the pope and for nothing else whatever:

We would like to take this occasion to tell you once again the esteem which we have for you as individuals, and for the high mission which you fulfill here with us.

This mission, as we see it, is ever a work done in common with the Holy See in the name of your governments to assure the true well-being of your respective nations. And in the light of current events this collaboration seems to us to be more important now than ever . . .

The Holy See has been, as you know, at the service of souls during every period of history. The Roman Pontiffs, in virtue of their spiritual missions, consider themselves the servants and the promoters of all those values which contribute to the moral elevation of humanity and to the reign of peace in the world. It is

6. *Discorsi . . .,* III, pp. 205-206.

towards this goal that they have always, through the course of history, oriented their activities and those of the sons of the Church scattered throughout the world.[7]

An even more beautiful insistence on the purely spiritual foundation and goals of the Vatican's diplomatic effort is found in the pontiff's Christmas message to his diplomatic corps of the previous year:

Gentlemen, you represent many, many nations before the lowly successor of Peter. We feel We can see the feelings and desires of all peoples, all their sufferings and their hopes, joined together in you, and We want to lay them before Jesus, the Son of God and son of Mary. It is to Him that We are lifting up Our humble prayer, which is that of all men, begging Heaven to grant what earth cannot give: brotherhood, love, and peace.[8]

One cannot but be impressed with the vast difference between this concept of Vatican diplomacy, so evidently verified in the concrete policies of Pope John, and the comparatively worldly orientations of the same See's diplomatic endeavors of a hundred years before. The change was made possible only by the loss of the papal states and the arrangements of the Lateran Pacts. But credit goes to John XXIII for having so fearlessly analyzed, expressed, and proven by action how basically reformed were the orientations of the whole Vatican Secretariat of State.[9]

The background changes had come about so gradually, and new orientations were so hidden by a completely traditional organization and operation, that it is easy to underrate their true extent. That the ultimate aims are spiritual has always been the contention of apostolic diplomacy. And history shows that this has surely always been ultimately true. But history has also left almost indelibly printed upon the minds of most men of public

7. *Discorsi* . . ., IV, p. 15.
8. *Discorsi* . . ., III, pp. 102-103 (cf. *The Pope Speaks,* Vol. VII, No. 1, 1961, 56).
9. Pope John's whole orientation was in the direction of responsible freedom.

affairs one conclusion: a purely temporal papal power (often positively worldly and unholy), however spiritual its ultimate justification may have been, almost invariably accompanied the pope's spiritual office. And this conviction in the minds of the pope's hearers very often sadly obscured and compromised the exercise of his spiritual influence. From a foundation well laid by Leo and Pius, Pope John effectively threw off this albatross which hung around the neck of the papacy. He realigned the aims and directions of the Church's diplomatic mission, and with it, the nature of its whole church-state system.[10]

To representatives of States with largely non-Catholic population, Pope John addressed messages which differed only in intensity from those offered to Catholic nations. For example, he said:

> By her doctrine and the love of her children, the Church brings without a doubt an efficacious assistance to the solution of the various questions of the rulers of your nation: demographic and economic development, financial stability, national cohesion and constructive relations with neighboring States as well as with all of the international institutions. The Church, as you will willingly concede, Mr. President, by her educational works, her social services, her hospital works, and the humane and civil formation which she gives, contributes willingly and effectively to the well-being of your people and to the growth of your institutions.[11]

He emphasized the civil benefits to be gained from relations with the Church. He also pointed out the general moral strength and resiliency which Catholic citizens, nurtured by an uninhibited Catholic Church, could bring to nations. Always the center of

10. This reorientation is succinctly described by E. Alexander: "This perhaps is the most stirring fact . . . Pope John formally initiated a dialogue between Catholicism and the whole of human society" (*Catholic Mind*, October, 1963, 44).

11. Address to the Hon. Hubert Maga, President of the Republic of Dahomey, September 25, 1962 (*Discorsi . . .*, IV, p. 547). See *The Pope Speaks*, Vol. VII, No. 2, 1962, 156.

attention was the communion and brotherhood which follows
upon the Prince of Peace:

> We are happy to recall all these past events in your presence,
> because We consider it rich in comforting promise for the
> development of good understanding and reciprocal friendship
> between Great Britain and the Holy See. This good understand-
> ing, We are happy to recognize, is facilitated by the high quality
> of the diplomats that the United Kingdom accredits to the Apos-
> tolic See; their distinction and capability We cannot fail to
> praise. Good understanding is facilitated still more by reciprocal
> good will and, we should say, by a certain community of efforts
> performed mutually for the defense of the fundamental values
> upon which the life of society rests.[12]

And again:

> Regarding your own person, Mr. Prime Minister, we have been
> following for a long time your activities as a statesman, and we
> know that they are inspired by a very noble and very elevated
> sense of loyalty to your country and to the great ideals of liberty,
> justice and peace, all of which forms a part of the traditional
> patrimony of Great Britain . . . The Catholic Church, on her
> part, labors without rest towards the coming into the world of a
> true and lasting peace founded on justice and charity. And she
> rejoices over all sincere efforts which tend towards this end and
> cannot but wish them full success.[13]

From the sum of these addresses to representatives of various
types of nations accredited to the Holy See, one acquires a clear
enough picture of Pope John's convictions regarding traditional,
formal, church-state relations. Three major components go into
the make-up of this picture. First of all, he unquestionably considered formal relations full of positive potentiality for good on
both the eternal and temporal planes. Secondly, with equal
clarity one perceives a mature and carefully thought out concep-

12. Address to Queen Elizabeth II of England and the Duke of Edin-
burgh, May 5, 1961 (*Ibid.*, III, pp. 268-269).

13. Address to Prime Minister Harold Macmillan of Great Britain,
November 23, 1960 (*Ibid.*, III, p. 36).

tion of the exact function which formal Catholic church-state relations should play in the modern world. This role is shorn of all purely political overtones and completely dependent on, and adjusted to, the spiritual office of the Roman pontiff. Thirdly, one sees a careful integration of this role with the wider one played by his program of globe-circling in formal relations which we have termed universalist.

The universalist principles of peace, freedom, and political equality remain the central theme of his formal relations. Suppression or prejudicial treatment of other religions by Catholic countries are not only not advocated as part of the traditional system: they are explicitly forbidden. As a result, the whole image (and direction) is changed. From the appearance of an apparatus for dominating and ruling, the Catholic church-state system takes on the appearance of a humble servant of the common good.

We noted how Pope Pius had shown considerable reserve and hesitation in bringing these two facets of his doctrine into harmony. The concept of freedom gave him particular difficulty. With John's great pronouncement in this field, the integration became smooth and relatively complete. A natural, ever narrower and more concentrated gradation of influence in church-state relations is visible. From his most universal international declaration to those addressed to States most closely united to him, the same emphasis, in humble, fatherly, peaceful spirit, shines through. It increases in intensity as the ties of faith between teacher and learner become more close. But universalist and traditionalist forms of teaching are adapted to the tasks they must perform, and the two form one whole church-state system, adequately tailored to the needs of the modern world.

2. *The Ideal System:* There remains for us to clear up one last question concerning the church-state doctrine of Pope John

XXIII: What was his position on the matter of the ideal system of relations between the Church and civil authorities? We have already seen that he was quite evidently in favor of formal relations. Does this mean that he therefore also believed the ideal to be formal union? Formal relations such as concordats or diplomatic relations are something vastly different from formal union, where the State weds itself to the Church.

Is Pope John in accord with the opinion of Pope Leo XIII, and the tradition of the preceding millennium, that the State always has an objective obligation to proclaim the Church formally as its official religion? Pope Pius XII was unquestionably in favor of formal relations. But we have seen how obscure he remained concerning formal union. Pope John, like his immediate predecessor, remained completely silent as to whether or not formal union was the ideal. He did not even treat church-state relations in general, much less this particularly thorny question. The battle among theologians on the point remained without any formal decision. Again, however, there abounds clear indications as to his opinion. The whole general trend of his teachings leads strongly away from the position holding formal and complete union as the objective ideal.

The most impressive indication against the formal union arrangement is constituted by John's detailed doctrine of religious freedom. In order to appreciate further the real bearing of religious freedom on the church-state union ideal,[14] let us compare closely Pope Leo's position on both problems with that of Pope John.

Leo's encyclical *Libertas* was based on the dignity and worth of the human person, just as was Pope John's *Pacem in Terris*. Close comparison reveals no contradiction whatever between

---

14. Cardinal Bea affirms this bearing of freedom on church-state relations in "Religiöse Freiheit," 331. John C. Murray says the same: see "Contemporary Orientations . . .," *Theological Studies*, X (1949), 182.

the principles on which the two letters are based.[15] They are the same: the natural law considered in the light of Christ. But how different are the practical conclusions. Leo refuses categorically to do more than tolerate as a necessary evil freedom of speech, press, religion, and conscience. Error should not be spoken or printed, and above all, religious error must be carefully controlled by both Church and State. Pope John, on the other hand, declared these freedoms to be fundamental human rights. He is not making exceptions for a faithless world. He declares that the natural law demands that these freedoms be accorded every human being.

This opposition between the practical conclusions of the two popes poses no great problem if one is cognizant of the rapid development in the doctrine of conscience and freedom during the half-century separating the two pontiffs.[16] Leo considered public, State-guaranteed freedom of conscience to be based on a belief that truth and falsehood were relative, and so, equal. And, for his day, he was right. That was the prevailing opinion.[17] Furthermore, the common good of many countries in Europe, including Italy, really demanded the position which Leo took.

But western society in general, and Pope John in particular, had another foundation for these freedoms. It was the one called the natural law. Pope Leo had also, of course, founded his position on the natural law. But Pope John's inclusion of the four freedoms in the natural law did not violate Leo's conception of that law but rather extended it. Even St. Thomas had taught this

15. "Whoever, therefore, finds Pope John's position too liberal or even revolutionary, especially as it implies the possibility of a dialogue and a kind of coexistence with Socialist or Communist nations, would do well to study these two encyclicals of Leo XIII (*Au Milieu des Sollicitudes* and *Notre Consolation*). They are neither mentioned nor dealt with in collections and commentaries on the Leonine encyclicals edited by Catholic conservatives" (E. Alexander, *op. cit.*, 43).

16. See Roquette, *op. cit.*, 405 ff. See also Leclerq, *op. cit.*, pp. 175-218.

17. See John Courtney Murray, "Contemporary Orientations . . .," 214 ff.

position, only the socio-political structure of his time forbade
that it be applied even to non-Catholic Christians. But the
modern socio-political structure, as well as modern civilization,
demanded that it be so applied. Hence, then, Leo was still so
much a part of the medieval world that he made the traditional
application. John, on the other hand, was so much a part of
the new world that he made the opposite, and more logical,
application.[18]

But (and here we arrive at the central point) the application
of the principle of freedom of conscience was nothing else than
our central church-state problem. Leo demanded that the State
"embrace" the Church, and that it police the community, the
press, and the public forum, against the spread of religious
error. Granted that both corrupt politicians and religious fanatics
need to be policed lest they gravely endanger the common good
and public order; nevertheless, Leo was demanding that even
sincere dissenters be prevented from following their upright
conscience.[19]

Thus it was that Leo's ideal of union between Church and
State necessarily presupposed a large degree of suppression of
real freedom and equality before the law for members of dis-
senting religions. He did not even mention the possibility of sincere and upright dissenters. Only when to suppress them would
have caused greater harm than good did he permit "tolerance"
to be applied. In this respect Leo was more moved by the argument of his medieval forebears than by the few theologians of
his day who already were arguing for freedom of conscience. By
the same token, Pope John's espousal of the four freedoms subtracted from the unionist cause its chief *raison d'être*. Since sincerely erring individuals have an inalienable right to follow

18. See John T. Ellis, "The Issue of Religious Freedom," *op. cit.*, 509 ff.
19. For his own times this may well have been a prudent choice of "the
lesser of two evils." But Pope John was not handicapped by such
circumstances.

their convictions, the State is under no obligation to the Church (indeed is positively prohibited by the Church) to furnish its "secular arm" for repressing or hindering heresy.[20]

Only time and further development will tell to precisely what extent Pope John's declarations will affect Catholic church-state doctrine and practice. But there can be little doubt that they were a definite step away from the position holding formal and total union as the church-state ideal in this world of ours.

There are other indications pointing in the same direction. Several of them are only negative. For instance, he never praised the union systems of the past as did Pius and Leo. Indeed, he had harsh words for them on more than one occasion. He constantly debunked the prophets of doom, and emphasized the positiveness of present trends which led to ever greater freedom of expression and of conscience.

A positive indication that John rejected union is found in an address made one month before the opening of the first session of the Vatican Council. It was the closest he ever came to addressing himself specifically to church-state theory. Discussing matters needing the attention of the Council, he asked the question: "What should we say about the relations between the Church and civil society?"[21] With his usual incisive wisdom he went to the very heart of church-state problems in his answer. He claimed full liberty of religion as being the very essence of the matter. He grieved over the widespread denial of this right, and ended with a most profound observation:

What shall we say concerning the relations between the Church and civil society? We live in the time of a new political world. One of the fundamental rights which the Church cannot renounce

20. "Religious freedom, like every other right, carries with it a duty. It presumes that the individual man, *and especially the political community,* watches over and protects this freedom" (Cardinal Bea, "Religiöse Freiheit . . .," *op. cit.,* 228).

21. Radio message to the faithful one month (September 11, 1962) before the opening of the Council, *Discorsi,* IV, p. 524).

is that of religious liberty, and not merely liberty of cult . . .
Truth and liberty are the two foundation stones upon which the
edifice of human society is built.[22]

His primary emphasis was, in fact, freedom for his own Church.
But he did not limit his concept of liberty in any way when he
proclaimed it "the foundation of human civilization." For him,
therefore, liberty and truth are the center of the church-state
problem of today. Not only was all mention of Leo's center of
emphasis, union, totally lacking—John's thought was going in
the other direction.

From the evidence at hand, therefore, it seems safe to conclude that Pope John's conception of the ideal in church-state
relations was not identifiable with that of Pope Leo XIII. The
ideal remained cooperation, beyond a doubt. Not only cooperation, but truth and love and a mutual receptivity. But John
wisely refrained from even hinting that such cooperation could
best be achieved by formal union. John's ideal remained generic.
Historian as he was, he was well aware that individual modes
of cooperation are always too dependent on passing political
circumstances to be made into an unchanging ideal.

Pope John XXIII's contribution to our theme was, then, of great
import when seen in the perspective of the historical currents
which he brought to maturity. He solidified and intensified Pope
Pius' universalist orientations in church-state relations. He laid
to rest with a strong but gentle hand the lingering tradition of
papal political power. To a large extent he fused the universalist
and the traditionalist tendencies of his immediate predecessor.
Finally, he swung sharply away from the view of those who
would claim formal union to be the ultimate, unchanging ideal
for Catholic church-state relations. All these things he accomplished without any great hue and cry. By simply preaching and

22. *Loc. cit.*

practicing love and respect for all men to the leaders of both Catholic and non-Catholic States, he moved mountains of tradition and fear. He is known by all as the pope of the Church's *aggiornamento*. In no other area did he earn this title more justly, by insisting on religous freedom in church-state relations.

4. DECLARATION ON RELIGIOUS FREEDOM

Pope Paul VI has been highly successful in continuing Pope John's church-state teachings and policies, developing them and bringing them to fruition. He has, by his successive statements on international morality and policy, continued along the way of the new informal, universalist system. By his speech before the United Nations he epitomized the role of a moral leader in appealing to all men's consciences. By far the most important of his achievements in this field is, however, the promulgation of the Second Vatican Council's Declaration on Religious Freedom.

The Declaration on Religious Freedom, though scarcely ten pages in length, and not specifically a statement on church-state relations, is the key document of our whole study. We must therefore examine carefully its contents and significance.

Although the declaration has but two chapters, it may be divided into four major parts: 1) a declaration of principles; 2) religious liberty as part of man's natural right to seek freely after the truth; 3) religious freedom in the light of revelation and of Church history; 4) the freedom of the Church in fulfilling her divine mission.

1. *A Declaration of Principles:* After a brief introduction, the document lays down its central principle in crystal clear terms:

> This Vatican Synod declares that the human person has a right to religious freedom. This freedom means that all men are to be immune from coercion on the part of individuals or of social groups and of any human power, in such wise that in matters

religious no one is to be forced to act in a manner contrary to his own beliefs.[1]

The heart of the declaration, then, is a clear statement of man's natural right to follow his conscience in religious matters, and to be free from outside interference with this right. But flowing directly out of this central statement comes what can be interpreted as a clear and epoch-making pronouncement on church-state relations:

> This right of the human person to religious freedom is to be recognized in the constitutional law whereby society is governed, and thus it is to become a civil right (679).

Here is a clear demonstration of the close connection between the two doctrines we have been studying: religious freedom and church-state policy. The one flows naturally and necessarily out of the other. Religious liberty in any society would be relatively meaningless unless the State refrained from violating it. In fact, reasons the declaration, the dignity of man demands that "constitutional law" *protect* this right. The classic concept of man as a social animal necessitates that any real right be a social right and therefore that the State, as the natural guardian of all social rights, protect this one with its laws. What we see here is a simultaneous flowering of the doctrines of both religious liberty and of church-state relations. The principle of the absolute binding force of conscience, which was taught by St. Paul and philosophically explained by St. Thomas, is here finally being applied to the area of man's religious beliefs.

It is very interesting to note that the Council itself considers its declaration to be the outcome of a slow doctrinal evolution:

> Thus the leaven of the gospel has long been about its quiet work in the minds of men. To it is due in great measure the fact

---

1. *Declaration on Religious Freedom*, in *The Documents of Vatican II* (ed. by Walter Abbot, S.J., New York, 1966), pp. 678-679. Page numbers to this edition will be given in parenthesis for citation in this chapter.

that in the course of time men have come more widely to recognize their dignity as persons (693).

2. *Religious Freedom as Part of Man's Natural Right to Seek Freely after Truth:* The second part of the declaration begins with an explanation of the foundations upon which the whole document is built. Then it applies the principles of the declaration to various concrete situations. First, it explains the source and the extent of religious liberty; next it defines the moral and legal limits of this liberty; and finally, it clearly outlines the role of the State as public custodian of religious rights. This last section is the heart of the declaration's church-state content, but the first two points are very much relevant to our investigation.

The section begins by simply presenting the classic doctrine of the "eternal law" and its potential for being known by man. This doctrine has its roots deeply embedded in scriptural, patristic and scholastic tradition:

> Further light is shed on the subject if one considers that the highest norm of human life is the divine law—eternal, objective, and universal—whereby God orders, directs, and governs the entire universe (680).

God has written this law in man's heart "through the mediation of conscience," whereby man can come to know it by his natural reason and be led ever more deeply into the divine truths. Conscience, this great gift, is a source of man's dignity, and by its very nature demands that it be allowed to pursue its quest of truth without any repression. The conscience finds truth by free investigation and embraces it by free assent, and therefore a condition of free dialogue between men must be maintained so that they may help each other in the pursuit of truth:

> On his part, man perceives and acknowledges the imperatives of the divine law through the mediation of conscience. In all his activity a man is bound to follow his conscience in order that he may come to God (680).

The notion of the eternal law expressed here goes directly back to Augustine. The notion of conscience, however, is clearly that of Thomas. It differs essentially from Augustine's notion. Augustine's Stoic-based notion would be quite unfit to support a declaration of man's right to follow his conscience in religion even when he is in error. The applications made in the declaration, though outlined by Pope John, are the Council's own:

> The exercise of religion, of its very nature, consists before all else in those internal, voluntary and free acts whereby man sets the course of his life directly toward God. No merely human power can either command or prohibit acts of this kind (681).

The statement is referring to the individual's personal rights. Next, the same concept is broadened out to include man's right to express his religious convictions externally and publicly, in community with his fellows:

> The social nature of man itself requires that he should give external expression to his internal acts of religion . . . Injury, therefore, is done to the human person . . . if the free exercise of religion is denied in society, when the just requirements of public order do not so require (681).

There then comes a statement which, in one bold stroke, decides an issue held in abeyance for centuries. The Council declares that the State would clearly overstep its jurisdiction if it either commanded or prohibited any religous actions. This clearly rules out all the coercions and prohibitions which former unionist regimes perpetrated in the name of Christianity.

> The religious acts whereby men . . . direct their lives to God transcend by their very nature the order of terrestrial and temporal affairs. Government, therefore, ought indeed to take account of the religious life of the people . . . However, it would clearly transgress the limits set to its power were it to presume to direct or inhibit acts that are religious (681).

What a long time was required to make this simple application of Christ's own "render to Caesar the things that are Caesar's." Yet, as the Council itself admits, only time and the experience of centuries made it possible for these bounds to be seen more clearly and described in our day. This is one of the outstanding church-state progressions of the declaration. We have seen time and again in our study how often obscure boundaries between Church and State authority caused quarrel, confusion, and bloodshed. Now, finally, we have a clearly marked frontier. The State can never go beyond a general favoring of religion. True, the document does not openly declare that the State is prevented by its very nature from making an act of faith in true religion. But the citation above seems clearly to favor this interpretation. At least the State can never use its force to "establish one religion and inhibit the free exercise of another."

> It follows that a wrong is done when government imposes upon its people, by force or fear or other means, the profession or repudiation of any religion, or when it hinders men from joining or leaving a religious community (685).

This, of course, will not automatically solve all church-state problems. What about the "mixed areas" such as marriage and education, where both Church and State have legitimate claims? Difficulties and obscurities in this matter are by no means totally solved by the Council. But this statement remains an achievement of truly monumental proportions.

We indicated in the beginning of this work that the central problem of Catholic church-state relations was whether or not the State is objectively obliged to embrace actively and to support the true religion whenever possible. We have seen the twisting paths which this question took down through Christian history. The primitive Church seemed to answer "no" to this question, and the medieval answer was a resounding "yes." We have seen how much the experiences of centuries have taught Christians on this subject. Now, we witness something quite rare in the history of doctrine: the moment when the slow growth process of centuries produces a flowering. With the last quoted statement the Church by conciliar decree settled the central question which had been the subject of most of the heated debate during the past half century. The State does not have any objective obligation to embrace one religion as true and inhibit others. In fact, it has an obligation *not* to do so. Many would have liked to see a further declaration that the State, as a purely natural entity, does not have the power to judge on supernatural matters. This is only hinted at. But at least the abuses of former ages are rather frankly repudiated.

> In the life of the People of God as it has made its pilgrim way through the vicissitudes of human history, there have at times appeared ways of acting which were less in accord with the spirit of the gospel and even opposed to it (692).

Next, section seven of the declaration deals with the limits of religious liberty. The first to be enumerated is the limit placed by the moral law. Freedom of religion stops short of allowing one's religious inclinations to lead him into practices clearly at variance with universally accepted standards of morality. The second limit complements this first criterion in marking the frontiers. It admits that it is the State's duty to regulate by law the limits of legitimate expressions of religious conviction.

On the surface, perhaps, these two statements seem contradictory. If the State has no legitimate share in the things by which man is ordained to God, how is it competent to make laws preventing abuses of man's religious liberty? The contradiction is only apparent. The State does have legitimate control of public order, and must protect all of men's rights. When the religious practices of any individual or group go contrary to either of these interests, it is the State's right and duty to step in and regulate the matter with its law.

The declaration then develops this principle and, in doing so, sets in place an important stone in the edifice of Catholic church-state relations. It entrusts to the State the guardianship of religious liberty in general. Since it is of the very nature of the State to protect man's inviolable rights, it falls to the laws and the enforcement agencies of the civil power to safeguard man's right to religious freedom:

> Furthermore, society has the right to defend itself against possible abuses committed on the pretext of freedom of religion. It is the special duty of government to provide this protection (686).

This same principle of State guardianship is also applied to the rights of religious groups or "communities." What is true for individuals applies also to men bound by common belief into religious groups or churches. It is a part of man's natural religious freedom that the communities into which the individual is drawn be given the right to govern themselves, teach their members and set up institutions for propagating their belief. It is up to the civil authority to protect these rights also. It is likewise immoral for any civil government to itself impede or suppress these inalienable rights:

> Provided the just requirements of public order are observed, religious bodies rightfully claim freedom in order that they may govern themselves according to their own norms, honor the Supreme Being in public worship, assist their members in the practice of the religious life, strengthen them by instruction, and promote institutions in which they may join together for the purpose of ordering their own lives in accordance with their religious principles (682).

It is interesting to note how closely these declared rights parallel those enumerated and safeguarded in the United States Constitution's Bill of Rights. Here we see an individual State coming to recognize and declare a set of natural rights centuries before the Church did so. Likewise many Protestant churches came to recognize and defend these rights before the Catholic Church. It has always been the teaching of the Church that it has the right to such protection and immunity. This is even taught in the New Testament. But never before has such a solemn pronouncement been made admitting religious rights and immunities to all men and all religious communities.

In pre-Constantinian times, Lactantius made a similar claim but, until Pope John, this natural right of all men had remained under the cloud of the old Roman uniformism. With this statement the last vestiges of the medieval system disappear from Church teaching. It may take some time for practice and legal structures in some countries to catch up with the Church. But gone at last are the old uncertainties and vagueness which helped so many well intentioned people to fear the Church as essentially authoritarian.

The State, the Council declares, has no power whatever to use its force to sway a man's or a group's religious convictions one way or the other, much less to repress them. Just as its duty is to stand back and not interfere with man's freedom of speech and of the press, and to guard this freedom with laws, so too it must not in any way block man's religious freedom or allow it to be blocked. This includes, continues the declaration, the parents' right to give their children a religious education, and the right of all groups to use whatever means they choose to propagate their faith.

3. *Religious Freedom in the Light of Revelation and Church History:* The first principle on which the declaration's affirmation rests is the dignity of the human person. But the document hastens to point out that this first principle carries with it the weight of divine revelation. We have already seen this in our study of the Church in the New Testament. It shows how God, in revealing himself and his truth to man, always showed the most loving respect for man's dignity and freedom. Having given man the priceless gift of a free will, God always revealed himself in a manner carefully in keeping with this gift.

Since this facet of religious freedom and church-state relations has already been treated in a manner substantially the same as that of the declaration, we will not dwell on it here. A few observations are, however, in order.

It is important to recognize the solemnity and binding force which these scriptural proofs add to the Council's statement. This doctrine is not merely a matter of temporary policy. It is the result of the slow evolution of a truth which God himself revealed. The Council is not, of course, saying that these scriptural references make its teachings directly "revealed." They do, however, give it such weight and solidity that it could certainly never be changed under any circumstances which we can at present imagine. Christ's doctrine lives and grows, but it does not die.

A satisfying conciliation is made here between the traditional insistence that everyone is bound to follow the truth of Christ, and the principle of religious liberty. It is pointed out that Christ himself used the greatest forbearance when announcing his "good news."[2] He taught his disciples and apostles to employ the same humble, respectful methods.

As his people continued to refine themselves down through the history of the Church, their realization of man's dignity slowly expanded. Slowly, too, the respect which men showed one another likewise increased. The declaration admits that the activities of some Christians in history were not in keeping with this spirit. But it reminds us of the Church's constant teaching that no one should be forced into the Church.[3]

It is not easy to miss the striking emphasis which the declaration places on the notion of development of doctrine as the key to understanding the true nature of this new teaching and policy. This growth is seen to have been the dynamic principle behind the progress of God's people, both in the New Testament and in the Church. It is this truth which we have been highlighting throughout our study of church-state relations.

2. *Declaration . . .*, p. 680 ff.
3. *Loc. cit.*

4. *The Church's Right to Freedom in Fulfilling Her Divine Mission:* Next, the statement begins to draw conclusions from these scriptural roots. Since God so carefully respected the freedom of his children, today the individual's freedom to accept or reject the true faith must also be respected. On the other hand, the Church itself, as the assembly of God's people, has a right to follow the attraction of the Spirit in a manner absolutely uninhibited by any social or civil pressures.

Lest anyone receive the wrong impression from all this talk of freedom, this third part of the declaration ends by reaffirming the duty of all Christians to go out and "teach all nations" (Mt 28:19-20). Man's inviolable right to freedom is in no way damaged by hearing God's word preached, and by feeling the resulting attraction of its truth. As "mistress of the truth" the Catholic Church has the duty not only to teach the truth, but "by her authority to announce and make firm the principles of the moral order." Human dignity in no way eviscerates the force of the Christian's duty to help in this even to the shedding of his blood. The Christian's duty to learn and to preach Christian truth, and his duty to respect other's consciences, are not contradictory but complementary:

> The Church should enjoy that full measure of freedom which her care for the salvation of men requires . . . In human society and in the face of government, the Church claims freedom for herself in her character as a spiritual authority, established by Christ the Lord (693).

Finally, the declaration, besides summing up its teachings, takes a clear step in the direction of what I have chosen to call "universalist" church-state relations:

> The disciple is bound by a grave obligation toward Christ his Master ever more adequately to understand the truth received from Him, faithfully to proclaim it, and vigorously to defend it, never—be it understood—having recourse to means that are incompatible with the spirit of the gospel (695).

The universalist trend in Catholic church-state relations works toward establishing mutual friendship, peace and understanding between the Church and all nations of the world. The very heart of this effort is the protection and furtherance of true religious liberty. This is what the Council urges:

> All nations are coming into ever closer unity. Men of different cultures and religions are being brought together in closer relationships. There is a growing consciousness of the personal responsibility that weighs upon every man (694).

It is a good omen for future church-state relations that the conciliar Declaration on Religious Freedom ends on this broad note.

The Second Vatican Council's Declaration on Religious Freedom is no less than the crowning achievement of two thousand years of Christian thought and experience as to man's religious rights as an individual and a member of society. No previous statement by either pope or council on this subject can compare with it in importance. But it is clearly a product of history.

It is the latest fruit of that long, living, growth process whereby the seeds of Christ's light and truth sprouted, took root and produced guidance toward peace within the family of man. Christ's seeds of love and respect for man fell first into the Roman world: a human field not particularly amenable to the rapid, healthy growth of such liberty. But grow it did, slowly and tortuously, the dead leaves of its own growth efforts imperceptibly fertilizing that rocky soil. No one obstacle gave the doctrine of religious liberty more resistance than the old Greco-Roman legacy of fusion between religion and politics. Christ's "render to Caesar" was one of his seeds of love and respect. The declaration brings the resulting plant into a new season of fruitfulness.

We have, throughout our study of church-state doctrinal development, emphasized the close interrelation between religious freedom and church-state relations. We have seen how— in the New Testament, the Fathers, the middle ages and modern times—a progress in one meant progress in the other. Nowhere is this mutual dependence more evident than in the Council's declaration. The phrase "church-state relations" never occurs there; but the problem is, as we have seen, directly and thoroughly treated. In fact, there is no more important church-state statement in the history of the Church. Here religious freedom, as well as the distinction between Church and State, reach a definitive state of development.

It is very interesting to note how the major pronouncements of the declaration parallel other historic Christian church-state pronouncements: the Edict of Milan, the statements of Pope Gelasius, the Concordat of Worms, and Pope John's encyclical, *Peace on Earth*. The same elements are emphasized in all of them. Of course, it also contradicts another tradition within the Church. It replaces the church-state teachings of Augustine, Hildebrand, Boniface VIII, and even Leo XIII. But this is by no means the first time that two opposing doctrinal conceptions have vied for centuries only to have one wither eventually and be cast aside. The Council's declaration leaves little doubt that State involvement in doctrinal matters, particularly when it entails coercion of any kind, was never in full accord with Christ's spirit.

This does not totally negate the merits of the medieval system. When humanity was younger and less mature, it spoke and acted as one younger and less mature. But it illustrates how the rejection of the "total union system" is properly interpreted as an upward curve of growth rather than a simple reversal of position. We have seen how the basic church-state principles enunciated in the New Testament (distinction of powers, friendly cooperation, and mutual respect) were maintained and reinterpreted in each era of Christianity. Sometimes the job was done very imperfectly, but these principles were always in evidence. Never have they been so beautifully developed as in the Declaration on Religious Freedom.

Chapter Eight

Foundation for Progress

In pre-Christian times, religion and politics were generally fused into a single structure, and rarely did individual beliefs receive freedom of expression. Christ preached his kingdom as the definitive religion, and accepted into it only those who freely chose to follow him. For the first three hundred years, relations between the State and Christ's Church were nonexistent, and the only constraint on a Christian's conscience was his own freely accepted faith. The Constantinian era began a church-state system which was much more Roman than Christian. This system evolved into the medieval one, still as much politically as religiously inspired and sustained. Little concern was given to the rights of individual consciences, because the authentically Christian concept of conscience had been only vaguely grasped.

However, the close coordination between Church and State in the middle ages was achieved by a system of relations geared to the needs and susceptibilities of the age. In its foundational principles it corresponded to the ideals held by both the Church and the political authorities. Religion needed and wanted close support from the State, and the State, in turn, relied heavily on the political strength always present in religious support. Crude communications, relative ignorance of other possibilities, and the comparatively undeveloped level of society, all tended to effect a minimalization of the system's disadvantages in the face of sheer necessity.

But, by the dawn of the twentieth century, this old constellation of relative advantages and disadvantages had been destroyed.

313

The French and American revolutions had made the common citizen equal to the aristocracy before the law. The Industrial Revolution was fast bringing self-respect and security, even if not plenty, to the masses of Europe and America. Modern communications and universal education had awakened the traditional downtrodden three-fourths of populations everywhere in the West. This revolution was primarily a sociological and civilizational, not a religious, phenomenon. Mankind, only indirectly influenced by Christ, had come of age. It recognized its natural freedom.

We have seen how profoundly this affected the Church, especially in its relations with States who had taken up the revolution's principles. When the Church continued to demand a relationship which excluded equality before the law for all citizens, it furnished the already hostile civil authority a fine excuse for breaking off all relations. This stand likewise alienated even further whole non-Catholic populations. It antagonized citizens of States (for example, the United States) whose anti-union stands were not inspired by hostility to organized religion.

The abyss which separated the political ideology of the majority of western States from that of the Church was not, of course, caused only by the Church's clinging to tradition. It was dug by an infinitely complex number of forces. But the important point is that at the beginning of Leo XIII's pontificate it existed. Even the wholly Catholic populations of Italy and Spain supported their governments, which were at that time at loggerheads with papal political doctrine and practice. The result was an almost total neutralization of papal efforts to enlighten the civil authority and political processes with the light of Christ. For the governments of Christian nations, after breaking so many formal ties with the Vatican, had little inclination to heed even informal advice from the popes.

Leo XIII, however, saw the many positive qualities of the national political world which was opposing him. He changed the direction of papal policy by striving mightily to come to terms with his opponents and bridge the ideological gap. His encyclicals on the condition of the working classes, on liberty, on citizenship and on the State were giant steps in this direction. A real bridge appeared with the signing of the Lateran Pacts.

Pius XII labored diligently at strengthening the foundational principles of this new bridge. But, more important, he began to use the bridge for communicating Christ's principles to national and international political endeavors. He used the traditional formal ties and formal union where they existed, and praised their function, but he utilized also the informal new media provided by radio addresses and the international organization of States. He delimited the old formalist framework which tradition decreed to be the only field wherein a church-state dialogue was possible.

In its place he forged the universalist doctrine that we have described, whereby relationships were governed not by protocol and formalities only, but by the natural law and theological principles which linked the two societies together. Without supplanting the need for relations with individual States, the new medium offered new capabilities and complemented the relatively narrow, individual relations which were in effect up to that time. This new type of communication removed the last remaining barriers which had kept modern democratic regimes and the Holy See apart.

Slowly, papal political and social doctrine gained new prestige and importance among the States of the world. Formal relations continued and even increased. But the invisible substance of church-state accord—mutual trust and respect—was more the result of the disappearance of papal political power and the appearance of the new universalist relationship than it was the result of formal diplomacy.

Pope John gave great impetus to the effectiveness of these new media in church-state relations. His Christlike simplicity, and his charity for all men, drew the attention of the world back to the Vatican. His resolute renunciation of all non-spiritual motivations did much to lay to rest the yet strong suspicions lingering in many minds and hearts. He returned to the Church and to the world the possibility of a mutually acceptable, effective coordination which had not existed since the middle ages.

The Second Vatican Council brought to fruition a long doctrinal development. It succeeded, for the first time, in laying down principles of church-state relations which were in full accord with Christ's respect for the dignity of the individual conscience.

Church-state doctrine has not yet reached full maturity in this new age. The Council has only furnished guidelines. Indeed, no final solution, or system, will ever be able to offer a concrete "ideal" in this regard. But the foundations for progress are so soundly laid that society can look forward confidently to continued fruitful development in the future.

Bibliography

Acton, J. *Essays on Church and State.* London, 1952.

Alkin, L. E. *Apologie pour l'humanisme chrétien.* Luttich, 1941.

Arquillière, H. R. *L'Augustinism politique.* Paris, 1934.

Bardy, G. *La théologie de l'Eglise de saint Clement de Rome à saint Irenée.* Paris, 1945.

Barker, I. *Social and Political Thought in Byzantium.* Oxford, 1957.

Barry, C. *Readings in Church History.* Westminster, 1959.

Bates, M. S. *Religious Liberty, An Inquiry.* New York, 1945.

Bayet, J. *Histoire politique et psychologique de la religion romaine.* Paris, 1957.

Bea, A. Cardinal. "San Paolo araldo et eroe della libertà," *Civiltà Cattolica,* IV (1960), 3 ff.

Bouman, C. A. *Sacring and Crowning.* Gronigen, 1957.

Brooke, Z. N. *Lay Investiture and its Relation to the Conflict of Empire and Papacy.* Oxford, 1934.

Buché and Leclercq. *L'intolérance religieuse et la politique.* Paris, 1912.

Cadier, J., *et al. Unité chrétienne et tolérance religieuse.* Paris, 1950.

Calvez, J. and Perrin, J. *The Church and Social Justice: The Social Teachings of Popes from Leo XIII to Pius XII.* Translated by Kirwan. London, 1961.

Carlyle, R. W. and Carlyle, A. J. *A History of Medieval Political Theory in the West.* Six volumes. London, 1930-1938.

Chambers, R. W. *Thomas More*. Second edition. London, 1948.

Combés, G. *La doctrine politique de Saint Augustin*. Paris, 1947.

Congar, Y. "The Historical Development of Authority in the Church. Points for Reflection," *Problems of Authority*. Translated by R. F. Trevett. Edited by John M. Todd. Baltimore and London, 1962.

Cullmann, O. *Dieu et César*. Paris, 1956.

Curtis, L. *Civitas Dei*. London, 1949.

D'Arcy, E. *Conscience and its Right to Freedom*. London, 1960.

Dawson, C. *Medieval Essays*. London, 1939.

Deman, T. *Le traitement scientifique de la morale chrétienne selon Saint Augustin*. Paris, 1957.

Dickenson, J. *The statesman's book of John of Salisbury*. New York, 1927.

Duchesne, L. *Histoire ancienne de l'Eglise*. Paris, 1908.

Dupont, J. "Syneidesis, Aux origines de la notion chrétienne de conscience morale," *Studia Hellenistica*, 5. Louvain, 1948.

Easton, E. *Roger Williams, prophet and pioneer*. Boston, 1930.

Ehler, S. and Morrell, J., editors. *Church and State through the Centuries*. London, 1952.

Eschmann, J. T. "St. Thomas Aquinas on the Two Powers," *Medieval Studies*, 1958, 154 ff.

Gilson, E. *The Church Speaks to the Modern World, The Social Teachings of Leo XIII*. New York, 1954.

Glez, G. "Primauté du pape," *Dictionnaire de Théologie catholique*, XIII, col. 275 ff.

Goerner, E. A. *Peter and Caesar: Political Authority and the Catholic Church*. New York, 1965.

Goodenough, E. R. *Church in the Roman Empire*. New York, 1931.

Green, V. H. *Renaissance and Reformation*. London, 1952.

Greenslade, S. *Church and State from Constantine to Theodosium*. London, 1954.

Guardini, R. *Royaume de Dieu et liberté de l'homme.* Tournai, 1945.

Guterman, S. L. *Religious Tolerance and Persecution in Ancient Rome.* London, 1951.

Haller, W. *Liberty and Reformation in the Puritan Revolution.* New York, 1963.

Hernegger, R. *Macht ohne Auftrag.* Freiburg-im-B., 1963.

Hughes, P. *A Popular History of the Catholic Church.* Garden City, 1954.

Hull, J. *Medieval Theories of the Papacy.* London, 1934.

Jordan, W. F. *The Development of Religious Tolerance in England.* Four volumes. London, 1932-1940.

Journet, C. *The Church of the Word Incarnate,* I, "The Apostolic Hierarchy." London, 1955.

Kerwin, J. *Catholic Viewpoint on Church and State.* Garden City, 1960.

Kittel, G. *Christus und Imperator.* Stuttgart, 1939.

Lecky, W. *History of the rise and fall of the spirit of nationalism in Europe.* Two volumes. London, 1882.

Lecler, J. *Two sovereignties, a study of relationships between Church and State.* London, 1952.

Leclerc, J. "Bras seculier," *Dictionnaire de sociologie,* IV, col. 226 ff.

Leclercq, H. "Constantin," *Dictionnaire Archéologie Chrétienne,* III, col. 2632 ff.

Lottin, O. *Psychologie et Morale au XII et XIII siècles,* II. Louvain, 1948.

Maisonneuve, H. *Etudes sur les origines de l'inquisition.* Second edition. Paris, 1960.

Maritain, J. *Man and the State.* Chicago, 1951.

Marrou, H. *De la connaissance historique.* Paris, 1955. (Eng. trans.: *The Meaning of History.* Baltimore, 1966.)

Murray, J. C. "Pope Leo XIII and nineteenth century liberalism," *Theological Studies*, 1952, 423 ff.

————. *We Hold These Truths*. New York, 1960.

Murray, R. H. *Erasmus and Luther: their attitude to toleration*. London, 1920.

Pilati, G. *Chiesa e Stato nei primi quindici secoli*. Rome, 1962.

Rommen, H. A. *The State in Catholic Thought*. St. Louis, 1950.

Schlier, H. "L'état selon le Nouveau Testament," *Lumière et Vie*, 1960, 99 ff.

Schnackenburg, R. *Gottes Herrschaft und Reich*. Freiburg, 1959.

Seston, W. "Constantine as a 'bishop,'" *The Journal of Roman Studies*, 1947, 129 ff.

Setton, K. M. *A History of the Crusades*. Philadelphia, 1955.

Spicq, C. *Les épîtres Pastorales*. Paris, 1947.

————. *Charité et liberté selon le Nouveau Testament*. Paris, 1960.

Stelzenberger, J. *Syneidesis in Neuen Testament*. Paderborn, 1961.

Stephenson, C. *Medieval Feudalism*. Ithaca, 1956.

Stratman, F. M. *Jesus Christ et l'Etat*. Paris, 1952.

Sturzo, L. *L'Eglise et L'Etat: Etude de sociologie religieuse*. Paris, 1937. (Eng. trans.: *Church and State*. South Bend, Ind., 1962.)

Tellenback, G. *Church, State and Christian Society at the time of the Investiture Contest*. Oxford, 1940.

Tierney, B. *Foundations of the conciliar theory*. New York, 1955.

Toumanoff, C. "Caesaropapism in Byzantium and Russia," *Theological Studies*, 1946, 216 ff.

Ullmann, W. *The Growth of Papal Government in the Middle Ages*. London, 1950.

————. *The Origins of the Great Schism*. London, 1948.

Valente, M. *L'éthique stoicienne chez Cicéro*. Paris, 1956.

Voigt, K. *Staat und Kirche von Konstantin dem grossen bis zum Ende der Karolingerzeit*. Stuttgart, 1936.

Wals, G. G. *Medieval Humanism*. New York, 1942.

Willis, G. *St. Augustine and the Donatist Controversy*. London, 1950.

Winston, R. *Charlemagne*. London, 1956.

Ziegler, A. K. "Pope Gelasius and his teaching on the relations of Church and State," *Catholic Historical Review*, 1942, 412 ff.

Index

Abelard, Peter, 125-126

Age of transition; See Post-Reformation period

Alexander of Hales, 126

Ambrose of Milan, 35, 47, 49, 53, 55, 58, 59, 64, 65, 67, 72, 75-76, 82, 85, 125

Aristotle, 72, 80, 115

Augustine of Hippo, 35, 47, 50, 69, 85, 111, 127, 130, 131, 139, 282-283, 304, 312; erring conscience, theory of, 69-71; influence on later ages, 52, 80-81; interpretation of St. Paul, 73-76; on nature of Church, 52-54; on nature of State, 49-54; notion of conscience, 68-71; on religious freedom, 67-84; on relationship between Church and State, 53-61; relations with Donatists, 68-70; Roman influence on, 51-54, 66; Stoic influence on, 70-73

Avignon, papal captivity at, 106, 108

Balzan peace prize, 279

Barbarossa; See Frederick I

Bea, Augustine, Cardinal, 27, 28, 82, 271, 294, 299

Bellarmine, Robert, 169-170

Bernard of Clairvaux, 114

Bologna, University of, 110

Boniface VIII, Pope, 103-106, 114, 118, 124, 139, 188, 244, 273, 312

Brutus, Stephen, 160

Byzantine Empire, 89, 93

Canon law; See Law, canon

Canonists' theories of Church and State, 109-115

Canossa, 48

Carolingian Empire, 91-97

Charlemagne, 92-97, 108-109, 141, 224, 283

Charles Martel, 92

Cicero, 70-75

City of God, 49-53, 85, 125, 142

Clement of Rome, 36

Clement VIII, Pope, 159

Clovis, 92

Conciliar theory, 107-109

Concordat of Worms, 99, 101, 312

Congar, Yves, 101, 272

Conscience: erroneous, in St. Paul's teaching, 29, 32; in St. Augustine's, 69-71; in St. Thomas Aquinas', 127-128; freedom of: in New Testament, 26-33; in Fathers of Church, 67-84; in middle ages, 125-135; in post-Reformation, 156-165, 173-176; in Pope Leo XIII's teaching, 212-215; in Pope Pius XII's teaching, 232-239; in Pope John XXIII's teaching, 282-284, 298-301; in Second Vatican Council, 302-310; nature of: in Ambrose and Augustine, 67-71; in St. Thomas Aquinas, 127-133

Constantine, 40-44, 54, 60, 62-63, 89, 140, 265; sons of, 44-45; False Donation of, 95, 120, 150

Constitution of the United States, 165, 258

Copernicus, 153

Council: Nicea, 60; Ephesus, 89; Lateran, 102; Florence, 107, 108; Trent, 148; Second Vatican, 106, 144, 207, 233, 243

Cromwell, Oliver, 161
Crusades, 103
Cullmann, Oscar, 22, 25, 173

Dante Alighieri, 119-120
Daniélou, Jean, 267
Dark Ages, 96-97
Declaration on Religious Freedom
of Second Vatican Council: admission of past excesses, 306;
church-state significance of, 303-
306; condemnation of State suppression of religious freedom,
304-305; culmination of two
thousand year growth, 311-312;
natural law foundations, 302-304;
relations to St. Augustine, 304;
relations to St. Thomas Aquinas,
304; rights of Church, 310; rights
of individual in, 302-304; scriptural basis of, 302, 308-310; on
State support of religion, 305-
306; traditional basis, 308-310
De Lamennais, 174, 175
Deposition, of King Henry IV, 98-
99; of Popes Urban VI and Clement VII, 107
Descartes, 153
Diderot, 162
Direct power theory, 101-102
Dondeyne, A., 189, 262, 265
Donatists, 60, 68, 76

Ecumenism, 11-12, 315
Eleutheria, 27
Ellis, John Tracy, 267, 298
Enlightenment, period of, 155-156
Erasmus, 150, 152

False Donation of Constantine; See
Constantine
Fathers of the Church: apologist
fathers, 37-40; apostolic fathers,
36-37; appeals to natural law,
37-39; beginnings of church-state
union in age of, 40-47; blurred
frontiers between Church and
State in, 53-62; condemnation of
Roman totalitarianism in, 39-40;
early fathers on religious freedom, 37-38; importance of, 34-
35; influence of Roman civilization on, 43-46; notion of freedom
of conscience, 67-83; philosophic
foundations of, 70-76; scriptural
foundations of, 34-36; on suppression of heretics, 68-81; on
suppression of paganism, 41-44,
65
Freedom, religious, 12; in the New
Testament, 17-33; in the patristic age, 34-83; in the middle
ages, 126-135; in Leo XIII, 207-
217; in Pope Pius XII, 226-240;
in Declaration on Religious Freedom of Second Vatican Council,
301-312
Francis I, of France, 158
Francis of Vitoria, 168
Frederick I, Emperor, 101-103
Frederick II, Emperor, 102, 124
Florence, Council of; See Council

Galerius, Edict of, 42-43
Galileo, 153
Gelasius I, Pope, 63, 89, 184, 188,
312
Giles of Rome, 117-118
Gilson, Etienne, 52, 182, 185
Golden Bull of Charles of Bohemia,
107
Gospels; See New Testament
Gratian, Emperor, 45, 55, 65
Gratian, canonist, 110, 114, 123
Gregory VII, Pope, 98-101

Häring, Bernard, 13, 282
Harnack, Adolf, 82
Henry IV, Emperor, 109, 111
Hieratic theory, 100
Hildebrand; See Gregory VII
Hugh of St. Victor, 111-123
Humanism, 147

Humbert, Cardinal, 110, 123

Ignatius of Antioch, 37
Immortale Dei, 101, 183, 187, 193, 195-198, 203, 212, 246
Indirect power theory, 101, 104
Innocent III, Pope, 102, 136, 139, 176, 188, 274
Innocent IV, Pope, 102, 104, 113
Inquisition, 103
Inscrutabili, 182, 190, 193-195
Investiture, lay, 98-105
Ireland, Constitution of, 257

Jaspers, Karl, 182
James of Viterbo, 117-118
Jews, church-state traditions of, 18
John XXIII, Pope, 135, 148, 180, 191, 233, 243, 269, 300; attitude toward formal church-state ties, 288-292; attitude toward other Christians, 297-299; diplomatic experience, 269-270; emphasis on pastoral nature of Church in society, 274; friendship with political leaders of Italy, 288-289; natural law foundations of his teaching, 281-282, 297; on human dignity, 285-286; on religious freedom, 282-284, 298-299, 301; reception of Balzan Peace Prize, 279; relationship to teachings of Leo XIII, 295-298; rejection of papal political power, 273; support of United Nations, 286
John Chrysostom, 35, 47, 57
John of Paris, 120-122, 139, 141
John of Salisbury, 111-112, 114, 123
Julian the Apostate, 45
Justin Martyr, 38, 68, 81
Justinian I, Emperor, 90-91, 99, 109, 140

Kempf, Friedrich, 100
Küng, Hans, 170-171, 190, 202

Law: canon, 114, 117, 142, 244; civil, 114; divine, 129, 134, 182-183; ecclesiastical, 134; eternal, 72; natural, 69, 71, 73, 129, 134, 182-183, 200-201, 203, 238, 257, 281, 284, 297
Lactantius, 253, 301
Lateran Pacts, 191, 223, 263, 270, 275, 290, 292
Lecler, Joseph, 129, 166, 216, 232
Leo, the Great, Pope, 89, 93, 94
Leo IX, Pope, 98
Leo XIII, Pope, 101, 142-143, 166; advances in church-state doctrine, 188-190; on American system, 201-202; attitude toward democracy, 186-187; on autonomy of Church and State, 185-191; convictions on union of Church and State, 191-207; diplomatic experience, 181-182; on fear of State domination of Church, 190; on freedom of conscience, 214-215; on freedom of speech and press, 212-213; major church-state encyclicals, 182-183; natural law basis of doctrine, 203-204; opposition to the liberalists, 190-191, 199; scholastic approach of, 184-185; on separation of Church and State, 207-211; speculative approach of, 187-188; on State's duty to support true religion, 191-199; teachings on religious freedom, 211-212
Liberalism, nineteenth-century, 219-225
Logos, 71
Louis XIV, King, 154, 160-162, 170
170
Luther, Martin, 143, 152, 157

Machiavelli, 157, 160
Manichaean, 72
Marsiglio of Padua, 114-120
Medieval developments in church-state relations, 85-143

Middle Ages: blurred church-state frontiers, 85-87, 142-143; canonical influence on, 109-113; Church's concern for spiritual freedom, 93, 98-100; church-state union, 91-95; concept of origin of political power, 96-97, 105; decline of papal power, 103-108; dependence on Augustine, 85-86; dependence on Roman idea of State, 87-88; eastern emperors' caesaro-papism, 89-91; growth of papal political power, 91-105; need of pope for protection against kings, 93, 95-101; permanent church-state legacies of, 135-144; political control of spiritual, 93-96; pope as unifying force, 103; religious freedom, 125-135

Milan, Edict of, 40-42, 63, 150, 224, 312

Monophysitism, 17

Murray, John Courtney, 165, 179, 188, 201, 202, 209, 211, 219, 246, 294

Nantes, Edict of, 158-159

Napoleon I, 162-164

Nietzsche, Friedrich, 82

Newman, John Cardinal, 156

New Testament, 17-33; Apocalypse, 22; condemnation of atheist state in, 25-26; Christ and end of essential union of Church and State, 18-20; Gospel teachings on Church and State, 19, 22-26, 27; import of scriptural guidelines, 17-18; on erroneous conscience, 29, 32; on just authority, 30-32; on State's ability to recognize true religion, 22-24; on religious freedom, 26-33; St. Paul on Church and State, 19-20, 23; the trial before Pilate, 23-25

Newton, Isaac, 153

Nicea; See Council

Otto I, Emperor, 97

Otto II, Emperor, 97

Otto III, Emperor, 97

Papal States, origin of, 91-93; loss of, 165-166

Pacem in Terris, See Peace on Earth

Patristic age, 34-83

Paul VI, Pope, 301

Paul, St., 19-53

Peace of Augsburg, 157

Peace on Earth, 253, 277-287

Pepin, 92-93, 108

Peter, St., 20-21

Peter Lombard, 126

Philip the Fair, King, 103-105, 115

Pilate, Pontius, 23-33, 48

Pius IX, Pope, 174, 178-180, 189

Pius XI, Pope, 219-220, 222

Pius XII, Pope: attitude toward democracy, 226-229, 259-263; attitude toward feud over ideal church-state system, 241-243, 262-263; on freedom of religion, 232-238; influence of Leo XIII on, 243-246; notion of Church's rights, 245-246; notion of supranationality of Church, 229-231; notion of ideal church-state relation, 256-260; on religious tolerance, 250-254; political neutrality of, 229-230; rejection of papal political power, 263-264; support of United Nations, 228; treatment of the traditional system, 240-246; on union of Church and State, 246-250; universalist teaching on Church and State, 226-240; use of modern communications, 232-239; world situation at election, 219-222

Plenitudo potestatis, 114, 118

Poitiers, Edict of, 159

Policraticus, 112, 114

Politiques, 161, 167

Polycarp of Smyrna, 36

Pontifex Maximus, 18, 44, 65

Post-Reformation period: intellectual transition, 149-156; Humanism, 149-151; nineteenth-century thought, 172-176; political and sociological transition, 156-166; progress in religious tolerance, 157-166; Protestant Reformation, 151-153; Renaissance, 149-151; scientific revolution, 153-156; transition in Catholic thought and action, 166-176; United States Constitution, first amendment, 164-165

Preparation, Period of, *See* Post-Reformation Period

Rahner, Karl, 225, 259-260, 264, 266, 272

Reformation, Protestant, 108, 119, 147-148, 151, 156, 166, 169, 266

Religious Freedom; *See* Freedom, Religious

Renaissance, 147-156

Rerum Novarum, 182

Revolution, French, 148, 155, 163, 266, 314

Risorgimento, 164

Roman, emperors, 62; empire, 19, 22, 61, 66, 119; law, *See* Law, Roman

Sapientiae Humanae, 183, 193

Separation of Church and State: in New Testament, 19-21; in St. Augustine, 53-61; in St. Thomas Aquinas, 115-116; in age of post-Reformation, 158-166; in Pope Pius IX, 174-176; in Pope Leo, XIII, 207-211; liberalists' views on, 207-211; in Pope Pius XII, 246-250; in Second Vatican Council, 302-306, 317-318

Schism, Great Western, 107

Schlier, Heinrich, 23, 28

Scripture, 17-27

Soto, Dominick, 168

Stelzenberger, J., 70, 73

Stephen II, Pope, 92-93, 109

Stoic influences, 70-84, 304

Suarez, Francis, 169-170

Syllabus of Errors, 180, 189

Synderesis, 70, 131-134

State, notion of, 18-19

Tertullian, 39-40, 68, 81

Theodosius I, Emperor, 41-45, 55, 64, 86, 89

Theodosius II, Emperor, 86, 89

Tolerance, 147, 168, 267

Thessalonica, Edict of, 41, 57

Thirty Year's War, 158, 161-162

Thomas à Becket, 112

Thomas Aquinas, St., 72, 74, 81, 115-116, 123-124, 127, 128-135, 158; concept of conscience, 127-133; concept of synderesis, 131-132; on conscience as a natural power, 133-134; on conscience as part of human reason, 132-133; on conscience as ultimate religious guide, 126-129; on duty to follow erroneous conscience, 127-128; interpretation of St. Paul on conscience, 127-130; notion of natural origin of State, 115-116; on how rulers lose right to rule, 116-117; on union of Church and State, 115-116

Turrecremata, Cardinal, 120

Ullman, Walter, 63, 112

Unam Sanctam, 105

Union of Church and State: in pre-Christian times, 17-18; in New Testament, 19-27; in early fathers, 34-39; in fathers after Constantine, 41-54; in age of Justinian, 90; in age of post-Reformation, 155-161, 165-173; in Second Vatican Council, 302-308; Augustine's views, 49-56; De Lamennais' view, 174-176; Pope Leo XIII's view, 191-207; Pope Pius XII's views, 246-250; Pope John XXIII's view, 276-282, 295-300; crowning of Charlemagne, 94-97; Constantine's impact, 40-44; effect of ancient Roman tradition, 43-46; effect of *City of God*, 49-56, 86-87; hieratic theory and its effect, 100-106, 112-116; effect of loss of papal states, 221, 263, 273, 288-289; origin of papal states, 91-93, 96-97

Valentinian, 41, 45
Valens, 45
Vatican Council, Second; *See* Council, Vatican II
Voltaire, 154-155, 162

William of Ockham, 119